Sex lives of the
HOLLYWOOD
GODDESSES 2

First published in 2004 by

Prion
an imprint of the
Carlton Publishing Group
20 Mortimer Street
London W1T 3JW

10 9 8 7 6 5 4 3 2

A catalogue record for this book is available from the British Library

ISBN 1 85375 514 1

Printed in Great Britain
by Mackays

Sex lives of the HOLLYWOOD GODDESSES *2*

NIGEL CAWTHORNE

PRION

Contents

Introduction

I first started writing the *Sex Lives* ... series of books as satire. This can be clearly seen in *Sex Lives of the Popes*, *Sex Lives of the Presidents*, *Sex Lives of the Great Dictators*, and *Sex Lives of the Kings and Queens of England*. *Sex Lives of the Great Composers* and *Sex Lives of the Great Artists* fell into that category too, showing that world-famous maestros – or maestri if you want to be pedantic – had just one thing on their minds when they wrote their great symphonies and concertos – all right, concerti – and men became artists so that they could persuade young women to take their clothes off. Shocking.

Sex Lives of the Hollywood Idols, *Sex Lives of the Hollywood Goddesses* and now this volume, don't have that satirical edge. Of course, it is amusing to see that the erotic fumblings of the great sex symbols of the movie industry can be as furtive and inept as our own. But while popes are not supposed to have sex and politicians, heads of state, composers and artists are supposed to keep their minds on higher things – at least, that's what they tell us – Hollywood goddesses are supposed to have sex, and lots of it. Are these books just gossip? Nothing so trivial. My *Hollywood Sex Lives* books are more akin to *shunga*.

Shunga is Japanese erotic art that originated in the Yoshiwara in Edo (old Tokyo) and the red-light districts of other cities. *Shunga* paintings and prints depicted men and women having sex. Often the prints came bound in the form of "pillow books" with extensive, poetic and highly erotic captions. These were used to instruct young couples on what their partner expected of them in the bedchamber. They provide more experienced couples with an erotic menu to entice them on to more adventurous indulgences or simply to turn them on.

In a way, most of Hollywood's output is *shunga*, though it is rarely as explicit. Classic Hollywood movies carry elements of ritualized romance designed to promote romantic, if not downright erotic, feelings in the cinema audience. Who has not felt erotic stirrings – if not fumblings – in a movie theater with a date, or dashed off to make love after seeing a Hollywood blockbuster?

Shunga has strict rules. Although the sexual parts are shown – and often exaggerated to ludicrous, or lewdicrous, proportions – the participants are rarely shown naked. The sexual act takes place in what the Japanese call "the floating world" – a world free from care and far removed from everyday life. And the women depicted were often famous courtesans, often so famous that they would be used to model the latest fashions.

In *Sex Lives of the Hollywood Goddesses II*, we revisit the floating world of Hollywood, the Yoshiwara of old Los Angeles. Just as in *shunga* prints, we see beautiful women, famed for their erotic allure, who were frequently used by couturiers to show off their wares. Although in this book they are often naked in the physical sense, parts of them remain covered. We see little of their thoughts, hopes, aspirations, their intellectual interests, their homes, families or their work. Instead, we have the sexual part of their lives in graphic detail, exaggerated out of all proportion so that they can be better examined. This time we get up close and personal.

So there we have it. This book is not tittle-tattle, trivia or gossip. It is pure *shunga*. Pretentious? *Moi*? as I asked in the introduction to *Sex Lives of the Hollywood Idols*. I think the answer then was a resounding yes.

So who are these Hollywood goddesses? In the first volume they were largely the usual suspects, the Hollywood A-list, from Jean Harlow and Joan Crawford to Grace Kelly and Marilyn Monroe. This time the list is more idiosyncratic. That's why this time it's "up close and personal."

Largely, of course, the Hollywood goddesses are gay icons. It is nice that we can share, because there is plenty here for us straights, too. This book should come as a handy reminder to heterosexual men that it is far easier to pull a beautiful woman than an ugly one. They know how to handle it and reward us for our boldness. The goddesses know we have enjoyed their simmering performances on the silver screen. Now we can enjoy them again between the sheets … of paper … that make up a book. And there is also something for the ladies. Girls, if you are looking for ways to misbehave, you'll find plenty of guidance here.

So if you are young and inexperienced, learn. Otherwise dip in and pick a fresh delicacy. If these books inspire one person – or, better, two people – to make love one more time, then I have increased the sum total of human happiness. Not a lot of people can say that.

The sex lives of some of those playing cameo roles in this book are covered more fully in other books in the *Sex Lives …* series and I have employed a system of footnotes so that you can follow the daisy-chain from volume to volume. Enjoy.

1

The Girl Can't Help It

"Is Jayne Mansfield's Bust Legal?" screeched *Dare* magazine in August 1956. Her bust size, like her genius IQ of 163, was awesome and a matter of heated debate. At its peak, it rose to 46 inches. More modestly she alternately claimed 40 and 43 inches, sometimes 41. Let's settle on 42½, shall we?

Admittedly towards the end of her life she risked prosecution under FTC (Federal Trade Commission) regulations. She claimed an hourglass figure measuring 44-18-35, but, in 1967, the year of her death, she was sacked by British contractors when she failed to match up to specifications. Those who saw her said she had floppy breasts, a none-too-thin waist and "disfiguring black and blue marks from her knees up." The breasts were 40 plus – but their shape and projection were a miracle of wire, posture and padding.

Nevertheless, she burst on to the scene after winning a poolside battle of the boobs with, of all people, Jane Russell[1]. Jane herself had come to prominence in *The Outlaw* (1943) because of her breasts. Movie producer and aircraft engineer Howard Hughes[2] had designed a special cantilevered bra to show off her magnificent bosom to the best effect. His specification was that the "brassiere should hold the breasts upward but should be so thin that it takes the perfect shape of her breasts."The idea was that it should look on-screen like she

8

was not wearing a bra. In fact, Russell later claimed that she had not been wearing a bra in *The Outlaw*. She said Hughes' bra was uncomfortable so she did not wear it. Hughes then held the picture back for three years, claiming that he was being banned by movie censor Will Hays and the Legion of Decency. The resulting publicity guaranteed it would be a hit.

In 1954, Jane made another bra-busting epic for RKO. Called *Underwater*, it was merely an excuse to squeeze Miss Russell's considerable chest into a skin-tight swimsuit. To launch the film, Hughes flew the Hollywood glitterati to Silver Springs, Florida, where he had planned an underwater premiere in a theater built at the bottom of a lake, with the first-night audience decked out in aqualungs, flippers and goggles. Afterwards, handpicked showbiz scribes would get to interview Jane Russell, Debbie Reynolds and a saucy array of eager starlets while they were still dripping wet. However, the party was gatecrashed. A 21-year-old, brown-eyed blonde from Pennsylvania had cadged a ticket from columnist Earl Leaf. On the plane out to Florida she sat beside the editor of *Variety*, Joseph Schoenfeld, who was so impressed with her possibilities that he had already made a mental note to give her "a puff in his columns." After the screening, as the press assembled to await Jane Russell and the other celebrities, the blonde, wearing nothing but a pair of high-heeled shoes and a tiny red bikini that was straining at the seams, appeared.

"It was the most voluptuous sight I have ever seen," said one reporter.

The photographers had a feeding frenzy. The stars and Hughes's other Hollywood hopefuls were lost in the scrum. Then, in a fitting climax to the proceedings, the blonde dived into the pool, bursting her bra as she went. Five minutes later, when Jane Russell appeared, the pressmen had run out of film.

"Who's that blonde tomato?" asked Russell.

Angry that his star had been upstaged, Hughes's publicity guy begged Jane to don a daring bikini. She refused.

"Hell, no," she said. "I wear a one-piece. This isn't a cheesecake competition."

It was – and she had already lost. The picture of the near-naked Jayne Mansfield bobbing around in the pool, ineffectually clasping her giant boobs, made the newspapers across the nation.

"Get that girl," yelled Hughes. "For a thousand a week, if necessary."

Jayne was to become Hollywood's self-styled queen of the cleavage, but was she really that well endowed?

"When I first met Jayne, she was very normal in that department," said photographer Frank Worth, a friend and one of the architects of her pool exposure. "I showed her how to push them up using a special bra."

Jayne herself admitted that when she met Frank Worth, she was 38–21–35. But 38 ain't bad. She had inherited her breasts from her mother.

"When mama was growing up," Jayne explained, "it was fashionable to tape and strap breasts to make them flat. Women with large breasts were considered base and vulgar."

Perish the thought.

"I'm glad I did not grow up then," she added.

At 11 she was sent home from school with a note for her mother, suggesting that she might like to start wearing a brassiere. Her mother apologized to the school and Jayne, who liked her tits to swing free, was forced to comply. In retaliation, she pulled the straps up as far as they would go. It made her shoulders red and sore, but her breasts stood to attention like two inverted ice cream cones.

"I wore brassieres until I was 14," she said, "and then I abandoned them for ever to be free. I like to feel my body free as though I am floating in air. I hate underthings. I loved to sleep nude."

This shocked her mother, who insisted that she wear a nightgown. Even so, each night before donning it, Jayne indulged herself, undressing slowly in front of the bedroom mirror.

Although Jayne always liked having big breasts – and showing them off – they attracted trouble from the beginning, and not just from boys. During a sleepover, a girl friend got over-familiar and pounced on her. Another girl at school followed her into the lavatory.

"She put her arms around me and kissed me on the mouth," said Jayne. "I made so much noise it attracted one of the teachers."

Indeed, she attracted the attentions of the swimming teacher. After admiring the older woman's tanned and athletic body, the mermaid returned the compliment in a rather more physical manner. Jayne fled.

Her swelling curves were also attracting the attention of men. She soon noticed that a male teacher at school was finding excuses to put his arms around her whenever he talked to her. This time she did not flee and allowed the innocent touching to turn into "passionate petting."

At school, she said, fellow students "were forever trying to fondle my body." And in the swimming pool she found that, every time she "fell in" the deep end, she would get rescued by a husky, blond lifeguard. So fall in she did. She also enjoyed the wolf-whistles she got in the street when she stuck out her chest and swung her "booty". It was not just the men who took notice. Every woman in the street, she could see, envied her figure.

"My dresses became tighter and I loved the attention," she said. "Momma kept trying to get me to wear a larger dress or sweater or skirt to grow into. But I liked the tight feel of clothes on my body. It was like a caress."

At 12, Jayne was so forward that she called a handsome 14-year-old to ask him to take her to a dance. He said he had to ask his mother, who gave her approval, but he came down with the measles and Jayne had to stay home with Momma on the night of the dance and play Old Maid.

"And that's just what I felt like," said Jayne, "an old maid."

At 13, she had her first kiss with a French boy named Robert on a hayride. She responded to his European manner and figured it would be okay as she could see her other friends happily necking.

"I didn't want to be left out then," she said. "And I'm happy to say I haven't been left out since."

In the following months she kept a diary recording how many times she had been kissed each day. But she was still naive about sex. The helpful little book her mother had bought called *Growing Up* had not prepared her for the realities. One day she was playing jacks with Robert on the front porch, when the ball rolled up between his legs. As she reached for it, she was shocked to find something hard and erect protruding from Robert's Bermuda shorts.

By the time she was 14, and bra-less again, boys were hanging around outside her house. Jayne loved all the attention they gave her and the candy bars they brought, but her mother was outraged – or jealous perhaps. She was a libidinous woman herself. When Jayne was three, her father had died of a coronary and her mother shocked small-town Pennsylvania with her fervent desire to remarry. Before long she had two suitors, then ran off to Dallas, Texas, with a salesman, with Jayne in tow.

Jayne was soon giving Momma the slip. She would go to the rest room of a nearby service station to put on make-up when she was going out, then stop off there on the way home to wash it off. Although she was going steady with Robert – even wearing his ID bracelet – she was also seeing an older boy named Leland, who wore one of the Davy Crockett hats that were popular at the time. He invited her out on a picnic – but Momma insisted on coming along as a chaperone.

With Robert she had a special song, "Cuddle Up a Little Closer." With Leland it was "For Sentimental Reasons." She also used a senior boy in the school orchestra who her mother trusted as a front so she could go out with other guys. Ever adventurous, she went to the novelty shop owned by an older man who had tried to touch her up in a movie theater. He said that he liked pretty, young teenage girls and had some of his own. He offered her toy planes and other presents. But when the situation "became sticky again," Jayne said that she had better call her mother. He showed her the door and she left empty-handed.

"I decided then and there that, in future, I would get the merchandise first," she said.

Although the teenage Jayne tried to base her girlish appeal on Shirley Temple, she was genuine jailbait without a doubt. When her mother chided her on the tight shirts and Lana Turner[3] sweaters she wore, Jayne said, "Oh, mother, for heaven's sake. This is the twentieth century – not the Middle Ages."

Jayne was already starstruck. She loved the movies and she had a picture of Johnny Weissmuller, the first talkie Tarzan, on her bedroom wall. He had the kind of beefcake body she admired. At 14, she went on a trip to Hollywood.

"My real thrill was a tour of 20th Century Fox Studios," she said (one day she would be one of their biggest stars), "but that afternoon I was excited when we stumbled upon Rory Calhoun changing trousers on set."

She never looked back. (Neither did Rory. His wife named Betty Grable, the girl with million-dollar legs, as one of numerous correspondents in her divorce suit.)

At home again in Texas, Jayne fell in love with a young man named Sean, who was half Irish, half Ecuadorian and six years older than her. Mother approved because he was a Christian Scientist, but he did not take her to the reading room. Instead they spent a good deal of time smooching on the couch. After that she was "engaged" constantly. But when she told her "fiancés" that there would be no heavy petting until their wedding day the engagements became shorter than she intended. She also began deliberately dating men her mother would not approve of. One was a 24-year-old gas station attendant named Inky, for his coal-black hair. He took her to parties and introduced her to booze in the form of a Tom Collins. After three of them, she passed out and he drove her home. There is a divergence in accounts of what happened next:

"I can't remember the details, but I was raped," Jayne told May Mann, friend, adviser, Las Vegas columnist and Jayne's biographer (though some of the interview she cites in her biography seems to have been conducted by psychic means, after Jayne's death).

However, to Raymond Strait, aka. Rusty Ray, her press agent and general amanuensis for ten years, Jayne painted a much more romantic picture.

"On the way home we stopped in the park," she said. "Inky kissed me. All the rest followed. I was certainly ready and willing. It was my first time."

Strait says that Jayne was never remorseful about her first sexual experience and never blamed Inky for it. "Her life was her responsibility," he said. Afterwards Inky drove Jayne home, where she was reprimanded for drinking. It never occurred to her parents that anything else had gone on. It did not seem likely to them that a boy who had "ruined" a girl would drop her off at her parents' front door and say goodnight. However, Jayne was grounded and did not see Inky again.

"I wasn't afraid of having a baby," Jayne told May Mann, "because people had told me you couldn't get pregnant the first time. But I felt used and alone."

Then her period stopped. She panicked and called Inky. He manfully offered to marry her, but that was unthinkable. She was going to be a Hollywood goddess. She could not marry a pump jockey. But marry she would. An abortion was out of the question and she wanted her children to be legitimate. She was an old fashioned girl.

"Marriage also gave a girl the key to a lot of things that single women can't get," she said, "not without giving something in return."

There were plenty of candidates. She settled on Paul Mansfield – "a sort of junior Mr America ... blue eyes, blond hair ... the most handsome boy in class." She had met him at the local Baptist church, where his family was a pillar of the congregation. She made a play for him, walking out of church at the same time he did. Then she invited him to a party. He misunderstood and turned up with a date, an older woman of around 20. To Jayne she looked ancient. Nevertheless she continued to throw herself at him and got herself introduced to his parents.

Eventually Jayne summoned up the courage to tell Paul she was pregnant and, after knowing each other just two months, they married secretly in Fort Worth. She lied about her age. Paul was now a freshman at the University of Texas. They rented an inexpensive apartment together, though Jayne scuttled home each night in time for her parents' 11 o'clock curfew. They had no idea that she was married.

Jayne was now the envy of all her school friends. Her husband would visit each day so the two of them could have lunch in the high school cafeteria. But the situation could not last. Jayne was beginning to show. Then, one night at the country club, Paul publicly announced that they were married and were about to have a baby.

Jayne's mother almost died. She did not believe that her baby was married, until she saw the certificate. Then she wailed that Jayne had ruined her life. Jayne fled to the loving arms of Paul, but Momma soon came round when she realized that, by marrying Paul, Jayne had done rather well for herself. There was a second wedding. This time, ironically, the bride wore white.

Jayne herself gave three dates for this marriage: January 28, 1950, May 6, 1950 and May 30, 1950. She regularly shaved years off her date of birth, and her obstetric history has also been airbrushed. According to Ray Strait, after she first got married, she discovered that she was not pregnant after all. But within a month she was pregnant by her husband. That was a bit lucky then.

Jayne and Paul spent their second wedding night in the Texas Hotel, five minutes from the Baptist chapel in Fort Worth where they had first got married.

"I suspect everyone thought we were just shacking up," said Jayne. "There wasn't a lot I could do about my pooching stomach. But I knew I was truly married – twice married – so to hell with everybody else."

They planned a night of champagne and dancing.

"We never made it to the ballroom," she said. For obvious reasons.

Her baby girl, Jayne Marie, was born in November. Although money was tight for the newlyweds, the baby brought one tangible advantage. Giving birth had made Jayne's breasts even bigger. This attracted even more men, but when they realized that the baby in the baby carriage she was pushing was hers, they lost interest.

Jayne was not content to be a dutiful housewife to the unambitious Paul. She wanted to use her brains and enrolled in college, majoring in drama at the South Methodist University. She also worked hard to get her figure back after giving birth, and brought in a little extra money by modelling nude in the best-attended life classes in the history of SMU. Paul objected, but for the wannabe movie star it was an unbeatable confidence-boosting experience.

The Korean War broke out and Paul was drafted. Jayne accompanied him to Camp Gordon in Augusta, Georgia, on the understanding that, after the war was over, she would get her shot in Hollywood. In the meantime, she was determined to keep her figure in trim. She practised pirouettes and bust exercises in a skimpy leotard on the barracks lawn and often swam in the camp pool. A complaint was lodged with the camp commandant. She feigned innocence.

"It's a good thing that I wasn't an enemy agent," she said. "I could have turned Camp Gordon into a ghost town if I had accepted all the invitations extended to me."

Perhaps it is fortunate for the United Nation's war effort that Jayne did not go with her husband when he was posted to Korea – though she could undoubtedly have undone an entire Communist battalion with a single mammary. Before the men left, Jayne featured prominently in the camp's parting production of *Anything Goes*. She gave the appreciative audience more than a glimpse of stocking. The applause she received in return had her hooked.

While Paul was away, Jayne returned to Dallas and supported herself by modelling. She was Miss Photoflash 1952. More accolades followed. In small town newspapers across the South, she appeared as Miss Standard Foods, Miss Four Alarm Fire, Miss 100 Percent Pure (syrup), Miss Nylon (sweaters), Miss Texas Tomato, Miss July Fourth, Miss Queen of the Chihuahua Show, Miss Orchid, Miss One for the Road (coffee), Miss Blue Bonnet of Austin, Texas, Miss Electric Switch, Gas Station Queen, Best-Dressed Woman of the Theater and, more revealingly, Miss Negligee. "Miss Mansfield is the most interesting person who depicts what negligees are for," said the sponsors.

"The only thing I ever turned down was Miss Roquefort Cheese," she said. It didn't smell right.

The editor of the *Dallas Morning News* introduced her to Baruch Lumet, the father of Sidney, who had just set up the Dallas Institute of the Performing Arts. He succumbed to her considerable charm and gave her a part in his debut production, Arthur Miller's *Death of a Salesman*. He also coached her in a scene for *Saint Joan*, though how Jayne was going to cope with wearing male armor has never been explained. Surely the breast-plate alone would have presented insuperable problems.

Good to his word, when Paul returned from Korea he took Jayne to California. By this time, Jayne had bleached her hair blonde and Baruch Lumet had given her an introduction to the Hollywood producer, Milton Lewis. at Paramount Studios. As soon as she arrived in Los Angeles she phoned his office.

"My name is Jayne Mansfield and I'm here to be a star," she said. "I just arrived from Dallas where I won a beauty contest."

Paul had agreed that she would call herself "Miss" for professional purposes in Los Angeles, though she used his surname, Mansfield, because, she thought, it had "star quality." Lewis saw her the next day. She turned up wearing a strapless top and a red flared skirt, and gave him a few lines from *Saint Joan*. Lewis suggested that she lose some weight and showed her the door.

"It was the end of me at Paramount," she said. "I think maybe I wasn't ready for George Bernard Shaw. But I was very large with Steinbeck."

On another occasion, she reflected: "Somehow, I've always suspected it was something to do with the skirt."

To make money she sold kitchenware door-to-door and toured the model studios, where she found that aspiring starlets were expected to pose for free – or nude.

"Whoever hired you always had sex on his mind," she said. "I was a married woman, although I never said so. And I had no intention of becoming an adulteress."

However, this did not seem to bother her when Paul left to go back to Dallas. She soon found comfort in the arms of another TV host. It did not seem to bother him either. He was a married man.

Whether Jayne posed nude at this point in her career is a matter of conjecture. She told May Mann that she had applied to a model studio on Santa Monica Boulevard where men photographed girls for $20 an hour. She was told that she had to pose nude and, when she was overcome with nerves, was bundled into the studio with the punter in her robe.

"I stood there, while he got his camera ready," she said. "I knew I was supposed to drop my robe, but I couldn't do it."

She began to cry. According to Jayne, the man took pity on her, told her to put her clothes on and drove her home by way of the supermarket, where he bought her a bag of groceries. He paid the $20 fee and gave her a ten dollar tip.

"He never even kissed me," she said.

But she told Ray Strait different story: When they were discussing the famous nude calendar that got Marilyn Monroe[4] started, Jayne confided that she had posed nude, explaining that she had needed the money for her Hollywood debut.

"I have often wondered why those photos haven't come back to haunt me – or help me," she mused.

She took a night job selling popcorn and candy at Grauman's Chinese Theater. It was not stardom, but at least she was in the movie business. But still the size of her bosom was bringing her problems, although not because it was too big. One day, when Grauman's was hosting a premiere, she bumped into a press photographer outside who told her, "You are a sexy broad, but you need big apples." At that moment, Loretta Young arrived and he threw himself into the scrum.

Jayne kept wondering what he had meant by his "big apples" remark and, with her IQ of 163, she decided that he must have meant that she should carry a big apple so that she would look like Eve starting the action in the Garden of Eden. The next day, she bought a great big shiny red apple from the supermarket and she was walking down the sidewalk polishing it when a newsboy whistled. Jayne, delighted with the compliment, handed him the apple.

"Are you the Apple Queen?" he asked.

Jayne explained that she had been told that she needed big apples for luck or something. He laughed. There is no record of the 15-year-old newsboy's IQ but, quick as a flash, he figured it out.

"He meant you need to put some falsies under your bra. All the starlets do," he said.

"But I'm pretty good as I am," she replied.

He put her straight.

"All the dolls with big boobs get photographed," he said. "Yours could be bigger."

As she walked on down the street, she looked at her reflection in the shop windows and decided that he was right. Soon after she met Frank Worth, who showed her how to make her 38 a 40 and even more.

Jayne's apples got another showing when she entered the Miss California pageant, part of the Miss America contest. If she won the national contest she would get a prize of $50,000 and, she felt sure, would be sure to get a movie contract. A friend at the *Los Angeles Daily News* bought her a tiny pink bikini and gave her the five dollar entrance fee, but when she appeared on page eight posing as a Miss California contestant, Paul got to hear about it in Dallas and put his foot down. If she did not pull out of the contest, he would write and tell the organizers that she was married, which meant she would be disqualified. In tears, she apologized to her friend at the *Daily News* for wasting his five dollars. He said it was okay, provided she let him see her in that bikini – though I imagine that he wanted to see her without it.

Near to Jayne's house at 9840 Wanda Park Lane, which was already being known as "Mansfield's Madness," lived the B-movie actor Steve Cochran, who had risen to prominence in *Storm Warning* (1950). She gatecrashed his Li'l Abner party, and they became friends, then lovers. Some expected a permanent relationship to develop, but Cochran enjoyed his bachelor freedom. His ocean-going yacht had a ten-girl crew. Jayne did not mind. It amused her. She had fun with him.

"He wanted to bite into life and enjoy every morsel," she said. There was one problem though: "He was not a good lover." Maybe he was tired out splicing all those mainbraces.

Cochran had great contacts in the business and she got a walk-on part in a Lux Video Theater television play called *The Agent Went AWOL*. Then Frank Worth got her a part as a "sexy girl of the streets, sensual and bad" - a nymphomaniac - in the movie *Hangover*, released under the more enticing title of *The Female Jungle* (1956). She got $100. Afterwards she found a job at the Hollywood nightspot Ciro's that gave her a chance to see the movie stars in action. She met influential men who offered to help her. They usually invited her back to their apartments for dinner, but she knew what the price tag for their assistance would be.

"I declined," she maintained. "I wasn't a whore."

However, she did admit to being a "swinger" after Paul left.

"I began dating lots of men," she said. Unable to afford a babysitter, she would take her daughter, Jayne Marie, along on dates. This did not seem to dampen her suitors' ardor. "Some tried to make it with me, even when she was on the back seat of the car."

From working at Ciro's, Jayne realized that a key element in becoming a star was knowing how to handle the press. To do that, she had to be seen in the right places, with the right people, wearing the right outfits. But she had no money to spend on clothes. Most of the time she wore sweaters and blue jeans. To remedy this, she went to Emeson's, a chic clothes shop, and propositioned the proprietor and designer Walter Emeson. She told him in her sexiest, breathiest, little-girl voice that she had come to Hollywood to be a movie star and that she had no clothes except the ones on her back. Emeson was frosty. She said that she needed something to wear for a screen test the following day. Emeson said that he did not give clothes away, but when she smiled, he melted. She promised to pay him back when she got a movie contract. He took her to the bookkeeper to fill out a credit card application, then took her into the changing room.

He later recalled: "She removed the man's white shirt and torn, old blue jeans and thongs she was wearing." Then, with shaking hands, he measured her. "Her bust was 40 and her waist 23 and her hips measured 37. She had practically no underwear on at all."

"I don't wear them," she told him innocently.

Not only did Emeson kit her out with a high-necked black dress that left her back bare, he was so impressed by what he had seen that he took her down the street and bought her shoes, stockings, gloves, a purse, costume jewelry and a pair of panties – which he insisted that she wore. He did not waste any money on a brassiere though, as actor Jim Bishop discovered when taking her to a premiere.

"She saw the fans behind the sawhorses," he said. "She told the driver to pull close to the curb and slow down. She threw off the white mink, wriggled the shoulder straps lower and smiled as the idiots aimed their cameras into the windows."

Soon Emeson got the pleasure of seeing his gowns in the newspapers at the chicest places in town, with Jayne on the arm of Greg Bautzer,[5] Hollywood's "attorney to the stars" who was famous for having slept with Joan Crawford,[6] Rita Hayworth[7] and Lana Turner,[8] Bautzer denied ever bedding Jayne.

"There was something overblown about her figure," he said, "something not sexy but pathetic. I would rather have gone to bed with Agnes Moorehead."

However, Bautzer admitted that as her attorney he never charged her a fee, so one wonders how he was recompensed for his legal services. In fact, his associate Jerome Lipsky handled much of the work. He recalled that Jayne dropped by his leather-lined law office one day. A light had fallen on her one day during filming and she asked if she could sue.

"Were you hurt?" Lipsky asked.

"Yes, it burned my right breast," she replied.

"Did it do any damaged?"

Quick as a flash, she got out her breast and showed him. He got the giggles and when he called for help, five volunteers rushed to assist in the examination.

With her insatiable craving for column inches, Jayne got herself a hot-shot press agent called Jim Byron. Christmas was coming so he dressed her up in a skimpy, low-cut, red Santa Claus outfit and sent her round the newsrooms. She was to kiss any newsman she saw, reach in her sack and pull out a bottle of whiskey. She also extended her largesse to the typesetters, who promptly dropped their linotype – she then bent down to help them pick it up. It was a coup. Jayne's picture appeared in every newspaper in the country. Byron's reward was a five-year contract and they became lovers.

Byron then cooked up the *Underwater* stunt, only the bikini top was not supposed to burst – Jayne was supposed to take it off and throw it at the cameramen. As it was, the next day, everyone in Hollywood was asking: "Who is Jayne Mansfield?"

Byron arranged a lunch with Hollywood agent Bill Shiffrin.

"When I first saw her, I honestly thought I saw two miniature dirigibles followed by a gorgeous blonde in a golden dress," said Shiffrin. "Can you imagine? A table for three and two dirigibles."

Although Shiffrin was in his 60s, Jayne made a play for him as soon as her divorce came through. She suggested she play Doris Day to his Marty Melcher, Doris's husband and the agent who made her movie career. Shiffrin pointed out that he had a beautiful young wife and three kids. He later said she never understood that sex and business were two different things. If any one of her advisers did something that was successful, she would offer sex as a reward. Nevertheless he took her on as a client.

"The reason I started with her was that we had a Novak and a Monroe and I thought the town could use another blonde," said Shiffrin. "We needed a new glamour girl."

Jayne went up for *The Seven Year Itch* (1956) – which Marilyn got – and *Rebel Without A Cause* (1955). Shiffrin turned down an offer from Howard Hughes[9] as he was well known to have 40 or 50 pretty young actresses under contract stashed in houses around Los Angeles. He slept with them, but rarely got them parts. Instead she started at Warner Bros for $250 a week. She appeared in a few low-budget movies, including *Illegal* (1955), where she was compared to Marilyn Monroe in *The Asphalt Jungle* (1950). After filming *The Burglar* (1957) in Philadelphia, she was dropped. Byron blamed Shiffrin and Bautzer, who tried to tone her down. To Byron, Jayne was a satire of all dumb blondes. He even posed her by a sign on a crane that said: "Excessive Frontage Overhang." But Shiffrin drew the line when Byron made a deal with a rubber company to produce Jayne Mansfield hot-water bottles.

To make up to Jayne for the loss of the Warner Bros contract, Shiffrin put her forward for a Broadway play based on an incident in the life of Marilyn Monroe called *Will Success Spoil Rock Hunter?* Shiffrin called the writer-director George Axelrod and told him that, short of Marilyn herself, he had the girl for the part. He sent Axelrod picture of a saucily posed Jayne and received the reply: "If she can talk, she's got it."

Jayne did not want to be a Broadway actress. She wanted to be a Hollywood goddess. Even so, she went to the audition wearing a black satin dress that fitted "like spray paint" with a built-in brassiere to give her that extra uplift. Everyone agreed she looked the part and when George Axelrod confirmed she had got it, she grabbed him and hugged and kissed him.

The play opens with Jayne lying on a massage table, only partially concealed by a towel. She was supposed to wear a body stocking, but dispensed with it and wreaked havoc with scene shifters, running about naked backstage. The script played directly into her sexpot image.

"I'm lousy in bed," ran one line, "everybody says so."

"This isn't written for Jayne," wrote one Boston reviewer, "This is Jayne."

From that first glimpse of her on-stage, the first-night audience wanted more and when the final curtain fell they were on their feet demanding another sight of her. The show was sold out for months in advance, largely because the audience often got more of Jayne than they paid for. Jayne began pounding the pavements of Manhattan wearing nothing but stilettos and a fur bikini. The *Saturday Evening Post* reported that she had been found nude the bathtub, splashing around while a handful of fortunate aficionados took pictures. When Jayne was urged to issue an injunction to stop these nude shots being traded, her response was to put out more revealing pictures.

"There may be somebody somewhere who doesn't have one," she said.

"She ... suffered so many on-stage strap and zipper mishaps that nudity was, for her, a professional hazard," wrote the *Los Angeles Times*.

Now she was the toast of Broadway, Hollywood wanted her back. 20th Century Fox snapped her up and paid $100,000 to spring her from the play. Fox also had to buy the movie rights.

Jayne, the queen of publicity, had life-sized pictures of herself all over New York, made the cover of *Life* twice and made the centerfold of *Playboy* two years running. She was seen out with director Nicholas Ray, Oleg Cassini, the dress designer and former lover of Grace Kelly and producer-actor George Jessel.

Jayne claimed that, at the time, she was so busy being a sexpot she did not have time for sex. Besides, she lived with her daughter in a one-room apartment with no doors. However, she was often seen to check in Jayne Marie with the maid in the ladies' room at El Morocco when she was out with a date. This brought allegations from Paul that she was a bad mother, much to the dismay of the studio.

In the press, Jayne cooed over everyone from Johnny Ray to Adlai Stevenson. Her perfect man, she said, would be between 48 and 50 with charcoal gray hair and blue eyes. Not quite fitting the bill was Robby Robertson. He was 36 with brown eyes, but he did have charcoal gray hair. He was an airline pilot and she had met him on a plane in April 1955 when he came back to invite her to see his cockpit. How could a girl refuse?

"All the other men, including some pilots, were making these huge pitches," she said. "But when he walked through the plane – he was flying it – I thought, 'I've got to have this.' He's the only person in my whole life I ever gave my phone number to the first time he asked for it."

His job took him out of town four nights a week, so she had plenty of time to fool around. He also had a high-pitched speaking voice. Jayne could not stand anything less than rugged masculinity in men. Robertson later married veteran movie actress Linda Darnell, who died in 1965 while watching one of her own films.

Jayne told the press that she would like to marry a prince, like Grace Kelly. She also included in her wish list Clark Gable,[10] Tyrone Power,[11] Robert Wagner,[12] Robert Stack, Marlon Brando and – of all people – Liberace. Instead of a prince, she found a penniless Hungarian refugee – instead of a mother's boy, she got a muscle man.

One night Jayne went with Jules Styne, the composer and producer of *Rock Hunter*, to the Latin Quarter to see Mae West's show which featured a chorus of muscle men. She was immediately taken in by former Mr Universe, Mickey Hargitay, who was Mae's beau at the time. Despite his poor grasp of English, Jayne was impressed, perhaps because his chest measurement was even bigger than her's.

"Ooooh, he's so gorgeous and so big," she cooed. "And in

bed, he's so great. He has the biggest pectorals this side of the world."

And they had similar interests.

"Like Jayne," said Mickey, "I like to keep my waist down and my chest up."

But on the dance floor things weren't so easy.

"Mickey has a 52-inch chest," Jayne explained. "I measure over 40 inches and we both have short arms. All this makes dancing difficult."

Mae West was not best pleased. After all, blonde sexpot Jayne was already stealing her act. Now she was stealing her man. She gave him hell over that "phoney Hollywood blonde." Jayne retaliated with: "I wonder when was the last time anyone took her picture in a bikini?" The answer to this you will find in the next chapter. Mae West fired Mickey after a press conference in which a fight broke out and Mae got knocked down.

"You can't do this to me, I'm an American institution," she said, from her undignified position on the floor. She dismissed Mickey as "the old Mr Universe, last year's model."

"If I'm the old model, what is she?" was his response.

Jayne was more gracious.

"I have been told to respect my elders," she said. "If I look that good at 64, I'll have no problems whatever." And so Mae lost what she had previously billed as "the most perfectly built man in the world."

Jayne and Mickey flew to Los Angeles where she was due to star in *The Girl Can't Help It* (1956), a movie that aimed to cash in on the new craze for rock'n'roll, featuring Little Richard, Fats Domino, Gene Vincent, Eddie Cochran and The Platters. Only Elvis was a no-show, after his agent, Colonel Tom Parker, priced him out of the picture.

"When I first saw Jayne I thought here was one of the world's great romances – a girl and her bust," said Frank Tashlin, producer-director of *The Girl Can't Help It*. But the studio began to have second thoughts. Paul Mansfield's allegations that she was a bad mother was bad enough, but now that she had a muscle man in tow, when the studio liked their stars young, free and single. Jayne was aghast that Darryl Zanuck[13], head of 20th Century Fox, was prepared to drop her after he had paid $100,000 to buy her out of Broadway.

"So he wants me to date lots of men," Jayne said, "all for publicity."

In a heated meeting at the studio, Jayne agreed to be seen to have lots of romances for the press, during studio hours.

"But," she said, "Mr Hargitay will be in my bed waiting for me at night. And no other man will be. Because I am going to marry Mickey."

The studio thought it had won.

"Career-wise, I know I shouldn't marry," she told a columnist. "But he has the biggest… and I am not going to let go of it." So in the next day's paper Jayne blew the studio away by putting her side of the argument.

"What can a girl receive dating a dozen different men, but ten dozen different mixed-up situations and men who expect a girl to go to bed after a first date," said the bruised innocent. "Champagne for breakfast may sound great, but it gives you a hangover. Men who go with you because you are a sex symbol get draggy. I've been actually miserable when I was fantastically happy. Now I feel clean, wholesome and poised with just one man who loves me."

A studio publicist chided her for talking to the press about "unmentionable things."

"The girl can't help it," quipped a columnist.

It then came out that Mickey was married, so the studio forbade Jayne to live with him. Mickey was forced to take a house nearby. However, *Whisper* magazine reported that Mickey's car was seen parked outside Jayne's house at all hours. One night he went up the steps into Jayne's front porch like a husband sneaking home after a wild night out with the boys.

Despite the studio's displeasure, Jayne continued to get exposure, pulling stunts like visiting her local supermarket in a leopard-skin bikini (and somehow finding a press photographer on hand to snap a picture). At the Screen Publicists Association's Ballyhoo Ball in October 1957, she found herself up against stiff competition for the photographers' attention in the form of Barbara Nichols in a sheer negligee and Mamie Van Doren clad in black fishnet stockings. But Jayne appeared in a tiny leopard-skin bikini and stole the show by being carried around by Mickey dressed in matching trunks. She called him "Peachy," he called her "Oochy." I think I feel ill.

When the statuesque Sophia Loren[14] breezed into town as the next big thing on the back of *Boy on a Dolphin* (1957), Jayne crashed Sophia's exclusive welcome-to-Hollywood party at Romanoff's in one of her most low-cut Emeson gowns. Grabbing a seat next to Sophia, she innocently wiggled her top until her nipples popped out. The newspapers went wild.

Jayne also had a run in with the Gabor sisters at a cocktail party in New York. Zsa Zsa took one look at Jayne and said: "I don't see what you've got that's so devastating."

Jayne took a sip of champagne and replied icily: "Honey, beside me you look like Tony Randall."

She confirmed her star status by playing opposite the Hollywood icon Cary Grant[15] in the far from iconic *Kiss Them For Me* (1957). She celebrated by publicly cavorting in the heart-shaped swimming pool Mickey had built, which was filled with pink champagne for the occasion. There wasn't a parking space for four miles.

"You people like to compare me to Marilyn or that girl – what's her name? – Kim Novak," she said. "Cleavage, of course, helped me a lot to get where I am. I don't know how they got there."

Jayne paid a flying visit to England where, billed as "America's Queen of Sex," she was presented to her counterpart, the Queen of England, at the Royal Command Performance. Mindful that Marilyn Monroe had been criticized for her daring décolletage when she had been presented to the Queen a few years before, Jayne wore a high-necked jersey dress.

"I know experts say a girl can be just as sexy in a high-necked dress, but that's the hard way," she explained. "If handled tastefully, cleavage seldom fails. It's the easiest way to get eyes focused on the right places."

So, her cleavage hidden, Jayne was forced to provide another focus. She wore a split skirt, which provoked a roar from the crowd when she curtseyed.

In her first nine months at Fox, Jayne had clocked up 122,000 lines of press coverage. The visit to Britain added another 2,500 column inches, almost all of them about sex. Newspapers published another 2,500 pictures of her, largely what picture editors refer to, with good reason, as "tit shots." And there was ample room for every one of her $42^1/2$ inches.

"I am not padded," she said. "I wear normal bras, the ones everybody buys." To make her point, she sued a Hollywood clothier who was using her name to sell padded bras and falsies.

Back in the US, with the help of an inheritance, Jayne and Mickey married. They moved into the "Pink Palace" at 101000 Sunset, built by Rudy Vallee for his bride, Fay Webb, the beautiful daughter of the Santa Monica Police Chief, though they never lived there. Pink was not Jayne's favorite color, but she used it as a means to promote herself. I don't think it takes an IQ of 163 to work out why.

She had a pink Cadillac, a pink Jag, pink phones in her house, and she dyed her poodle pink – she said she was never happier than with a dog in her lap, if you take my meaning. When they married, she wore a pink wedding dress and drank pink champagne from a pink slipper, before reading the reviews of the ceremony. Jayne and Mickey eschewed the obvious venue, the ostentatious Rodeo Room of the Beverly Hills Hotel, for the small, all-glass Wayfarers' Chapel overlooking the Pacific Ocean at Palos Verdes. The reverend worried about marrying two divorced people, but was talked round by Jayne, who satisfied him that it would be a quiet, dignified wedding with no publicity. Plans for Jayne to get married in a white satin bikini with Mickey and the congregation similarly attired were dropped. But Jayne had hundreds of pink cards printed up saying "See Jayne Mansfield Married Under Glass" and with the time and date of the ceremony and the address of the chapel. Byron had these dumped from a helicopter over LA while every news outlet and radio station was bombarded with press handouts.

They had been well primed. At her bridal shower, Jayne posed poolside in a sheer yellow negligee, with only the tiniest pair of panties hiding what Mickey was going to enjoy on their wedding night. He got so jealous of the photographers that he swore at them, swooped Jayne up in his arms and carried her inside – giving them all the photograph they had wanted.

"Mickey's so in love with me," Jayne gushed to the reporters. "He's so physically exciting. I am so turned on by him. I wouldn't trade him for all the millionaires or titled men I met in London." Besides, "Mickey is not only powerful and gentle, he's deep ... I wish all girls could be movie stars and all men could look like Mickey." I am beginning to feel that tickling sensation in the back of my throat again.

The pink-lace wedding dress she wore was so tight that she could hardly walk to the altar. At the "no publicity" wedding, she spent an hour posing for photographers. The police had to be called to prevent the glass church shattering from the crush of 10,000 fans; and traffic was held up for miles around. The reverend was indignant about this publicity circus, but he still described Jayne as "a very decent, sweet and spiritual young woman."

Jayne was condemned from another pulpit though, by none other than evangelist Billy Graham.

"This country knows more about Jayne's statistics," he said, "than the Second Commandment." That's the one about graven images. I had to look it up, too.

Jayne responded by saying that she lived up to the Ten Commandments "one hundred per cent" – though she did not go into any detail about where she stood on graven images. She pointed out that she devoted a lot of time to good works, especially to boys' clubs and got more mail from the seven to 12 age group than from the army and navy put together.

"That proves I have more to offer than my figure," she said, though it may also indicate the effect she was having on the hormones of adolescent boys. "I feel there is an overemphasis on sex." But Billy Graham would not be told.

During the wedding, Bob Hope pulled faces at Jayne and someone leaned over to Bill Shiffrin and said: "Don't worry, you're not losing a client, you're gaining an adviser."

The ceremony did not take long – just six minutes. It was followed by a 12-hour booze-fuelled reception that kept the gossip columns buzzing for days. Then the couple headed off for Miami Beach where the city fathers rolled out the red carpet and planned to name a street after her.

The ostentatious wedding brought with it a suit from the former Mrs Hargitay for an increase in child support. "Mickey has aged 15 years since he took up with that woman," she told court reporters. "I don't understand it, the way he keeps trailing her and fawning all over her. That's not the Mickey Hargitay I married."

The newlyweds pleaded poverty and the press ran a picture of them sleeping on the floor of their new home. They were so poor, "even the two servants sleep on the floor," Mickey complained. This prompted the Laguna Beach Police Department to have a whip-round to buy their favorite pin-up a bed.

"What marvelous men, how understanding," said Jayne. "They are really noble to buy me a bed so another man can sleep in it with me. Few men are so generous. That proves they really love me. They care for my comfort."

I think they probably got off on it. Their imaginations must have worked overtime conjuring the delightful visions reflected in the pink mirrored headboard Mickey added to their gift, especially when they found out that the walls of Jayne's bedroom were also mirrored.

The newlyweds then got more exposure, putting their double act on stage at the Tropicana in Las Vegas, where Jayne played a dizzy blonde called Trixie Divoon, while Mickey flexed his massive pectorals.

"Jayne waggles and warbles and does some acrobatic maneuvers with Mickey Hargitay," wrote the *Las Vegas Sun*. The surprising thing is that he did not pop out of his gold lamé underpants. Although Jayne said that her costume had "elegance, charm and dignity," it was, in fact, a skintight, transparent sheath. The only thing that got it past the Legion of Decency were a few strategically placed sequins. "I designed it myself. I wanted to be completely covered," she said. "I don't compete with the nudes here," she added, drawing a distinction between her performance and the other girlie shows in Las Vegas. "They have been through the war, those poor German and French girls in the nude lines. After all of that hardship, they are not as healthy as I am. And I am covered and in good taste." However, as she wiggled about on stage, the sequins quickly became misplaced.

The management complained that Jayne spent most of her days signing autographs poolside in a tiny bikini, effectively giving away during the day what she was supposed to be selling in the evening. Despite the presence of Mickey, so many would-be lovers tried it on that other Las Vegas headliners jealously suggested that she had paid the front desk to have herself paged every couple of minutes, 24/7. But Mickey more than held his own and, before Jayne headed off to England to star in *The Sheriff of Fractured Jaw* (1958), opposite Kenneth More, Robert Morley and Sid James, she was pregnant with his child.

The Swedish press named her "America's Sex and Bosom Queen" and the United Nations invited her to make a week of personal appearances on the Gaza Strip and to visit refugee camps.

Although the studio were not pleased that Jayne was having another baby, it did not slow her down. At the time it was said that she did not need to get out of bed to get publicity. When she went into hospital to have the baby, she proved it was true once again. Within minutes of giving birth, she was on the phone to Louella Parsons extolling the joys of motherhood. If nothing else, she was a pro.

However, Jayne's devotion to Mickey began to get in the way of her career. When the notorious womanizer Darryl Zanuck invited her over for an intimate dinner *à deux*, she took Mickey with her. Then when Zanuck made it clear what his real intentions had been, she trumped him. She had brought Mickey along, she said, because "I thought Mrs Zanuck might be lonely."

Of course, Mickey had to put up with being called "Mr Mansfield." According to Jayne he turned down a movie with Hedy Lamarr[15] to be with her and he was relegated to the role of househusband, looking after Jayne Marie and Jayne's growing number of pets. "Mickey is a hard worker. He takes care of the house, looks after my animals, and satisfies me," said Jayne. "What else can one expect of a man?"

Jayne continued to lose her clothes by accident. She was kidnapped one night in her negligee, burst out of a kimono in Tokyo, split a pair of riding breeches at the Palm Springs Desert Rodeo, caused a three-car pile-up when she posed in a bikini on Copacabana beach, and had her dress torn off her by the crowds at the Rio carnival. And in her autobiography, actress Liz Renay said that she saw Mickey and Jayne balling at one of her parties.

At the West Berlin Film Festival, she burst out of the top of her low-cut dress and the actress Laya Raki burst out of the bottom of hers. At Cannes it was still Jayne who was billed as "the girl with a thousand curves, and every one of them enticing" after posing for the pressmen on the Croisette. Her nude publicity shots often showed her pubic hair – which was very advanced for that time.

Her career then seemed to hit the skids. Playing a stripper in an art-house movie called *Playgirl After Dark* (also released as *Too Hot to Handle* (1960)), the censors objected to her revealing gowns and an animator had to be hired to paint sequins over Jayne's naked nipples. Then she filmed a topless bedroom scene in *It Takes a Thief* (1960), released in the UK as *The Challenge*. Both were disasters. Jayne began drinking too much, taking uppers and fooling around, though she managed to get it together enough to perform a bedroom scene on-stage at the Dunes in Las Vegas, in a show called "House of Love." There were more sequins that shifted and shoulder straps that burst.

"The skill which went into the design of Miss Mansfield's bras probably impressed the audience the most," wrote columnist Colin McKinlay.

On the back of this, she released an album called, tastefully enough, "Jayne Mansfield Busts Up Las Vegas." There was also literally a bust up in Las Vegas. Jayne was "having fun" with an agent and a young chorus boy when Mickey and the agent's wife walked in on them. Jayne simply told Mickey to get lost. When she heard later that the agent's divorce settlement amounted to $100,000, Jayne was ecstatic, boasting that no other star was worth $100,000 for an hour in bed.

*

Mickey hung on in there and managed to get himself the lead part in *The Loves of Hercules* (1960), with Jayne co-starring. During the filming, Jayne got pregnant again. After she had had the baby, she sent her old maternity dresses off to a young woman who was pregnant and had no idea where the father of her baby was. In her covering letter, Jayne said that she was outraged by the way "some men are" and explained that "I could have been in the same situation a couple of times."

Jayne followed this with another tawdry toga part in *It Happened in Athens* (1962). There were now four flops on her resumé, so she did the only thing a girl could do under the circumstances – she announced her divorce. Appearing for the press in tight-fitting gold lamé pants and a white sweater, scooped to the navel, she rehearsed a number of sexy and sultry poses for the cameramen, while telling the reporter, "I am sorry that our marriage has ended. It is due to irreconcilable differences." Then, blowing farewell kisses in Mickey's direction, she swept into the Pink Palace.

In fact, the "irreconcilable differences" were a young Italian. One night at Frascatti's, they had disappeared out into the parking lot. Raymond Strait found them in the back of her Cadillac, both partially undressed. His muscular young body was wedged between her legs and her dress was ripped, said Strait. He was slapping her around and she was hysterical. When Strait opened the car door the Italian stallion made off and Strait had to drive Jayne home with "one of her million-dollar breasts exposed."

Forty-eight hours after the press announcement that they were splitting, Mickey and Jayne were reunited with Jayne giving both Louella Parsons and her arch-rival Hedda Hopper "exclusives" on the reconciliation. Then they flew off to Rome where she was to film *Panic Button* (1964) with Maurice Chevalier.[16]

In Rome, she immediately fell for the producer Enrico Bomba, who Jayne imagined would play Carlo Ponti to her

Sophia Loren.[17] She wrote home to Strait:"Nobody ever turned me on that way. We made love on a couch in my dressing room. I knew after him I would never be satisfied with Mickey again."

Upset, Mickey reminded her that their luggage was marked with a crest bearing the initials "J and M" – "meaning Jayne and Mickey," Mickey said.

"Shut your fucking mouth," said Jayne. "That doesn't mean Jayne and Mickey, it means Jayne Mansfield. Now get out of here."

She and Bomba were seen out together on the town in Rome. Doing the twist, which was all the rage, her dress fell down twice in the same evening. This delighted the paparazzi, whose pictures appeared under the banner headline: "Striptease by Jayne Mansfield."

"It wasn't striptease," she protested. "I just happened to be wearing a very loose-fitting dress. Occasionally it came apart. I tried to hold my dress together."

Unable to stop Jayne twisting, Mickey returned to Los Angeles. But without her husband's jealousy fuelling her passion, she seemed to cool towards Bomba. Returning to the US, she was seen crying on the plane. Back in LA, she began spending her nights picking up young men in the discotheques of Sunset Strip – having fun for the first time in her life, she said. It was reported that Mickey beat up a hairdresser and a 21-year-old UCLA student, both of whom Jayne was openly dating. She was photographed crying and distraught after an altercation in a nightclub between Mickey and a young stud.

A close friend named Nancy Bacon remembered driving Jayne home from a party. Jayne stripped naked in the car. Stopped at traffic lights on Sunset Boulevard, she waved her bra out of the window and yelled to the guy in the next car:

"Hey, you want to make it with me? I'm Jayne Mansfield."

Fortunately it was someone Nancy knew.

"It's Griff, Jaynie," she said.

"You mean the one with the big cock?" said Jayne.

"The same."

"Hey, Griff," yelled Jayne. "You want to fuck?"

Then came the news of the death of Marilyn Monroe at the age of 36. This really shook Jayne. There had been so many parallels between their lives – not least their involvement with President Kennedy.[18] Jayne was a close friend of the actor Peter Lawford,[19] who was Kennedy's brother-in-law and the man who arranged JFK's affair with Marilyn. According to Ray Strait, Jayne would get calls from a mysterious "Mr J" when the president was vacationing in Malibu or Palm Springs. A black limousine would then whisk her away to a secret rendezvous. Strait said he recognized the voice on the phone. Then, one time, Jayne received a phonecall while they were drinking in the Polo Lounge. The conversation became heated and Jayne suddenly yelled: "Look, you'll only be president for eight years at the most. I'll be a movie star forever," and she slammed down the phone.

Jayne announced that she was going to marry Bomba the following April. Mickey agreed to a Mexican divorce. Meanwhile, Jayne was seen out with Brazilian bandleader Ivan Morice, though, when questioned, she said: "I have never heard of such a man."

Jayne and Bomba spent Christmas together in New York. But Jayne suddenly walked out and returned to Mickey. It seems that Bomba, a Catholic, could not divorce. "And I would never be his mistress," Jayne told May Mann. "I always get married to the man I love. In that way, I am very old fashioned." There seems to have been a lot of this type of old-fashioned girl around in Hollywood.

The press were waiting at LAX. Mickey was there too and he told them: "I have never been with another woman since we were first married." But Jayne refused to kiss him for the cameras. She told the press that Bomba was "the most wonderful man in the world, with a beautiful soul and a wonderful heart," but "a woman has a right to change her mind and I am a woman." There were no arguments about that.

She got Mickey a small part in her next movie *Promises, Promises* (1964). It was the first movie in which she was going to do a nude scene. Although the set was supposed to be closed, the sound stage was as busy as Grand Central Station. As well as every scene shifter, electrician, carpenter and focus puller who could find the slightest excuse to be there, there were photographers from *Playboy*. Slightly tipsy, Jayne bared it all to the camera. At least one of the spectators thought that this revelation was historic. He grabbed the comb that Jayne's hairdresser Marc Britton had used to tease up her bleached-blonde pubic hair, saying that he was going to donate it to the Smithsonian. *Playboy*'s June 1963, featuring Jayne's spread, was a sell-out worldwide. Publisher Hugh Hefner found himself charged with obscenity. Nude pictures appeared of Jayne rolling about on her bed in the Pink Palace, apparently masturbating. She insisted that the only thing that was rude was the caption. Meanwhile *Promises, Promises* was banned in Cleveland where a judge ruled that her performance was "lewd."

"There are two scenes in which I appear nude for a brief moment," she said coyly. "And the only objections I have heard are that they were not long enough."

The photo session in the Pink Palace rocked her marriage. Although she could roll around naked in the presence of 18 men – all, it seems, vital to the success of the shoot – when Mickey entered the room, she covered up. Halfway through, she was caught on the phone speaking Italian. And after the filming of *Promises, Promises* was over, Jayne went off to Palm Springs with producer Tommy Noonan.

Nudity was to be her new thing. She incorporated a "satire on strip" into her stage act and went on tour. She would also wander among the audience in a dress that seemed to have been sprayed on. One night she sat on the lap of an older gentleman. As his eyes zeroed in on her magnificent bosom, his face went red and Jayne fished out her left breast and thrust it into the man's mouth.

Another old man, possibly with a weak heart, asked her to get off.

"But I'm a sex symbol," she cooed.

Jayne was already becoming a gay icon. Why? Perhaps because the overemphasis on her milky paps attracted those with a mother fixation. Perhaps because she confirmed that gay men were right to be afraid of voracious female sexuality – any lover risked being suffocated by those tits. Perhaps because she came on like a drag act. I don't know. If you want psychology, go read some other book.

Separating again from Mickey, Jayne started spreading her assets around more widely. One night in Atlanta, Strait said that she threatened to go out on the street to find someone unless he slept with her. She was lonesome. Although Strait was a friend of Mickey's, he said: "When a beautiful woman like Jayne Mansfield offers herself to you, the niceties of protocol easily dissipate with the night."

Later in Atlanta, nightclub singer Nelson Sardelli sashayed into the club where she was performing. Jayne spotted him and said to Strait: "Get me that Italian." After one drink with Sardelli, she told Strait: "That is going to be the father of my bambino. My beautiful little Italian baby I've always wanted."

She went on tour with Sardelli. He was shocked that all such a big star had in her repertoire was a strip act. Jayne had other worries. One afternoon she called Strait into the bathroom. She was standing naked, scrutinizing the black stubble in her pubic area.

"Last night some guy yelled that I had black roots, the son of a bitch," she complained. "Get me the razor, Cooz." She called Strait "Cooz" – slang for the vulva. He handed it to her.

"No, don't give it to me," she said. "I might cut myself. I want you to do it."

Strait, taken aback, was just getting down to work when Sardelli returned to the suite.

"What the hell is going on?" he wanted to know.

"Oh, nothing," said Jayne. "The Cooz is just shaving my snatch."

Sardelli took this in good part.

"I want to marry him, Cooz," said Jayne. "He's Mr Right for me." She wanted the wedding to be in St Peter's in Rome. Seriously.

Sardelli was pictured kissing Jayne's ankles and sipping champagne from her high-heeled shoes. Mickey's Mexican divorce came through, but by then the affair cooled and she started seeing Bomba again.

"Nelson Sardelli?" she said. "We had such a beautiful romance. He was young and virile and sexy and wildly in love, and sweet. I really believed we would be a big thing – but then I heard he was married all along. I called him long distance to ask him the truth, but Nelson didn't even return my call."

However, Jayne was carrying another baby. So, after recording the album "Jayne Mansfield Meets Shakespeare and Tchaikovsky" on which she lisps the Bard's love poetry to the accompaniment of strings – all in the best possible taste – she skedaddled back to Mickey on the grounds that, although they were divorced in Mexico, they were still married in California. To seal the deal, she brought his mama over from Budapest and installed her in the Pink Palace.

The press began to speculate on whose baby it was: Mickey's? Sardelli's? Bomba's?...

"I pray that Mickey won't hear too much of this," Jayne told reporters, ensuring he would.

Once the baby was born, Jayne was out on the town again.

"Jayne Mansfield starred in a couple of sizzling scenes on different nights at the Whiskey-a-Go-Go," one paper said. "Jayne got terribly affectionate while teaching Richard Boone some sexy rock'n'roll dances. Mrs Boone flipped furiously. Another night Jayne strolled in with a handsome young UCLA student who didn't even resemble her husband, Mickey Hargitay." This was 21-year-old Jim Goldstein with whom Jayne was having a "friendly affair." Jayne also liked to strip off in Hollywood clubs. It set the tills along Sunset Strip ringing. Although the owners tried to stop her when she got down to her bra and panties, which was as far as the law allowed, Jayne insisted on going all the way.

Having made the front covers of 500 magazines worldwide – "Look, I am even very big in Istanbul," she said – the world's press voted her "The World's No. 1 Sex Symbol." She, naturally, protested.

"I'm a mother first, and a good mother," she said. "Then I'm an actress. And finally a sex symbol." Yeah, well keep your clothes on, girl. Besides, she said, she was giving up being a sex symbol and becoming a Catholic. God was calling her to become "a fine dramatic actress." She felt an Oscar in the offing. However, she said she did not feel the need to pare down her sex life for the sake of her new religion. She had seen how men and women in Italy fooled around.

"I love sex," she said. "Since it is one of God's gifts to everyone, there should be no shame in saying so. It gives me a glow of happiness all day… When it is honest, it enchants, it captivates, it amuses, it fascinates. It arouses within you the desire to protect and shelter."

There were more scuffles in nightclubs. Mickey complained about Jayne's penchant for "latin-lover types." They split up once more, but this time on intellectual grounds.

"I'm a girl with an IQ of 163, and I need someone with whom I have an intellectual attachment," she explained. "For instance, I wanted to study Italian and French literature and Mickey couldn't care less about things like that."

With Marilyn dead, Jayne expected to inherit her mantle, but this was the 1960s and the busty, bleached blonde look had gone out of fashion. Jayne headed back to Rome to film *Primitive Love* (1964), in an attempt to revive her movie career. There she delighted two waiters when she did a private striptease for them in her suite. She then assuaged the passions she had aroused – on the proviso that they would tell the newspapers about their good fortune. They did, but no one believed them. So Jayne restaged the whole event, this time with the paparazzi present.

It was rumored that Jayne made two hardcore porn movies in Rome, but they have never surfaced and it is possible that Jayne started the rumor herself in a desperate attempt to gain news coverage. Nevertheless, God was telling her to give up being a sex symbol, so pursuant to her ambition to become "a fine dramatic actress," she opened at the Yonkers Playhouse in *Bus Stop*, playing Cherie, the part Marilyn Monroe had made famous onscreen. The director, Matt Cimber, boasted a IQ of 165. It was a match made in heaven. They were intellectually compatible. But Jayne did not take to him straight away.

"I was really turned off when I met him the first day," she said. "By the second day he had turned me on." Soon they were seen out dancing together.

When *Bus Stop* ended, Jayne went on tour playing the Monroe role in *Gentlemen Prefer Blondes*. Mickey was outraged when she decided to take Cimber on tour with her, especially as he was a latin-lover type. His real name was Tomaso Vitale Ottaviano and he was, indeed, an Italian. The inevitable confrontation followed. Cimber had his arm broken. Asked by the press what she intended to do about Mickey, Jayne said she was going to "kick him around until he gets lost. Know anybody who wants a washed-up Mae West chorus boy?"

Jayne said she was in love like never before.

"After Matt kissed me, I didn't believe I had ever been kissed before," she said. "I felt like I had been a virgin all my life."

Meanwhile she was constantly on the phone to Nelson Sardelli.

By this time Jayne was lost in bourbon and uppers. She laid on a disastrous party for the Beatles at the Whiskey-a-Go-Go in LA, which broke up after George Harrison sloshed a glass of scotch in Mamie Van Doren's face. Afterwards Paul McCartney called her "an old bag" in his 1965 *Playboy* interview. Having run nude spreads of her every year since she first stripped off in 1955, *Playboy* dropped her. She could not take the hint. In her next movie, *Spree* (1967), Jayne did a strip act while singing "Promise Her Anything." She got a standing ovation for the dress – or rather, undress – rehearsal.

"It's wonderful," she said. "I've always thought it's the role of women to spread sex and sunshine in the lives of men. This was the perfect way to do it." However, she did not seem to be spreading sunshine in Cimber's life. Those close to her began to notice bruises on her body. May Mann asked her about them in front of Cimber.

"Matt beats me, but I love it," she replied, cuddling closer to her lover man.

They married.

"It's just too, too wonderful, almost unbelievable, but it's all real. It's not a dream and I won't wake up sobbing on my pillow," Jayne said, three seconds after exchanging vows with her 28-year-old director.

This time the wedding was a private affair, largely because one of Jayne's eyes was swollen shut. One newspaper called it "the marriage least likely to succeed," but, for Jayne, it was a career move.

"He will be to me what Carlo Ponti is to Sophia Loren," she said. "He'll manage me and direct me in the more serious things I'll do now in the Fellini/ De Sica vein."

It was all getting very pretentious. When the Russian magazine *Soviet Culture* called her "a Philistine with a huge bust who has no need of acting talent," with Cimber's coaching she responded: "I must remind the Russians that it was their great stage figure, Konstantin Stanislavsky, who said an actor's greatest success in the final analysis is his audience appeal." She undeniably appealed. She then volunteered to star in Chekhov's *The Seagull* at the Moscow Arts Theater – presumably as the seagull itself. Cimber later admitted that Jayne had never heard of Chekhov or *The Seagull*, but she did know how to make babies, and a few months later she presented Cimber with a son. She began to fancy herself as a modern-day Isadora Duncan,[20] having a child for each of her great love affairs.

After the birth, Jayne condemned other glamour queens for having abortions, pointing out that her predecessors, international sex symbols Jean Harlow,[21] Mae West (see the next chapter) and Marilyn Monroe had all "forfeited their divine, God-given right to bear children... They were afraid, I guess, that it would detract from their 'image.' My children enhance mine." They enhanced the size of her tits at least.

She also had the recipe for domestic bliss:

"Once a man's happy in the bedroom, the kitchen and the living room are a cinch," she said. "Any intelligent girl knows that." She just could not keep that IQ in check.

However, things were far from blissful at home. According to Cimber, Jayne Marie acted bartender while Jayne's two sons were employed to massage oil into her naked body.

After more movie flops and bit parts, Jayne ended up on Broadway again in *The Rabbit Habit*. Then she went on a singing tour of South America where, according to testimony given at her divorce hearing, she enjoyed "an astonishingly energetic and varied sexual trip." She returned with VD and a 20-year-old handyman named Douglas Olivares, who spoke no English.

"He won't be 21 for two-and-a-half months yet, so we have to be very, very careful," she said. "I am his first love."

Cimber was not surprised. Jayne had always been free with her favors.

"If she didn't dig you she wouldn't have anything to do with you," he said. "And if she did, you could be the bus boy and you'd score." But then she dug at least half the population. According to Greg Bautzer, "She never met a man she didn't like."

Douglas had protected Jayne in Venezuela. She feared that someone might bribe the bell-boy to put something in her drink and that she would wake up having been raped, so he volunteered to sleep outside her door.

"You can't imagine what men, even highly respectable men, will do to try to go to bed with me," she said. "My sex symbol image has gotten out of hand. I seem to be an international challenge." Soon Jayne figured that she would be just as safe if Doug slept inside the door.

But when she took him back to the States with her, there was a problem. Sixteen-year-old Jayne Marie, bursting with hormones, also fancied Douglas. Jayne had already seduced several of her daughter's boyfriends, so Jayne Marie decided to get her own back. One day, when Jayne was having a massage by the pool, she went over to him in full view of mommy dearest. In an imitation of her mother's provocative screen image, she put her arms around his neck, looked deep into his eyes and drew her body tantalizingly toward his. Like a rabbit caught in the headlights, he tried not to react, but the bulge in his swimming trunks could not be concealed.

Jayne leapt up to separate them.

"I'm shocked," she said to Jayne Marie.

"You're shocked!" said Jayne Marie. "You're standing there naked mother. I'm shocked. He's my age. You're too old for him."

Jayne Marie was packed off to her grandmother in Dallas who was instructed to have the girl examined by a doctor to see if she was pregnant. Meanwhile Jayne began dating heartthrob crooner-turned-actor Bobby Darin.

"Douglas is very jealous," she said. "But he has to know that I can't confine myself to any one man right now."

Sick of the whole business, Cimber ran off with his son.

"I was determined to get Tony away from her before she had him massaging her body in her drunken stupors like she was doing with Miklos and Zoltan" – her two sons to Mickey. "I wanted my son to have a chance to grow up and be a normal human being," he said.

He tried to discuss the matter sensibly with her, but when he arrived at the Pink Palace he found her sitting on Douglas's lap, drunk.

Determined to get Tony back, Jayne hired lawyer Sam Brody and immediately fell for him, though he was a short, balding, fast-talking Jew – hardly her type. Brody sent Douglas back to Caracas with a couple of hundred dollars in his pocket to prevent him being subpoenaed as a hostile witness, and set about trying to prove Cimber was a fag. Meanwhile, Brody himself was petitioned for divorce. His wife claimed he had committed "adultery with 40 women in ten years of marriage" and named Jayne as the 41st. This was, perhaps, understandable. Thirty-six-year-old Mrs Brody was wheelchair-bound with multiple sclerosis.

"Miss Mansfield has telephoned me on a number of occasions and has very freely discussed with me her current love affair with my husband," she told a reporter.

Jayne retorted that accusations of adultery were "unfounded and ridiculous. Mr Brody is my friend as well as my barrister. He's just a friend, and I have many friends." She struck back by suing Mrs Brody and Matt Cimber for harassment.

Brody also pushed Bobby Darin out of her life. He was a jealous man and beat her savagely. But again, she did not seem to mind.

"An orgasm with Sam is like being in heaven and hell at the same time," she said.

Brody quickly took complete control of her affairs. She told May Mann that he had all her business papers and would not give them back. "He has a terrible picture he'll blackmail me with too," she said.

According to May Mann, the attention Jayne's beauty drew drove Brody insane with jealousy. He said he would kill her rather than lose her and he had a sinister plan to hold on to her.

"Sam got me drunk one night and took pictures of me naked with a strange man I never saw before or since," Jayne said. "I never knew until Sam showed me the pictures. He says he will give them to the judge and release them to the press and the scandal magazines to prove I am an unfit mother. He'll take my children away from me."

Emotionally Jayne began to unravel. Even in front of her mother, she would whip her tits out. And when she objected, Jayne banned her from the house. She turned up at custody hearings smelling like a brewery and wearing miniskirts and skimpy tops, revealing bruises on her arms and legs. The judge was sympathetic, but while she was trying to prove that she was a good mother, her second son, Zoltan, was mauled by a lion on a visit to the zoo and lost his spleen.

She moved into a suite in the hospital where she dropped LSD and was seen wandering about naked with Brody's legal partner Melvin Belli (the two of them, Belli and Brody, had defended Jack Ruby, the slayer of Lee Harvey Oswald, the accused assassin of John F. Kennedy[22]). When he heard about the incident with Belli, Brody had a characteristic fit of jealousy.

Jayne was then banned from the San Francisco Film Festival for wearing a sideless dress that left her nearly naked.

"Sideless is better than topless, isn't it?" she told the press. In your case, Jayne, no it isn't. Apparently Brody had trashed her other clothes in a rage.

Brody was so jealous he even closed his law office.

"I'm afraid to let Jayne out of my sight, or some other man will steal her away," he explained.

But still, in public, she continued to play the sex goddess. When asked how many lovers she had, she said: "With me, it's like Catherine the Great of Russia. My heart cannot rest one hour without love."

In San Francisco, Brody and Jayne met Anton La Vey, the founder of the First Church of Satan. According to Eric Ericson's book, *The World, the Flesh, the Devil*, "Jayne attended the Friday rituals of the innermost circles for an act of worship performed over the naked body of a woman as altar. Though it cannot be known for certain, it would be very much in character if she volunteered herself as the altar."

Brody grew angry and jealous, and La Vey, it is said, cursed him. Apparently he told Brody that he would die violently in a car accident within a year and, if she did not get away from him, Jayne would suffer the same fate.

Jayne was up for the title role in *Fanny Hill* (1965), but Brody failed to clinch the deal. Instead she went on a cut-price tour. In England, she was sacked for turning up for shows late, in an "unfit condition" and with bruises on her legs which made it "impossible for her to wear the miniskirts called for in performances."

She talked of her forthcoming marriage to Brody, but that did not stop her consoling herself with affairs. Her name was linked to Engelbert Humperdinck's – quite a linking – and she had an unbridled affair with "mod" club owner Allan Welles.

"I love Englishmen and Allan in particular," she told the press. She also talked of becoming a British citizen and living there so her kids could have British accents.

Predictably, Welles and Brody came to blows at Jane's leaving party and a guest who tried to separate them found himself sitting in a huge chocolate cake inscribed: "Farewell Jayne, Love Allan."

In Ireland, Jayne was mobbed at the airport, but condemned from the pulpit for a Sunday booking in Tralee. The Dean of Kerry wrote a statement to be read out at all Sunday Masses. It said: "This woman boasts that New York critics said of her, 'She sold sex better than any performer in the world.' I appeal to the men and women, to the boys and girls of Tralee to dissociate themselves from this attempt to besmirch the name of our town for the sake of filthy gain."

She responded by saying she was a good Catholic, but admitted: "I am a sexy entertainer."

The good people of Ireland boycotted her shows. She did little better in Paris, Germany and Stockholm. In Canada, she held a mock trial as a publicity stunt, when her dog was accused of sexual misconduct. The story ran in the Canadian papers under the headline: "Doggone It Jayne."

Back in LA, she played Hollywood goddess one last time with a cameo role in Gene Kelly's *A Guide for the Married Man* (1967). However, a series of car accidents – nine in as many months – began to get Jayne and Brody spooked. Then Jayne Marie turned up at the office of Cimber's lawyers covered in bruises. She claimed that Brody had beaten her on her mother's instructions. Jayne countered that her daughter had been beaten because she took drugs and hid a naked boy in her closet, who she tried to palm off on to her mother, assuming Jayne would find him attractive. As a result, Jayne was not allowed to take Tony with her when she went to Biloxi, Mississippi to perform at Gus Stevens' Supper Club. But she did take Miklos, Zoltan and her new daughter, Mariska. In New Orleans they were picked up by Ronnie Harrison, a 19-year-old employee of the club. Brody very firmly sat between Jayne and Harrison in the front of the Buick, while the kids sat in the back. Heading down Route 90 at around 2.30am, they were momentarily blinded by the light from the headlights reflecting off the mist from a mosquito-spraying machine. The car ran into a trailer, taking its roof off. The kids, who were lying down in the back, were saved. But Brody and Harrison were flung from the car and killed, and Jayne was decapitated. And Anton LaVey said, I told you so.

Even though it was now headless, the battle over Jayne's beautiful body was not yet over. Matt Cimber wanted to ship her back to LA and have her buried like a Hollywood goddess at Forest Lawn. Mickey contended that, as their Mexican divorce was invalid, he was still legally her husband, and whisked her north to Argyle, Pennsylvania. She was buried under a heart-shaped headstone in a private ceremony attended by so many spectators that 3,000 policemen had to link arms to restrain the crowd. There was also a memorial service in Hollywood, where one eulogist remarked that she had died as she had lived – on page one.

The California courts then found that Matt Cimber was the legal husband. He went on to make *Butterfly* in 1979 with Pia Zadora and a series of porno movies with such tasteful titles as *The Sensuous Woman*, *He and She*, *Man and Wife*, *Delirium* and *Black African Sexual Power*. Mickey stuck to what he knew and opened a topless bar. It failed, presumably because none of the staff could match up to Jayne. The fate of Paul Mansfield went unrecorded.

Of Paul, Jayne herself said: "He was too young to know what I was doing. He was a nice wholesome boy, but not for me." And of Mickey Hargitay and Matt Cimber, she said: "It would have been less costly to hire them than to marry them."

The Pink Palace was bought in turn by Ringo Starr, Mama Cass Eliot and Engelbert Humperdinck. Starr and Humperdinck tried to repaint it but gave up when, each time, the original pink kept showing through.

I must apologize to the reader if this chapter seems a bit long, but then Jayne Mansfield was a big girl.

2

Goodness Had Nothing
To Do With It

Jayne Mansfield was the last of the pneumatic blondes. She stole Mae West's boyfriend and, indeed, her whole act. For Mae was the first of the pneumatic blondes.

Like Jayne, Mae first found fame on Broadway. Born Mary Jane West in Brooklyn in the hot summer of 1893, she was known from the start as May. She swapped the last letter for an "e" because she did not like to see the droppy tail on the "y" – or anything else. Her mother, Matilda or Tillie, was a Bavarian immigrant, whose stunning, hourglass figure led to a brief career as a corset model. Her marriage at 18 to cigar-chomping, prizefighter John "Battlin' Jack" West was not a happy one, and Mae was determined from the start not to fall into the same trap. Tillie claimed to be a relative of Harry Thaw, the wealthy wastrel husband of beautiful model Evelyn Nesbit[1] who caused a sensation in 1906 when he killed his wife's lover, the architect Stanford White. Battlin' Jack called her "Champagne Till." She was Jewish. Battlin' Jack was an Irish Catholic, but he had a cousin who was a Ziegfeld girl. As a child, Mae liked to hang out in the gym where her father trained. She always loved muscle men and, later, would cruise the gyms of New York looking for sexual partners.

She also had a thing about grizzly bears. In her book *On Sex, Health and ESP*, she relates that, as a child, she had a vivid, yet comforting, dream where she had sex with a bear, which gave her her first orgasm. She also boasted about being sexually precocious.

"I first heard about sex when I was nine, through a medical book," she said. "It'd have been better had I not seen that book until I was 12 or 13."

She claimed to have seduced a handsome young teacher at school at the age of 12. Her deflowering took place, she said, on the classroom floor after school was out. On another occasion, Mae said she first had sex at the age of 13, before she had her first period, with a 21-year-old actor. He had walked her home after an amateur show and made love to her on the stairs in the vestibule of her house with her fur coat wrapped around her. This had an effect: at the amateur shows Mae began singing "novelty" – that is, saucy – songs with lashings of innuendo, the way only a girl with some experience knew how.

"Even as a little girl, Mae's character songs were risqué," said her older sister Beverly. She now rammed home the point by wiggling her hips suggestively.

Her mother encouraged her.

"My mother thought I was the greatest thing on earth," Mae said, "and she liked me to play with the boys."

Mae considered friendship with girls a waste of time and she liked the fact that testosterone-fueled gangs of youths fought over her. One young man presented himself to her battered and bleeding and was duly rewarded with milady's favors. Throughout her life she loved to have sex with boxers on the night they fought, and often did so. She also liked being the only female at all-male parties where games included catch-as-catch-can kissing and more.

"I'd play with their – umm, you know," she said.

When her father found out about this, he went wild, but her mother told him to leave her alone.

"Mae's different. She's not like other girls," she said.

Indeed she was not, thanks to Momma.

"Mother pointed out other married couples to me," Mae said. "She showed me how their lives were wasted. She didn't nag me. She never did. But when I saw her face, how unhappy she was, I couldn't get round that. I knew I'd be unhappy, too."

Her first steady boyfriend was the pianist Joe Schenck. She also claimed to have slept with the trumpet player and the drummer in his band – though she later said that the affair with Joe Schenck "wasn't a sex love affair." But by then she was claiming not to have had sex until she was married. She said she had done nothing more than "neck and hug and kiss and play with each other," but she was already an aficionado of the condom (made in those days from thick unyielding rubber). She herself practiced the "sponge method." She would soak a sponge with warm water and insert it into her vagina before intercourse, a method she recommended to Fanny Brice. In her 20s she used condoms because she was afraid of VD. Later she would have her lovers tested before she slept with them.

Another of her school teachers was Ned Wayburn, who moonlighted as an agent. He later represented Marion Davies[2] and Broadway star Marilyn Miller, and got Mae jobs in the "pony lines" dancing on Broadway. She also branched out into burlesque as a fan dancer. Gypsy Rose Lee made fan dancing balletic and tasteful. But according to one eyewitness, in the hands of Mae West, it was both revealing and suggestive:

"The fan was big and red and she shook her bare body behind it. Her body was simply saturated with powder. When she shook herself, the powder would fly all over the stage and down onto us in the front rows."

The audience stamped their feet, yelled for more and got it. She liked to give them their money's worth – and an eyeful.

Later she denied appearing in burlesque, but Mae was proud of her body. "She'd drop her clothes at the drop of a hat," recalled Hollywood photographer George Hurrell. Marlene

Dietrich's[3] daughter, Maria Riva, remembered seeing her nonchalantly lifting one milky white breast out of its whalebone cage. The ghostwriter Stephen Longstreet recalled turning up on the first day of work on her autobiography, *Goodness Had Nothing To Do With It*, at her Ravenswood apartment to be greeted by a life-size nude statue of Mae in the foyer and Mae herself in a negligee.

"Feel these," she said, thrusting out her breasts, "they're hard as rocks."

One thing about a fan act was that the men backstage saw more of the performer than those in the audience. Mae attracted the attention of a comedian named William Hogan and they started a double act. Then a 19-year-old dancer named Frank Wallace, probably at Momma's behest, took Mae on the road. They did a ragtime dance act borrowed directly from the African-Americans Mae lived among in Brooklyn.

"It was the black man's sound and we copied it because it was the greatest," she said.

This passionate, uninhibited form of dancing caused a sensation – and was condemned by both church elders and social reformers, always a good sign. *Variety* called their act "pretty close to the line" – of good taste, presumably – and remarked that Mae West "may develop." Something was certainly developing off-stage and Frank soon wanted to marry Mae, but Momma was against it.

"She explained that I was young and full of emotions," said Mae. "She said that was natural, but that I could use them to help me be very famous or I could waste them on the first man. It was an awful struggle."

Mae was happy just to sleep with Frank. Once the first flush of passion had passed, she went out with any attractive man who asked. She became the scandal of the company. However, a singer named Etta Woods, an older woman on the bill who kept a maternal eye on Mae, advised her to marry just in case she got pregnant. So on the morning of April 11, 1911 in

Milwaukee she married Frank. At 17 she was under age, so she lied about it.

"I did it because I was scared," said Mae. "Getting pregnant was a real disgrace in those days."

She married Frank on the proviso that he would never tell her mother.

"I had a beautiful close relationship with my mother and I never wanted to do anything to hurt her," she said.

He never did. Later, she said that she suspected some connivance between Frank and Etta Woods. He had bought her a dress to use her influence.

Now with the thin veneer of respectability a marriage licence lent, she went back to her old ways, going out to clubs every night to pick up men. She treated Frank so cruelly that the company turned against her. The manager chided her that she was behaving disgracefully. After that she tried to be more discreet.

Fearful that her mother might find out about the marriage, Mae insisted that they live apart when they returned to Brooklyn. Frank was relieved. Soon after, he left town on a 40-week tour which she claimed to have arranged. Rumors about her marriage eventually did get back to Momma. When she confronted Mae, Mae denied everything. Momma never did find out.

Mae was also frightened that marriage might harm her career. Managers steered clear of married actresses on the grounds that audiences liked their temptresses to be available. And Mae was available. She would have carried the secret to her grave if an officious clerk in the Milwaukee County Register of Deeds had not unearthed the licence in 1935. Marriage simply did not suit Mae.

"I was born to be a solo act," she said, "on- and off-stage."

She was famous for her quips about marriage.

"Marriage is a great institution," she said. "But who wants to live in an institution?"

In *I'm No Angel* (1933) Mae's character, Tira, is asked: "I don't suppose you believe in marriage?" She replies: "Only as a last resort."

But there was one good thing about being married to Frank. Now she could not marry anyone else.

Mae was not big on love either, except in the physical sense.

"I saw what it did to other people when they loved another person the way I loved myself, and I didn't want that problem," she said.

With Frank out of the way, Mae headed for Broadway, stealing the show at the Folies Bergère in red harem trousers and a bare midriff. She also came to the attention of Lorenz Ziegfeld,[4] famous for his casting couch. Mae was sacked from her next show after a riot which, *Variety* speculated, she instigated.

With two well-built male dancers, she went on the road as "Mae West and the Girard Brothers." She sang songs like "Cuddle Up and Cling to Me," "Isn't She a Brazen Thing," and "It's An Awful Easy Way to Make a Living" while "making interesting movements in a seated position" and shaking her body "in devastating slow motion." In New Haven, students from Yale University trashed the theater, getting her sacked, but headlines such as "Her Wiggles Cost Mae West Her Job" made her a name. New York was now at her feet, partly because she had taken the precaution of sleeping with her agent, Frank Bohm.

"I learned that one man was about the same as another," she said. "I learned to take 'em for what they were – stepping stones. If a man can help me… Men can be a lot of help to a girl in more ways than one."

Bohm took out a big ad in *Variety* pitching "Mae West, 'The Scintillating Singing Comedienne,' Late of Ziegfeld's Moulin Rouge" while Mae posed in a nurse's uniform for the cover of the sheet music for "Good Night, Nurse" – another song she incorporated into her act. However, critics complained that she could not sing, that her humor was too crude for vaudeville and perhaps she should go back to burlesque, and that she did not fill out her costumes. In her 20s she had a boyish figure. The magnificent 43¼-inch bust she later boasted had not arrived yet. But she was already a gay icon. She gravitated toward effeminate vaudevillians. She took them home with her.

"Mother loved them because they'd fix her hair and her hats," she said.

In turn, her little posse of poofs loved her and copied her every move.

"It's easy for them to imitate me," she said, "'cause the gestures are exaggerated, flamboyant, sexy."

Mae stole much of her screen persona from the camp drag act of Bert Savoy, who played an overdressed hussy with a penchant for large hats at the Greenwich Village Follies. Savoy died as freakishly as he had lived. During a storm he shook his fist at the heavens and cursed "Miss God" – and was struck down by a bolt of lightning in true Biblical style.

Mae began to get into trouble with the censor, who even made her cut the word "chicken" – meaning "pretty young girl" – from her act, presumably because the chicken was ripe for plucking. Sorry. But somehow she managed to get away with a song called "And Then," which is a step-by-step account of a hot date. It went:

First we had a talk – and then,
We sat by the fire – and then,
It was getting warm and so,
We drew our chairs away from the fireside glow.
Mother said: "Good night" – and then,
We turned down the light – and then,
We cuddled close together,
And we talked about the weather,
Yes we did (Yes we did) – not then.

Steamy stuff, I am sure you will agree. But let's compose ourselves... "And Then" was a big hit. One critic in Detroit said that it hardly seemed possible that Miss West was allowed to sing such a song. She was "plainly, vulgar," but he noted that "the audience howled for more."

A pattern emerged: censors cut, critics chided, managements restrained her, but audiences loved every moment. By now Mae was writing her own material. One of her songs was called "I Want a Cave Man," which she performed draped in a leopard skin. The final couplet went:

I learned to bill and coo from a turtle dove
And a grizzly bear taught me how to hug.

There's that bear again. And it did more than hug.

Meanwhile Mae was having one of the *grandes amours* of her life with an Italian accordion player named Guido Deiro. This was unusual for Mae. Although practically every straight man she met in the theater made a play for her, she usually kept her lovers outside the stage door – "bankers, brokers, or merchant chiefs, or maybe just a push-face truck driver with oversize muscles." Guido had "a terrific personality and sensual Latin charm." She was bowled over.

"The sex thing was terrific with this guy," she said. "I wanted to do it morning, noon and night, and that's all I wanted to do." Even the dreaded "L" word almost came into play. It was "very deep, hitting on all the emotions. You can't get too hot over anybody unless there's something that goes along with the sex act, can you?"

In his memoirs, Nils Granlund, publicist for the Loew circuit, said that Mae and Guido got married. If they did they were both bigamists. Deiro was married to Julia Tatro who, according to *Variety*, had accused him of statutory rape but had withdrawn the charges when he married her in 1911. When he took up with Mae, he stopped sending her money and was arrested on a fugitive warrant when they were playing the Chicago Palace.

After two years of a high-intensity relationship, Mae came down with influenza in Hamilton, Ontario, and Guido did completely the wrong thing – he took care of her and her feelings quickly waned. Men should be men, she thought, sex objects who were only judged by their ability to transport her erotically. If she had wanted a nurse she would have hired one.

Momma was against the relationship, too, fearing it might damage Mae's career.

"She was right, and when I realized that, I got rid of him," she said. "It almost killed the poor guy. He started to drink. He would come around to our house looking for me, and my mother would say she didn't know where I was. He would cry and cry and say he was going to kill himself."

Mae fell straight into the arms of heavyweight boxing champion James J. Corbett, after seeing him fighting in the ring. This affair lasted, on and off, for several years. She also seems to have been having an affair with Joseph M. Schenck[5] (not to be confused with the pianist Joe Schenck, who schencked her early), the booking manager of the Loew circuit, who later became head of Columbia Pictures. Deiro smashed Schenck's desk in rage and Schenck arranged a booking for her safely out of town in Chicago. There she found a man she called "Rex" in her autobiography who she described as a character out of F. Scott Fitzgerald. He was a handsome, wealthy, socialite and he wanted to marry her.

"I felt that Mother would be happy with a marriage of this kind," she said, but decided that Rex was too domineering and would have wanted her to give up show business if they wed.

She had a fling with an opera singer too, but, after hours, she liked to hang out in African-American clubs on South State Streets where men had scars on their faces – something she always liked. There Mae learned dances such as the bump, the jelly roll and the "shakin' the shimmy" – that is, chemise – or "shimmy sha-wobble." She introduced the shimmy into her act. Shaking her top until the sequins flew off, she brought the house down. The dance had been declared "vile" by the Chicago Morals Commission and the management complained. But the applause was so thunderous Mae was not to be stopped.

Mae West also sang jazz at a time when the music had only recently emerged from Storyville, the red-light district of New Orleans, and the word still meant "screw" in the sexual sense. She anticipated the new "flapper" look, wore short skirts, discarded her corset and let her breasts swing free. According to an ad in *Variety*, she also became a "comedy gymnast" which must have been quite a sight.

Back in Brooklyn, Momma had changed her mind about marriage. She hired a lawyer named James A. Timony, who she thought might be a suitable consort for her daughter, though some said he was a gangster and he certainly had underground connections. She almost got her wish. A former football player, he was stocky, florid, round-faced and not conventionally handsome. Mae fell for him immediately. She liked "guys with busted noses and cauliflower ears and scrambled pans, especially … guys with faces that ain't handsome, but strong. Guess it's because I been in shows so much with handsome faces around me … that I go for the ugly ones who got something more than a face."

They became lovers, and Timony began divorce proceedings on her behalf, perhaps because he intended to marry her himself. He told Frank Wallace that the divorce had been granted, but no record of it has ever been found.

A successful "business man" and criminal lawyer who defended gangsters, hit men and bootleggers, he wore flashy clothes and drove Mae around in expensive cars. At Timony's behest, she left Brooklyn and set up home in an apartment in Jersey City. Jim did not live there, but was a regular visitor. She said that they did not live together because she did not want to be branded "immoral." In fact, she wanted her freedom. Timony had a jealous streak and was not a man to be crossed. She had many other lovers at the time and continued to accept diamonds from other men as tokens of their esteem.

Timony took over as Mae's business manager and began to mould her image as a sex goddess. He used his contacts in the press to plant titillating stories about Mae, but when the sports editor of the *New York World* wanted a picture of her in a bathing suit, she refused. Except for her fan dancing days and one frightening foray into miniskirts in the 1960s, Mae always kept her legs covered.

"If a gal has her legs covered she can concentrate on her hips and bust," she said, "and so can a fella."

As the movies, or "flickers," became regular features in vaudeville theaters, Mae began to incorporate movie characters into her act. One of them was Jazzimova, a shimmying take-off of the Russian Hollywood goddess Alla Nazimova[6] – the women, the publicity handouts said, from whom no man was safe. In fact, she was a rampant lesbian, complete with her own harem. Her all-girl orgies in Hollywood were legendary.

One night the heavyweight champion Jack Dempsey turned up in Mae's dressing room, fresh from breaking Al Jolson's jaw. Before Dempsey's championship fight with Georges Carpentier – the first million-dollar fight – Jolson's manager had organized a publicity stunt with Jolson and the champion sparring for a few rounds – not his best decision.

Mae described the Manassa Mauler as "a shy, young guy with muscle appeal." He liked her shimmy and made her an offer she couldn't refuse. He was going to make a movie with Pathé called *Daredevil Jack*. Her screen test was a love scene, which she felt he was approaching with a certain lack of ardor.

"Look, Champ, I won't break," she urged. "Hold me tighter."

Dempsey's manager arranged a pre-shoot vaudeville tour for Mae and the Champ, but Timony forced her to withdraw, knowing that she would never be able to keep her hands off the boxer. Instead, she put a new act together, which required a pianist. Harry Richman,[7] later a lover of Clara Bow,[8] turned up to audition.

"She did not speak. She did not even smile," he recalled. "Instead her eyes swept me from head to foot, a long, appraising stare."

Then she spoke.

"Are you versatile?" she asked.

He said he was. Very.

Timony warned him to keep his hands off Mae, but later he boasted to Milton Berle and other cronies in the Friars Club that they made love often, once to the accompaniment of a baseball game on the radio. Apparently Mae said she needed something to help her concentrate and music made her drowsy. However, she may have been fantasizing about all those hunky baseball players. In her play *The Ruby Ring*, the protagonist, Gloria, says that her ideal man is a combination of Jack Dempsey, the tenor John McCormack and the legendary baseball player Babe Ruth.

Years later, as guest of honor at a testimonial dinner for Richman at the Friars Club, Mae said: "You always had a great touch … even on the piano."

Their act included a scene called "The Gladiator," where Mae played an empress who wanted to hire a gladiator dressed in a squirrel skin – she wanted him to show some skin. The audience howled its appreciation, but there were also howls of complaint. Mae was summoned to see the general manager of the theater chain, Edward F.Albee, to run through her act in the front office. One of the lines that had been blue-pencilled was: "If you don't like my peaches, why do you shake my tree?" Mae performed it with such wide-eyed innocence, that Mr Albee declared that not even a priest could be offended by it. That night she performed the same line with a bit of a wiggle and brought the house down. And she added a lot more besides.

The front of house manager objected, but there was nothing he could do.

Her next show was called, brazenly, *The Ginger Box Revue*. At nights she would hang out in clubs in Harlem and, daringly for the time, incorporated master-and-slave material ino her act that hinted at sex across the color line – which was totally taboo in America back then.

On tour, Mae fell for a Texas-based reporter for *Variety* named Bud Burmester. Later in *I'm No Angel*, she sang "No One Does It Like That Dallas Man," which included the lines "He's a wild horse trainer/With a special whip." The song fell foul of the Hays Office. She also risked bigamy charges when he took out a marriage licence, but it remained unsigned and there is no record of a ceremony taking place. Afterward she talked about the affair, but never mentioned Burmester by name.

"His name is sort of sacred," she said.

After two months, Mae realized, once again, that she could not have both marriage and a career and she knew she had to give him up. She resorted to her old panacea – going out with other men. But she said, "I wouldn't go out with a man who didn't remind me of him."

Later she looked back on the break-up without remorse.

"If I hadn't made such a big success, I'd regret it," she said. "If I hadn't got to the top, I'd be sorry. But as it is, you can't do two things in life. Mother was right."

After love there was *Sex* – the play that really put Mae West on the map. In it, she played a prostitute who makes it from a rundown brothel in Montreal to the poshest part of Westchester County. Mae claimed she got the idea after someone pointed out to her a prostitute down by the docks who was servicing sailors at 50 cents a trick. Mae did not mind the woman selling herself. What she did not like was the woman selling herself cheap. So, she said, she wrote a play about a hooker who rises in the world.

In fact, Timony had bought a play for Mae for $300, which she then spiced up with the help of another collaborator. Anyway, *Sex* was the beginning of a writing career that would earn her the epithet of "America's Oscar Wilde" – not without good cause, which was all the more remarkable as her reading did not extend beyond *Variety*.

When the play was rejected by professional producers, Timony decided that they should put it on themselves. He set about raising the money and opened the ironically named Morals Production Company. One of its principal backers was the British-born underworld boss Owney "the Killer" Madden, owner of the Cotton Club – a man who had been shot at so often even the police called him "Clay Pigeon." Needless to say, Mae was one of Owney's lovers.

"So sweet," she said of him, "and so vicious."

In *Belle of the Nineties*, she sang: "He's a bad man, but he treats me so good."

The play was guaranteed to offend. Kisses abounded. Mae flaunted her body, stopping just short of nudity. The notices were universally awful. The play was condemned for "depravity" and portraying "not sex but lust – stark, naked lust." It was "disgraceful," "nasty," "vicious," "disgusting" and "infantile." It was, of course, a huge hit.

Having found a rich seam, Mae quickly set about writing another play. This time the theme was gay and transvestite men and it was to be called *The Drag*. Homosexuality had been hinted at in plays before, but this time Mae was determined that no one would miss the point.

"I've got 17 real-life fairies on stage," she boasted.

A week after *The Drag* opened in Bridgeport, Connecticut, New York's mayor, Jimmy Walker, a broadminded playboy who enjoyed the company of good-looking actresses and hoodlums such as Owney Madden, went off on one of his frequent junkets to Florida and the acting mayor, Joseph V. "Holly Joe" McKee seized his chance to close down *Sex* as part of his campaign to clean up Broadway. Mae West, Jim Timony, the director C. William Morganstern and 21 members of the cast – still in costume and in full make-up – were taken to the local precinct and charged with "corrupting the morals of youth, or others."

It was just what Mae had been hoping for. After a run of 41 weeks, box office receipts were falling off and the play needed some publicity. Mae appeared before a West Side night court and was bailed for $1,000. Minor players paid $500. The reason for the bust had nothing to do with *Sex*. Rather, it seems that McKee and others feared that if *The Drag* made it to the Great White Way it would cause a riot.

Even though Mae and the company had been busted, the State Supreme Court granted them an injunction to allow performances to run. Demand for tickets soared and the run extended. With Daly's still full of *Sex*, *The Drag* was blocked from moving into town. No other theatre would take it and efforts to stage *The Drag* in New York had to be abandoned.

The *Sex* trial began on February 15, 1927. The police inspector called as a witness for the prosecution was too embarrassed to repeat the coarse language used in the play so, when he read from the text, he bowdlerized it as he went. Titters ran through the court.

More laughs erupted when one of the arresting officers, when asked about the visibility of Mae West's navel during a seductive belly-dancing scene, testified that "something in her middle moved from east to west." Mae said that her *danse du ventre* was nothing more than a body-building exercise her father had taught her as a child, but she did her case no good when she repeated her line: "The audience wants dirt and I give them dirt." This was an obscenity trial after all.

In her autobiography, *Goodness Had Nothing To Do With It*, Mae said that it was her belly dance and the testimony concerning the movement of her navel that put her in jail.

"It was on this moron stutter alone that a conviction was secured," she wrote.

The ten-day sentence came as something of a shock, but Mae brazened it out. She told the press that she would spend the time writing more scripts. Prison would be, she said, "the making of me." She was taken to the Jefferson Market Prison, then to the Welfare Island Women's Workhouse. Told to strip and put on a prison uniform, she said: "What? I thought this was a respectable place."

Among the other inmates she was a celebrity. They would reel off lines from *Sex*, to show they had seen the show. She got on well with the other women, especially the prostitutes.

"If I hadn't started writing plays," she said, "I think I could have gone the other way and wasted my whole mentality and life on sex."

Warden Schleth also gave her one day's remission for good behavior. But then it was Mae who said: "When I'm good, I'm very, very good, but when I'm bad, I'm better."

Schleth certainly took a shine to her. "Mae West is a fine woman and a great character," he said on her release.

Mae said that, in jail, she had gathered material for a dozen plays, which was true. Her next production was *The Wicked Age*, about the bathing beauty contests that were sweeping the country. While it may have provided the opportunity to have lots of pretty young women in bathing suits on stage, it was not as controversial as *Sex* or *The Drag*. Mae and Timony had been warned that, if convicted again, they would face much stiffer sentences. Also keeping her in the public eye was the Grand Street Follies which featured a Mae West character in prison stripes who seduced every man in sight. The sketch was called "Stars in Stripes." Mae really was a star now.

Mae was now a little plump to play an 18-year-old bathing belle and was easily upstaged by younger, slimmer models. So next she played the eponymous Diamond Lil – "one of the finest women ever to walk the streets" – a play that returned to the theme of white slavery and prostitution, but put them safely back in the 1890s.

In *Diamond Lil*, Mae West had finally found her stage persona, which she later took to Hollywood. She even made her own corsets, buying regular whalebone corsets, turning them upside down and trimming them off. The script provided plenty of opportunities to show them off.

"I prefer to talk to men when I am not dressed," runs one line.

The British photographer Cecil Beaton[9] saw the show and described Mae as "a huge, blowsy, lustful blonde" who made him realize that the current craze for thinness was "unsatisfactory sexually." He said: "This fat, pink, creamy, fleshy creature looked so lewd and naturally, healthily, amorously, lustful that in one scene where a Spanish lover mauled her, felt her breasts and buttocks, one had to cross one's legs and scream hysterically with laughter."

It was a financial and critical success, with *The New York Times* calling it "almost Elizabethan." The only problem she had with the authorities was in Detroit when she distributed a mock-up of the *Police Gazette* as a publicity handout, featuring her picture with a caption comparing her to Madame du Barry, the legendary mistress of Louis XV.

She began playing the part off-stage as well as on. In her dressing room, she would recline on a gilded bed in the shape of a swan, which had belonged to the 1890s actress Amelia Bingham.

"Diamond Lil – I'm her and she's me," she said, "and in my modest way I consider her a classic. Like Hamlet, sort of, but funnier."

On-stage, Lil admits to being a "scarlet woman in a setting of white ice" and says: "When I die, I'm goin' to burn in hell." Indeed, she had no wish to go to heaven "where there's a lot o' people lookin' like they was brung up on a dill pickle." The God she was interested in was of the Greek Adonis type. She particularly did not like Moses and his Ten Commandments, especially the one about adultery, which she equated with sex unsanctified by marriage.

"What was the harm in skin to skin if you had a lot of fun and nobody got cut?" said Lil.

But even for Mae, life was a little more complicated than that. In her next play, *Pleasure Man*, a man who is having an affair with a married woman dies after being castrated by a young man whose sister he had also seduced. Mae, it is thought, was taking dramatic revenge on a Frenchman named Dinjo. They had been having a passionate affair, but he then turned out to be married.

"We met any place we could – dressing rooms, elevators, the back seat of his car or my limousine," she said. "A kind of hit-and-run affair, you might say." And she bragged about their stamina as lovers. "One Saturday night we were at it 'til four the next afternoon. A dozen rubber things. Twenty-two times. I was sorta tired."

When Dinjo's wife showed up, Mae dropped him. After all, it was not as if he was the only man in her life. At the same time, as well as Timony, she managed to make room for an unnamed boxer and a green-eyed hood who was sadly shot before their dalliance was consummated. And she was having an affair with George Raft. Later a Broadway hoofer and a movie star, Raft was a hoodlum who shot craps with Lucky Luciano and Al Capone and shared Owney Madden's taste for white ties, black shirts and gray fedora's pulled down over one eye. Mae also claimed to have spent a night with Al Capone, though her shows still had to pay protection money when she visited Chicago. Of Raft's love life, we shall learn more later.

At the try-outs, the critics dismissed *Pleasure Man* as "filth," though *Variety*'s reviewer urged: "Go early. Some of the lines can't last."

Hundreds were turned away on the first night, with the audience hoping to see some police action. They were not disappointed. During the drag party in the third act, the cops burst on to the stage with their truncheons drawn. The actors were carted off to night court still in their frocks. Some were spat on by the crowd outside.

On the second night, the show was raided again. This time Mae was arrested, too. Once more Mae bailed out the cast and she underwrote the defence costs of the other 56 people who were charged with putting on an "indecent" performance, which "paraded and glorified sexual perversion."

This time she appeared in court dressed in black and cut out the wisecracks, but she had to stuff a handkerchief in her mouth to stop herself laughing when one of the transvestites was called on to perform some of the "indecent" songs, which included "Officer, May I Pat Your Horse" and "I'm the Queen of the Beaches, (pronounced "bitches"). A team of German acrobats had to perform their act which the police maintained was "suggestive," but the star of the show was Police Captain James J. Coy who demonstrated a snake act that he found particularly objectionable. The defendants were acquitted among gales of laughter.

Meanwhile Wall Street had crashed. Mae was unaffected as her only investments were in diamonds and her shows.

"I didn't invest in something I couldn't sit and watch," she said.

The crash soon hit the takings of *Diamond Lil*, but Hollywood was putting out feelers. The inaptly named Colonel Jason Joy from the Hays Office, the movie censors, went to see the show at the request of Universal Studios to see if it was suitable material for a movie. According to Joy, it was unacceptable due to its "vulgar dramatic situations and the highly censorable dialogue." *Diamond Lil* joined the lists of productions considered unsuitable for film adaptation (which already included *Sex* and *Pleasure Man*) under the 1930 Production Code which specified that sex outside marriage was "impure" and consequently "must not be the subject of comedy or farce or treated as the material for laughter."

Mae then tried her hand at writing a novel about mixed-race sex. Initially entitled *Babe Gordon*, later *The Constant Sinner*, an ironic reference to Somerset Maugham's *The Constant Wife*. It was set in Harlem, which Mae called "the Paris of the Western Hemisphere" – though she had never been to Paris – and "a museum of occult sex, a sensual oasis in the sterile desert of white civilization" where you could see "the bodies of almost naked colored women, wriggling and squirming" and peep shows that featured "the antics of blacks, and blacks and whites, in tortured postures of cruel … soul-naked passion." She had numerous African-American lovers, including the heavyweight champion Jack Johnson, the former owner of the Cotton Club who stayed on as manager under Madden, whose predilection for white women was well known. When *Jet* magazine asked if she had ever seen Johnson in the ring, she answered: "No, but he came up to see me, several times."

She also had affairs with the featherweight Chalky Wright, who later became her chauffeur, and the middleweight William "Gorilla" Jones, who she managed. She loved athletes, both black and white, because, like her "they don't smoke, don't drink, and understand the importance of keeping their bodies in top working order," she said. After all, "a hard man is good to find."

She was often seen in the Jungle Alley on 133rd Street with Johnny Carey, one of the club's owners, and was one of the few whites allowed into the clubs along 140th Street which featured transvestite floor shows. She was also close to Duke Ellington, who played at the Cotton Club and appeared in some of her movies. He was a great womanizer and it is hard to imagine that he did not take the opportunity to come up and give her a seeing to sometime.

The idea for the novel came from the black actor Howard Merling. "Negroes had become the rage of society," he said. "Their vices charmed thrill-seekers." He provided detailed notes on the clubs, the clip joints and the fly characters –

along with much of the jive-talking dialogue. When the publisher expressed an interest in publishing it, she greeted him in an expensive negligee and invited him to join her on the bed. When he recommended certain cuts, she said: "Don't try to make me respectable. My public expects me to be bad."

The protagonist, Babe Gordon, is the wife of a white boxer named Bearcat Delaney. She takes a black lover, Money Johnson, a pimp and bookmaker with a magnificent body that both black and white women drool over. When Delaney quits the ring, Babe makes a living peddling morphine, heroin and coke, while indulging herself in opium with Money Johnson. One night, wealthy aristocrat Wayne Baldwin sees Money Johnson caressing "her cream, white throat." He finds the thought of "Babe's white body and Johnson's black body ... terrible, yet it gives him a sensual thrill."

Baldwin and Babe become lovers. Johnson goes to jail. When he is released, Babe and Johnson indulge in a drug-fuelled lovers' spree in a Harlem tenement. Baldwin bursts in, shoots Johnson, frames Babe's husband Bearcat Delaney, then hires him an expensive lawyer who gets him off by convincing the all-white jury that he "upheld the best traditions of the white race [and] the honor of its womanhood" by protecting her from assault by "a low, lustful, black beast." Babe gives Bearcat, anonymously, the money to go back into training. Meanwhile, she heads off to Paris with Baldwin, with no intention of being faithful to him. "Even if she decided to marry Baldwin, that would not prevent her having a lover, or lovers, on the side. That is Babe Gordon." As for Baldwin: "He cannot avoid thinking of Babe's white body and Johnson's black body, darkness mating with dawn..."

It is hard to imagine a more deliciously scandalous tale, especially for 1930. Mae obviously put a lot of herself into the book.

The book went through five editions and sold 94,000 copies. The stage version starred Greek-American actor George

Givot playing the part of Money Johnson in black face. Mae constantly invited him to her dressing room and made love to him both with, and without, make-up.

The first night audiences loved the play, but the critics once again dismissed it as "filth," though they were quite taken with the scene in which she crossed the dimly-lit stage in a thin chiffon gown and changed into a robe.

"I wasn't really nude," she said, merely adding to the titillation.

After a run of just eight weeks, she tried to take it on the road with a black actor in the lead role. But in Washington, DC, then an officially segregated city, it closed after two performances, when the district attorney threatened to jail the entire cast.

Former lover George Raft rode to the rescue, getting her a part in his latest movie *Night After Night* (1932). She signed with Paramount and Mae, Timony and sister Beverly jumped the Pullman for LA. Although she had never made a movie, or even seen a talkie being made, Mae made it clear from the outset that she was not some star-struck ingénue from the sticks.

"I'm not a little girl from a little town making good in a big town," she told the press at the Union Pacific railroad station. "I'm a big girl from a big town making good in a little town" – though she said she had never been an ounce over 119 pounds, "the rest is padding." She very publicly despised "bean poles." What men wanted, she said, were curves.

She also claimed to be 31 – she was 39. Movie magazines took this with a pinch of salt and *Movie Classics* said: "Hollywood wonders if she will be a sensation in Hollywood, where sex is a trademark and not a novelty."

Mae immediately went on the offensive.

"I can't say that I think much of your screen stars for sex appeal," she said. "The flat figure does not attract men and, in spite of styles, the figure of Venus will always be the world's love ideal."

Greta Garbo[10] was "cold – terribly cold. I can't imagine a man going crazy over her." Clara Bow[11] and Pola Negri[12] came in for some praise, but they were no rivals as their careers had been killed by the talkies. And Clark Gable,[13] the reigning king of Hollywood, "has as much sex appeal as a dish of leftover potato salad," Mae told *Screenplay* magazine, which commented that she seemed "entirely unconscious of the fact that she had just tossed a bomb into a million boudoirs."

Mae and Beverly moved into an apartment in the Ravenswood district. Timony took the adjacent flat. This complied with the morality clause in her contract. It also gave her the space to play around, though naturally she denied it. On Tuesdays, Wednesdays and Fridays she went to the fights – and it wasn't for the boxing. She said she would rather hang out with the "pugs" who gave her kicks than go to Hollywood parties.

In *Night After Night*, Mae had a minor, though key, part as a prostitute. But she sat at home earning $5,000 a week – even offering to repay it and buy herself out of the deal – until she got script approval. She then wrote her own dialogue and always gave herself the punch line.

"She stole everything but the camera," said George Raft.

A shot showing her sashaying up the stairs was too hot to get past the Hays Office, but in her first appearance on-screen she was surrounded by adoring men. Bedecked with diamonds, she checks her fur in a nightclub.

"Goodness, what lovely diamonds," gasps the hat-check girl.

"Goodness had nothing to do with it," replies Mae.

That line, loaded with innuendo, made Mae West an instant movie star.

Mae later explained that she had to write one-liners for her movies because they wouldn't let her sit on men's laps – "and I've been on more laps than a napkin."

She got away with other great lines in *Night After Night*. In one scene, she is asked: "Do you believe in love at first sight."

"I don't know," she replies, "but it sure saves an awful lot of time."

Cinema audiences had never heard anything like this. There had been strict censorship since the advent of talkies.

"There was a terrific explosion," said *Photoplay*. "A bomb had gone off in a cream-puff factory… Blonde, buxom, rowdy Mae – slithering across the screen in a spangled, sausage-skin gown! Yanking our eyes from George Raft and Connie Cummings" – supposedly the stars of the movie – "I dare say that the theater has never sent Hollywood a more fascinating, spectacular and useful figure than bounding Mae West, queen of the big-hearted, bad girls of show business."

To celebrate, Mae commissioned a nude portrait of herself being ogled by a monkey, which hung in her living room in Ravenswood. She also installed a huge bed with a brocade canopy. Above it was a mirrored ceiling. When asked what it was for, she said: "I like to see how I am doing." Adding: "I do my best work in bed."

The movie theaters were doing good business with *Night After Night* and clamored for another Mae West movie, this time with her in the starring role. Paramount was practically bankrupt and had no choice but to comply. Filming her stage hit *Diamond Lil* was the obvious solution. The studio's research department said that modern audiences did not want movies set in the 1890s, so it would have to be updated. What's more, *Diamond Lil* was on the Hays Office banned list. So they changed the title to *She Done Him Wrong* (1933) and watered down the plot. Mae responded by adding more suggestive one-liners, and collared Cary Grant[14] as her co-star, after she saw him walking across the Paramount lot in white uniform. "If he can talk, I'll take him," she said – a line echoed by George Axelrod 25 years later.

She was informed that he was playing Lieutenant Pinkerton in *Madame Butterfly*, hence the uniform.

"I don't care if he's making *Little Nell*," she said. His repressed upper-class Britishness was the perfect foil for her uninhibited, low-class American vulgarity.

"I learned everything from her," Cary Grant said. "Well, no, not everything."

He also said: "I have never worked with anyone who had so much 'she' as Miss West," and that she was "extremely helpful" during the love scenes.

Mae insisted on rehearsing the cast so that they were word perfect when shooting started and shot the movie in sequence. This was unheard of in those days, but she brought it in ahead of schedule and at a cost of just $200,000, more than half of which was spent on the woman Sherman called "America's wet dream."

Despite lines like – "When women go wrong, men go right after them," and "Haven't you ever met a man that can make you happy?" "Sure, lots of times" – the Hays Office's only comment was that it was a "hearty, if somewhat rowdy amusement."

Just weeks after Paramount had gone into receivership, *She Done Him Wrong* began breaking box office records across the country. It grossed over two million dollars in the first three months. "The Whole Country's Going 'West'" pronounced the headlines. *She Done Him Wrong* saved Paramount from bankruptcy, as well as helping out a number of old prizefighters and former lovers she hired for bit parts. It was just the tonic that the Depression-ridden country needed. It put the movie industry back on its feet, reopened closed theaters and changed the way people looked. Suddenly, after the flat-chested flappers, breasts and hips were back in fashion. Without Mae West there would have been no Jayne Mansfield, Marilyn Monroe[15] or any of the other pneumatic blondes. When she was told that Marilyn had been dubbed the new Mae West, she said: "Well, if you want imitation…" She later conceded that, of her imitators, Marilyn was the best. The rest

– and this presumably includes Jayne Mansfield – just had "big boobs."

She Done Him Wrong gave Mae the line: "Why don't you come up sometimes, see me?" This was translated in the popular imagination to: "Come up and see me sometime." The misquoted line became so popular that she used it in her next movie and adopted it as her catch-phrase.

However, there were those who were against her. She answered her critics in an article entitled "Who Says I'm A Bad Woman."

"Almost every woman (although she won't admit it) would like to be a scarlet adventuress – without any of the penalties, of course… Why should I be attacked as a menace to movie morals because I present sex on the screen as it really is? Is it not far less dangerous to do it that way than to give it a phonily romantic and mysterious label and a fancy foreign accent? … Love is a woman's stock-in-trade and she always ought to be overstocked."

The National Legion of Decency was formed six months after the opening of *She Done Him Wrong* and the Hays Office were on the case when she "displayed her wares again" in her next movie *I'm No Angel* (1933), the story of a girl who climbs to the top of the ladder, as Mae put it, "wrong by wrong." Lines such as "she'd give the old biological urge to a Civil War veteran" and "the only girl who satisfied more patrons than Chesterfields" had to go; black musicians were replaced by white ones; and the line "that's all, boys, now you can go home and beat your wives" was cut. But she was allowed to say of a young male acrobat, with feeling, "I'm not going to hurt him, I only want to feel his muscles." The song "They Call Me Sister Honky-Tonk" also got by – again, presumably, because of the ignorance of the censor, if that is not a tautology.

She even got away with the oft-repeated lines: "It's not the men in my life, it's the life in my men" and "When I'm good, I'm very, very good, but when I'm bad, I'm better." But the line that stole the picture was the simple instruction to her maid: "Beulah, peel me a grape."

During filming, Mae would disappear into her dressing room for an hour at a time with Boris Petroff. She had also become friends with Marlene Dietrich.[16] As Mae was Paramount's number one star and Marlene their number two they had adjoining dressing rooms and often compared costumes.

"You give 'em the bottom and I give 'em the top," Mae said to the leggy Marlene. She also said if she only had to appeal to men and not to women as well "all I'd have to do is take them out."

What effect this had on the bisexual Marlene we don't know, but Mae told a story about an encounter with a "Hollywood glamour girl." She was in her dressing room washing her hair when a woman entered. She felt a towel being wrapped around her head and hands rubbing it. When she turned around she found the woman in question staring at her and wearing nothing but a flimsy robe.

"You had better button up, dearie," Mae said. "You're going to catch cold."

It is widely believed that this "glamour girl" was Dietrich.

If there was no room for women lovers in her life, there were plenty of men, notably the welterweight boxer John Indrisano, who lived with her for some time, and her bodyguard Mike Mazurki. Mae started having a bodyguard after she was robbed at gunpoint, and it was to her bodyguard that she first used the line, for real: "Is that a gun in your pocket, or are you just pleased to see me?" She also hinted of an affair with Gary Cooper.[17]

She had a one-night stand with the boxer Max Baer. After they had made love, she noticed that he was standing at the bedroom window waving at someone in the street and asked what he was doing. He explained that he had had a bet with a friend that he could bed her and the wave was the signal that he had won. Mae burst out laughing. She had a thing about boxers. At one time she claimed to own part of the "Brown Bomber" – heavyweight champion Joe Louis. She didn't say which part.

In his autobiography, Joe Louis mentions that he was in a Buick showroom when a very important, good-looking white woman with blonde hair came in. The sales assistant left him viewing a car while he went over to talk to her. When he came back, he informed Louis that she had bought the car for him. He gave her two ringside tickets for his fight with Max Baer and she bought him a new Buick every Christmas for the next five years. He said she taught him the meaning of the word discretion and they were "discreet" on many occasions during those five years.

In another passage he says: "I'd see a big, beautiful movie star and wonder how she is in bed. We would find out very easily. These were just one night stands. But we both knew how to keep it cool."

There was also the exotically named Watson "Gorilla" Jones, another African-American whose mother was Mae's maid, and Speedy Dado, a Mexican bantamweight. Timony was on the rota, too. By now he had accepted that neither he nor any other man could completely satisfy Mae sexually. However, he protected his own interests, kept an eye on her, and tried to limit the amount of time she spent with any one man – though she never spent an entire night with a man, out of her own preference.

Mae complained that Timony had turned into her mother, preventing her from falling in love with anyone. But she liked being spied on. It gave her an illicit thrill. It also made her secretive about her affairs, which kept her out of the scandal sheets. However, the *Hollywood Confidential* eventually ran an exposé on "the Empress of Sex," taking her to task for her preference for "bonze boxers" and other "tan warriors."

While denying the details – and suing the *Confidential* – Mae flaunted her voracious sexuality in the press.

"I would swap all my diamonds for a good night's sleep," she told one reporter.

Still, she had to defend herself against the charge of loose morals.

"Loose morals," she said. "Why, after four years of Depression, you'd be lucky if you could find a loose nickel."

Privately, she accompanied Timony to Mass every morning, but she never accepted the Church's views on sex. And she denied having introduced sex into the movies.

"When were pictures ever without sex?" she said. "Have we forgotten the vampish writhings of Theda Bara[18] and Valeska Suratt? Sex is considered the strongest instinct next to self-preservation. When will humans lose interest in it?"

However, the Catholic Church led the attack on Mae West.

"I have never done anything to harm the Catholic Church," she told the local priest, "why does the Catholic Church start preaching against me."

He replied that men of all ages – young, old and middle aged – had come to him to confess "sins committed as a consequence of spending an evening at a Mae West movie."

She conceded proudly: "I stimulated sex all right."

She promised to tone it down, but critics implored her to keep it "spicy, straight from the shoulder, without compromise or one eye on the Woman's Club." Her sexual frankness was praised by everyone from Will Rogers to F. Scott Fitzgerald. D.W. Griffith ranked her alongside President Roosevelt[19] in prestige and the British author Hugh Walpole said: "Only Charlie Chaplin and Mae West in Hollywood dare to directly attack with their mockery the fraying morals and manners of a dreary world."

Nevertheless the studio tried to clean up her image. They signed her up for a radio drive promoting the local Community Chest.

"Love your neighbor," Mae urged, "and by that I don't mean his wife."

Mae could not help herself. In articles about her home, it was revealed that two new nude statues had been added. She always compared her figure to that of the Venus de Milo. "But," she said, "I've got it on her. I've got two arms and I know how to use them. Besides, I ain't marble."

When *I'm No Angel* came out, the NRA – President Roosevelt's[20] National Recovery Administration – was the topic of the day.

"NRA stands for No Regrets After," said Mae. As part of the New Deal, she said there should be a special code for single women. Their new deal should involve "jewelry, motor cars, flowers, furs and candy."

Mae had fans in high places, but there was a growing campaign to clean up Hollywood. "Film Morals – or Else," ran a headline in *Variety*. Italy's fascist dictator Benito Mussolini[21] cited her as an example of "virile, healthy womanhood" in his campaign for larger families. But in America, the film censors were talking about the "Mae West Menace." This gave the studio publicist Arthur Mayer a problem closer to home. His poster showing Mae's huge swelling bosom with the line "Hitting the High Spots of Lusty Entertainment" earned him a reprimand from Paramount boss Adolf Zukor for using such a "dirty word as lusty." Mayer explained that the word lusty was innocent. It came from the German *lustig* which meant merry or jolly.

Zukor, a family man, said: "Look, Mr Mayer. I don't need your Harvard education. When I look at that dame's tits, I know what lusty means."

At the premier of *I'm No Angel*, the radio commentator said: "Here's the lady herself. The star of stars makes her appearance. Every feminine eye follows her dazzling gown, every masculine eye … oh, well."

I'm No Angel was a huge success, breaking records in grosses and attendance. In Boston, police reserves had to be called out to control the crowds. *Variety* called Mae West the "biggest conversation provoking, free-speech grabber and all-round box office bet in the country. She's as hot an issue as Hitler."[22] Her secret, according to the *Chicago Tribune* was that "she really and truly doesn't give a damn."

Even so, she was famous the world over. Invited to the Jubilee of King George V,[23] she declined with a telegram saying: "Sorry George." She did not decline a similar invitation from 1934's Mr America, the well-oiled Richard Du Bois. When he visited her ranch, he was told to bring along 11 of his muscular colleagues and Mae entertained all 12 of them, well, royally.

She was even celebrated in France where her famous phrases entered the language. The painter Salvador Dali[24] immortalized her in gouache in the painting *The Face of Mae West Which May Be Used as an Apartment* and designed a sofa in the shape of her lips. Her form was used for the bottle of couturière Elsa Schiaparelli's perfume Shocking, and another Parisian perfume house produced Parfum Mae West – "Loaded with allure … dripping with sex appeal," ran the slogan. "A few drops behind your ears – and it's all over bar the wedding march."

Hollywood columnist Hedda Hopper asked her how she knew so much about men. Mae replied: "Baby, I went to the right school."

Despite the National Legion of Decency censor Joseph Breen banning *She Done Him Wrong* and *I'm No Angel* and excising all references to sex, prostitution, crime, drugs and gambling (in other words, the entire plot) from her next film, *Belle of the Nineties* (1934), Mae was not dismayed.

"I believe in censorship," she said. "If a picture of mine didn't get an X-rating, I'd be insulted."

Besides she knew how to handle it. She added "hot lines and jokes I knew they'd cut" to distract them from less obvious, but more suggestive, passages. "It's the sex personality, not the words," she said. "The censors could never beat that."

No one was going to stop her.

"I've never had a wishbone, where my backbone should be," she said.

After Mae's father died, she turned to spiritualism. At a séance with Amelia Earhart, Battlin' Jack advised that she should drop one lover – probably ex-acrobat and dancer Jack Durant who she had been seen around town with – and continue seeing another, a man who just happened to be at the séance. This is thought to be the heavyweight wrestling champion Vincent Lopez, who was her lover for many years and later became her bodyguard.

The movies still kept coming, but she had to be more subtle. Nevertheless, Paramount kept releasing wish-lists of men Mae wanted to meet. This included John D. Rockefeller; the Prince of Wales[25] "who's been looking for the right girl for 40 years," the pitcher Dizzy Dean "to find out if he's as good as he says he is"; the father of then-famous quintuplets Oliva Dionne; Melvin Purvis, the FBI man who tracked down John Dillinger; and the founder of modern Turkey, Mustapha Kemal,[26] because: "When he took Turkish women out of harems and out from behind their veils, he did a real service."

Then the 1911 marriage certificate and the 1924 Texas marriage license surfaced. Mae denied everything.

"I'm a single girl with a single-track mind – and it doesn't run to matrimony," she said.

And Frank Wallace? "I never heard of the guy."

Mae found that the best way to counter the story was to say that no less than eight men made matrimonial claims on her. She made light of it on Louella Parson's radio show, saying: "I hope all my husbands are listening in."

Still the press had a field day when they discovered Mae's real age – she had shaved seven years off it – and found out that she had once performed in burlesque. Frank Wallace went on the road with a new double act, billing himself as "Mr Mae

West." When that failed, he sued for maintenance. She counter-sued, eventually winning her divorce in 1942.

Mae now had a more powerful enemy than the censors – newspaper magnate William Randolph Hearst, whose 30 newspapers, he boasted, landed on 15 million American breakfast tables every morning. After an unguarded remark about the acting ability of Marion Davis,[27] Hearst's mistress, Hearst newspapers banned ads for Mae's movies and their editorials began asking: "Is it not time Congress did something about Mae West?"

"The nearest Congress came to that," said Mae in her autobiography, "was almost naming twin lakes, round ones, after me."

Despite Hearst's animosity, "rain, Lent and the elevator man's strike," her next movie *Klondike Annie* (1936) was a sell-out in New York and across the country.

Hearst found it particularly offensive that Mae played the "consort of a Chinese vice lord" – race was always more of an issue than sex in America. Breen banned any scenes Mae played with African-Americans in *Go West, Young Man* (1936), knowing that her real-life lover, her chauffeur Chalky Wright, was black. However, in the movie, her chauffeur is played by another real-life lover, John Indrisano, and the line: "A thrill a day keeps the chill away" stayed in.

In *Every Day's a Holiday* (1937) the producer, perhaps ironically, promised: "There are no sex situations that could possibly attract the criticism that her previous pictures received." So Breen went after two lines where Mae positively precludes sex: "I wouldn't lift my veil for that guy," and "He couldn't touch me with a ten-foot pole." Some people are never satisfied. They were duly cut

"Sex ain't what it used to be," concluded *The New York Times*, "or maybe Miss West isn't."

So Mae decided to put some sex on the radio, appearing with ventriloquist Edgar Bergen. Publicity for the broadcast showed her lying on a bed in a negligee with Bergen's dummy Charlie McCarthy, who Mae said she loved because he was "all wood and a yard long."

Mae was in a sketch set in the Garden of Eden. She played Eve as a bored housewife who tried to get sex out of Adam with a little forbidden applesauce. NBC were flooded with letters of complaint. "Mae West Pollutes Homes," wrote the *Catholic Monitor*.

She was duly banned from the radio, though that Sunday's broadcast had pulled an audience of 40 million, more had listened to the abdication speech of Edward VIII.

"Did they expect a sermon?" said Mae. "Why weren't they in church if they were so religious?"

To capitalize on the furore, Paramount rushed out *Every Day's a Holiday*. It found itself up again *Snow White and the Seven Dwarfs* (1937) and it bombed.

"I used to be Snow White," quipped Mae, "but I drifted."

Now 46, Mae was dropped by the studio and, gamely, went back to the stage where her act got even steamier. When her stage maid informs her that there are 400 men waiting for her in the lobby, she says: "Well, I'm a little tired, so one of those guys will have to go."

She went on the road again with *Diamond Lil*, which she took to England where, despite bringing her four muscular bodyguards of her own, Scotland Yard insisted on two of their men guarding her at all times. Interviewed on the BBC in London she had to say: "Who is this Big Ben? I'd love to meet him."

The actor Bruno Barnade recalled being auditioned for the British production. When he arrived at her suite in the Savoy he found her in a negligee.

"We'll just run through the bedroom scene," she said. "Come up behind me and put your hands on my bosom. Okay."

He put his hand on her left breast.

"I mean both breasts, honey," she said. So he put his script between his teeth, grabbed both of her breasts and gently rotated her hands.

"You're in." she said.

On stage, Mae purred with pleasure when Bruno rotated his hands, then she would turn so that he kissed her left breast in front of the audience. The Lord Chamberlain's office, which regulated the English theater, had something to say about this.

The negligee routine was par for the course when auditioning male actors. Bert Waller also visited her in her suite at the Savoy.

"She came waltzing out in her negligee," he said. "She always believed in everyone getting an eyeful… She had perfect skin, lovely firm breasts."

But Waller was not in luck. She had a young university student with her.

"Timony came back unexpectedly and she literally had to shove the student out onto the window sill and make an excuse to get Timony out of the room to get the boy in again," Waller said. "She was every bit as interested in sex as she claimed."

A rumor started with a make-up girl in England who said that Mae had scars on her breasts, the result of surgery to augment them. Mae told a different story. When she was leaving England to return to the US, Bert Barnabe, who had the good fortune to feel her breasts on stage every night, said jokingly, "I wonder if I will ever come across such firm breasts again."

She took his musing seriously.

"It is only because I exercise every day," she said. Then took him through the routine.

Back in the US she toured with *Come On Up*, *Ring Twice* and *Catherine Was Great*, based on the life of Catherine the Great of Russia. In it there is a scene where she inspects her male courtiers at crotch level. After passing several men, she stops with her eyes fixed on the bulge in his trousers and says: "You're new here." This scene was used again later in the movie *Myra Breckinridge* (1970). And, of course, when her leading man's scabbard accidentally stabs her in the abdomen, she says: "Is that your sword, or are you just pleased to see me?"

At the end of each performance she made a curtain speech. She told the audience: "Catherine was a great empress. She also had 3,000 lovers. I did the best I could in a couple of hours."

And she was not kidding. She used auditions to select muscular new lovers. Even though she was now in her 50s and practically bald under her wig because of the persistent peroxide abuse her hair had suffered, she was still sexually voracious. Yolande Donlan, whose father appeared with Mae in *Belle of the Nineties*, recalled going to visit her backstage with a couple of friends. Miss Donlan's friend suddenly noticed that Mae and her boyfriend were missing. They had only been gone a few minutes, but when she stormed into Mae's dressing room she found them locked together.

"I don't know if she was sex-obsessed all the time," said Miss Donlan, "but she certainly had a spurt of it then."

Then came her nightclub act, featuring Richard Du Bois and a squad of muscle men in loincloths. Mae was 61 at the time. At "Mae's cattle calls" – as her auditions were dubbed – hundreds of prime specimens, stripped to their shorts, paraded past her while she made notes. She was very selective. It must be remembered that in such auditions earlier in her career she had rejected the young Kirk Douglas. Even Spartacus could not pass muster.

"Why marry a ball player when you can have the whole team," she told the audience.

A singer she engaged, Steve Rossi, told *Globe* magazine: "She insisted on having sex every day, otherwise she wouldn't feel right."

"Tonight I feel like a million – but one at a time," was her line.

One of the musclemen she selected was Mickey Hargitay, who was Mae's beau before he became Jayne Mansfield's. Walter Winchell said it was a case of "Hello Jayne, goodbye Mae." One of her boys went off to India when she refused to marry him. Another left to join a monastery when he discovered that Mae – 40 years his senior – was two-timing him with one of his colleagues. He used to stalk the corridors of the hotel they were staying at in tears, lamenting: "She doesn't love me, she doesn't love me."

Rival muscle man Paul Novak, former Mr Baltimore, was not such a cry-baby. He went on to become her live-in lover and factotum for the rest of her days. They lived part of the time in her Santa Monica beach house, which had a Roman-style mural featuring naked charioteers with golden penises and unattached testicles floating like pink clouds across the sky. In her private suite she had a bedside table whose legs were four sculpted penises.

She could still shock. *Diamond Lil* was banned in Atlanta in 1951. A long, realistic televised kiss with Rock Hudson[28] at the 1958 Oscars, followed by a knee in the groin, caused a storm and CBS pulled her interview on Charles Collingwood's *Person to Person* because of its sexual content.

She turned down the opportunity to play Norma Desmond in *Sunset Boulevard* (1950) – what a different picture that would have been. Director Billy Wilder was obsessed with Mae and they used to get together at the commissary to swap dirty stories. To Wilder she represented the platonic ideal of "the whore." Her vulgarity and fleshiness reminded him of the Berlin and Viennese prostitutes he had enjoyed in his youth.

She also turned her nose up at the chance play opposite Marlon Brando in *Pal Joey* (1957) and Elvis Presley in *Roustabout* (1964). These two young men were both at their sexual peaks, but Mae refused to play parts where the woman does not come out on top. Mae also refused to appear in

Federico Fellini's *Juliet of the Spirits* (1965), which is odd, as Fellini said: "I think that her work was really her sex."

Certainly her sex was her work. Writing books like this one, I find myself in the same boat. She was tempted by a part in Fellini's *Satyricon* (1969), which cast her as a sorceress who guided adolescents through their first sexual experience. But then she discovered that the sorceress had children. There was no way that Mae West was playing a mother.

She did appear in Gore Vidal's X-rated *Myra Breckinridge*, where she plays a Hollywood agent who beds all her clients, in 1970 and *Sextette*, a film version of her own play about a woman's five ex-husbands trying to stop her bedding her sixth, in 1978. Again she personally auditioned all the men for their parts. At the age of 85, she was still playing the red-hot sexpot that no man could resist. This was the role she had played throughout her career. Fanmail from men often included nude pictures.

In 1979, the year before she died, a young African-American man, about 17, turned up at Ravenswood. Mae had him sent up. When he came down again an hour and a half later, he said to the receptionist: "I will never forget you and what you have done for me for the rest of my life." And he was seen to float, not walk, out of the door.

Her magnificent chest stood out to the end. Although her quips litter books of quotations – in foreign languages as well as in English – her proudest moment was when her name entered *Webster's Dictionary* as the name that the British Royal Air Force had given to their life preservers during the Second World War. It is not recorded how many lives these inflatable chests saved, but the real thing gave succor and comfort to millions.

3

The First Love Goddess of Color

While Jayne Mansfield and Mae West had their undoubted charms, I prefer women of a darker hue. So I welcome this opportunity to get up close and personal with Dorothy Dandridge. She was the first black Hollywood goddess, though she is now largely remembered for *Introducing Dorothy Dandridge*, the made-for-TV movie that first brought the incomparable, golden-skinned Halle Berry to prominence. Personally, I refuse to go and see any film that does not feature Halle Berry nude these days. She has now taken over from the glorious Robin Givens as the African-American actress guaranteed to get her kit off in a movie.

In the 1950s, the critics called Dorothy Dandridge: "One of the great beauties of our time, a sex symbol to magazine editors the world over, and Hollywood's first authentic love goddess of color."

Color was right. Dorothy described herself as "mixed American ... one-fourth English, one-fourth Jamaican (which is often a mixture of Indian, English and African), one-fourth American Negro, one eighth Spanish and one-eighth Indian." Her mother was the child of a West Indian man and a Mexican woman, while her father was the product of a British gentleman and an African-American woman who married, daringly, in the 1880s. But Dorothy's parents broke up when her mother, a well-known actress, was pregnant and she did not meet her father until she was nearly full grown.

As a child, she spent a great deal of time trying to keep other men from getting near her mother. While her mother worked, she was looked after by the minister's wife, Auntie Ma-ma, who beat her brutally and brought her up in the ways of Christian meekness, forgiveness and understanding.

"One day I would have to 'understand' producers, actors, agents, lawyers, psychiatrists, insurance agents, suitors, double-crossers, chiselers, parasites and greedy magnates in search of beautiful flesh," she said.

Dorothy and her two sisters formed a song-and-dance act called "The Wonder Kids," who went on tour with Auntie Mama in tow. The money they earned went, not to them, but to Auntie Ma-ma's church. A talent scout from MGM saw them and signed them. They moved to the coast and settled in Watts, the ghetto area of Los Angeles. There the pretty young Dorothy began to attract attention, not all of it pleasant.

One day she overheard one white laborer saying to another: "How'd you like to spin that little black bitch on your pecker."

"Those black kids have venereal disease from the day they're born," said the other. "You can count me out."

"As far as I'm concerned, it's worth a dose of clap to screw that little black bitch," said the first.

Dorothy ran into her house and cried on her pillow. She did not understand what the men meant, but their talk frightened her. Later, at 13, a man flashed at her and a girlfriend, and they fled.

She first fell in love at the age of 11 when she was on tour in Hawaii. Her beau's name was Istio Ull. He was half Hawaiian and half Japanese. After their first kiss on a palm-fringed Hawaiian beach, he taught her to hula. This, she said, was where she got her sinuous, writhing dance style which was later compared to "a caterpillar on a hot rock."

Then came the tearful and lei-bedecked parting.

"We exchanged a simple and plaintive kiss on each other's lips," she said. "There was a pureness and a quietness about that early love with Istio that I was never to have again."

Although she was still a child, Dorothy developed a slinky walk – and other things. Auntie Ma-ma began to notice the way boys looked at her and decided to bind her chest.

"Girls your age everywhere get bound up so they won't be big in front," she said. "It doesn't look right. Now's the time to keep you from getting as big as a cow. The way you're growing out, big men will stare at you."

Dorothy hated it, but her Auntie insisted she was doing the right thing.

"You aren't appreciative," she said. "You're just bad, bad."

Dorothy liked looking at her breasts. She liked the way they had blossomed and, now that she had reached puberty, her hips had widened. She compared herself with Auntie Ma-ma who was then the same height and noticed that Auntie Ma-ma's bosom was flat and shapeless, while her belly was round. But Auntie Ma-ma's word was law in the Dandridge household. She told Dorothy that she would have to wear a muslin band around her chest for two or three years "till they're flat and don't stand out." What a waste. If Auntie Ma-ma didn't have nice tits, no one was allowed them.

"My breasts felt flat and tight against my chest," said Dorothy. "This was not the first nor was it the last of the sexually inhibitory influences that Auntie Ma-ma would exert on me. Because of her I would come to marriage frightened, ignorant, bedeviled."

Dorothy worked as an extra on the MGM lot, where, she said, "Lap-sitting was my forte." She would sit on the knee of Leroy Prinz, then scoot over to Bill "Bojangles" Robinson and sit on his lap or that of his wife, Fanny. Bojangles told her she was pretty.

"Keep away from the wolves – like me," he said.

He knew what he was talking about. A few years later, Bojangles divorced Fanny and married a girl not much older than Dorothy who had also sat on his lap.

At 17, the beautiful and talented Dorothy Dandridge

dreamed of marriage. All her friends were getting married. She
wanted to marry and quit show business. She had already set
her cap at Harold Nicholas, of the famous Nicholas Brothers
dance act, who she first met performing at the Cotton Club.
She was just 14 at the time. Harold was a good deal older and
already an accomplished womanizer. He had been her
chaperone at a party given by the singer Etta Jones who, at that
time, was planning to marry and quit showbiz herself.
Throughout Dorothy's four-year romance with Harold, she
said: "Sex was limited to kissing and getting hot." But Harold's
thermostat did not work so well with other girls. A friend told
her that Harold had been out with many of the Cotton Club's
glamorous chorus girls.

"Oh, he's been down the line," she said.

This did not perturb Dorothy in the slightest. When her
father turned up out of the blue and asked if she had a
boyfriend, she said: "Yes, I do."

Her plans to marry Harold were interrupted by a tour of
Europe, where she dreamed of marrying an English duke or an
Italian count. But the tour was interrupted by the outbreak of
the Second World War. One of the girls in the company got
pregnant and Aunt Ma-ma, who was still beating Dorothy and
her sister three times a week, suspected that Dorothy might
have been fooling around, too. During an air raid, she pulled
down Dorothy's panties and pushed her finger inside her
vagina to see if she was still a virgin. The bombs were falling as
Dorothy tried to fight her off.

A similar incident occurred back in Los Angeles, when
Dorothy had returned late from the movies after a perfectly
innocent date. Auntie Ma-ma forced the sensitive young girl to
strip. Dorothy did not want to show her aunt her private parts,
and when she refused to take off her bra and panties Auntie
Ma-ma ripped them off and satisfied herself that she was still a
virgin.

After four years of cursory groping, Harold realized that the only way to go all the way with Dorothy was to marry her. It would be a disaster. Harold was a highly sexed young man who could not keep his hands off pretty young women. Dorothy, on the other hand, had been brought up in an all-woman household and had never even seen a man in his shorts. Later, she said that she thought boys and girls should be brought up together so that they grasped the rudiments of sex early on.

Dorothy was ignorant of real maleness, and afraid of what she called "the ultimate." As Harold pressed her to set a date, she grew afraid of what went on between a man and a woman in bed. For her it was a mystery and both her mother and Auntie Ma-ma had embedded in her a great fear of sex.

Looking back, Dorothy was certain that if she and Harold had gone all the way beforehand he would not have married her. As it was, she retained the aura of the unattained. She was what, at the time, every respectable bride should be – a virgin, untouched and unsullied. When they went out in Los Angeles and New York, either Harold's chauffeur or her mother would play chaperone. Because of their work commitments most of their courting took place by phone, across the Atlantic from England or from payphones in dressing rooms, hotel lobbies and nightclubs. Harold would supplement this with romantic telegrams and flowers.

"Occasionally," said Dorothy, "there were those hours of idling, me holding out like a good girl, Harold getting hotter and hotter for whatever he imagined he was going to get."

She did have one lapse – with another man. At the time the Dandridge Sisters, as they were then known, were touring with Jimmy Lunceford's band. They did one-nighters and cut records, moving from place to place.

"I had a small interim romance with a saxophone player named Joe," she said.

Joe was experienced. He was older than Dorothy and had already been married and divorced. In the tour bus, they would get together up in the back while Auntie Ma-ma was down in the front.

"He put his tongue in my ear, and I nearly went through the roof," she said. "The thrill was so intense that I wavered about Harold."

On the road, she thought that maybe she should marry a man who gave her such terrific aural sex, but Dorothy was a more calculating girl. Harold was talented and had money and a big career in front of him – "and he wanted me and I really wanted him."

"At 17, you might marry for a thrill in the ear," she said, "but at 30 – as I was to find out – you'll thrill as hard if a guy shows he can pay the rent."

The Nicholas Brothers were signed by 20th Century Fox and settled in Los Angeles. Harold and Dorothy began to see each other daily. Then one day backstage in a theater, Harold sat down on a piano stool next to her and whipped out a ring – "I said yes and we set a date."

Later Dorothy pondered Harold's motives. Certainly he wanted to get away from home. He was tired of giving most of his money to his mother. He wanted to be on his own, in his own home, with his own money, and with a girl who "had not been used by everybody."

In the light of what happened later, Dorothy could not be sure if he loved her, or even if he knew what love was. But "he knew what sex was, and he knew he wanted that with me as much as he wanted anything in the world," she said.

Dorothy longed for marriage. She did not find show business glamorous and wanted to quit to become a housewife. They bought a house together, which they remodeled and furnished. Alarm bells should have rung when Dorothy ordered separate beds.

"Why do you want twin beds?" asked Harold.

"I don't know," she said. "I think it might be nicer."

On reflection, Dorothy conceded that she was afraid of what might happen in a double bed.

On their wedding day, Harold was delighted with his virgin bride. Other men looked on jealously as he wed Dorothy who, at the age of 20, was already being recognized as one of the most beautiful women in the world. But on their wedding night, Dorothy delayed going to bed until after midnight. Then she took a long shower and stood naked and shivering under the water. Why was she so afraid, she asked herself. Being in show business she was surrounded by sex, but why did they have to have it now? Harold loved her and had been contented to go without sex up till now. He was relaxed about it. She knew that he was a swinger and had slept with lots of girls, some of whom she knew. Several were famous movie actresses. She wasn't jealous. She was afraid. What, she wondered, would Harold expect of her, and how could she hope to compete with the Cotton Club chorus girls?

She knew that he was in bed, naked, waiting for her to come out of the bathroom unclothed or in a flimsy negligee. And she knew she had to go through with it. Through the ordeal of sex, the pain and the blood, she could have everything she wanted, a strong marriage, a good home, children – and she could quit the world of entertainment.

"Dorothy, are you all right?" cried Harold.

"I'm just fixing up," she replied.

She turned on the faucet and made it sound like she was busy. By now it was two o'clock in the morning and she could not stay in the bathroom all night. She dried herself off and sprayed her body all over with perfume, a wedding present from a girl friend. Then she donned a sheer, powder blue negligee. Still, she found her feet glued to the tiles. When she finally made it to the bedroom door, she had a problem with the knob. She stood there with her hand on the knob, but could not turn it.

Inside, the lights were still on. Harold sat up in bed and told her that she was beautiful.

"What kept you so long?" he said, turning out the light. "Are you afraid?"

"A little," she said.

"Don't be."

What followed was bad, she admitted later. He asked her to take off her nightie and they lay together naked in each other's arms. Dorothy, fearful and inexperienced, was cold. As his hands began to explore her body, she felt ill. It was like what she had experienced with Auntie Ma-ma all over again. He bombarded her with kisses and told her how much he loved her, but she had withdrawn so deeply within herself that she barely heard him. Patiently, he managed to get her to spread her legs wide. He slipped on top of her and tried to enter her, but she was so tense that her vagina was too tight. It hurt.

"Don't," she said. "I don't feel like it."

But Harold had been waiting for this moment for four years and he knew that marriage without sex was a barrel of trouble. She would get used to it. He tried to force himself on her. She knew that she was obliged to give in to her husband's wishes, but still she fought back. Eventually, Harold relented. He was no rapist. It was her right to refuse him.

"We'll get an annulment," he said. "Why fight?"

They said goodnight and Harold went to sleep. Dorothy lay there in the dark, thinking. She did not want an annulment. She wanted marriage. She thought her way through the sex act. It wasn't so terrible and she thought she could numb herself enough to blot out the reality of what was happening.

She ran her hand across Harold's chest, woke him, and apologized. This was all very new to her. She had lived a very different life.

"I'm willing to try again," she said. "Be patient."

This time they managed to have sex, but Dorothy had no

recollection of it. She had managed to block everything that happened from her mind.

On the surface the marriage was fine. Dorothy enjoyed having a nice car, clothes and time to relax. Harold was a good provider and he liked to be seen out with his beautiful young wife. But from the very beginning he went out with other women, showgirls who were much more sexually experienced than Dorothy and could give him what he wanted in bed. He would come home late – two or even six o'clock in the morning – often with the tell-tale marks of illicit sex still upon him. This caused rows. He would tell her to stop nagging and complain that she was behaving like his mother.

Dorothy tried to hold his interest by cooking him splendid meals, but these did not assuage his other appetites. Then, after three months – never having had an orgasm or even knowing what one was – she fell pregnant.

With a child on the way, it was more important than ever to shore up her marriage. The way to do that, she decided, was to improve their sex life, and she began to try new things. It was too late. Harold rejected her attempts to put a little zing into that thing.

"He wanted me to stay as I was," she said. "He even expected me to remain sexually illiterate." That way, she would stay at home and play housewife while he went his own way.

However, on one occasion he found a little experimentation irresistible. He came across her barefoot, pregnant and in the kitchen, frying something on the stove. Harold said he was afraid that some of the hot fat would spit in her face. To protect it, he put a paper bag over her head, with two small eyeholes. Somehow he found this scenario so arousing that he made love to her there and then on the kitchen floor.

But the marriage was bust beyond repair. Harold went out to play "golf" when Dorothy felt the first pains of labor. He did not return until early the following morning. By that time the man next door had had to take her to the hospital. It was a forceps birth. Dorothy blamed the delay in getting to hospital for the fact that her daughter, Lynn, though she seemed normal enough to start with, was mentally retarded.

After the baby was born, Harold would rarely return before sunrise. Dorothy no longer cared, and focused all her love on the child. Soon she noticed that Lynn was slow to start talking. The diagnosis was brain damage and, while Dorothy trudged from specialist to specialist in the faint hope of finding a cure, Harold went off on a European tour.

"My love for Lynn was a little abnormal," she said. "She would jump into bed with me, and we would cuddle up, she naked against my naked breast." They would bath together. Lynn would hug her, crushing into her breasts.

"It was all warm, wet nakedness," said Dorothy. "I have known quite a few men since then, but I tell you, you cannot get that feeling from anything else in the world."

Dorothy sent Lynn to a carer and traveled with Harold as he toured. Harold found it convenient to have her along because he could discard the girls he bedded on the grounds that he was married. However, he took off to Europe where he found a cute Italian girl and signed a long-term contract to stay on. Soon he stopped sending Dorothy money.

"Like a gentleman," she said, "Harold allowed me to get the divorce."

Dorothy felt she had failed as both a mother and as a wife. Five years of marriage left her uncertain about relationships with men. Her father had left her mother before she was born, now her husband had moved on. Perhaps all men were like that. In that case, a girl had better know how to make a living.

She took to singing in clubs and teamed up with the composer Phil Moore, who had spent years working with Lena Horne. Their professional relationship soon became personal.

"From Phil I was able to learn about physical intimacy, and it was he who helped me to 'come out,'" she said. "With him I went about the details of lovemaking with a certain will, as if to end once and forever my ignorance."

With Phil she was able to reconcile herself to her own dichotomy – that she looked sexy, but felt she was not. They became passionately involved, though she denied ever being in love with him. Nevertheless, they moved in together.

In her dressing room after shows, Dorothy would often suffer paroxysms and shortness of breath. Referred to a psychiatrist, she learned that these convulsions were caused by her contradictory sexual feelings and her guilt over Lynn. With Phil's help, Dorothy began to put a new sexiness across on stage. But it was not Phil who would benefit.

Rather it was Harry Belafonte. When he came to see the show, Dorothy was instantly attracted. She said she found him "beautiful" and they found they had a lot in common – they were both seeing psychiatrists. They began seeing each other regularly and Dorothy told him that she would be happy to give up show business and become Mrs Harry Belafonte, if he wanted. It was not to be. Belafonte was distressed by the divorce he was going through at the time and much of their conversation was couched in psychiatric jargon. He accused her of "castrating" him. He would show up late for dates and became forgetful about things that were important to her.

Although the relationship continued for several years, he slowly disappeared from her life. He eventually decided that he had rejected her because she was too independent and too dominant a personality. She, on the other hand, felt that he overshadowed her. At the same time, she rejected a legion of other suitors – mostly white – who, she complained, looked on a black girl simply as a hot partner in bed.

The relationship with Belafonte caused a rift with Phil Moore. She also began to overshadow him in the act. The *Los Angeles Mirror* called her: "The satiny, sexy songstress with starlight aura. She has beauty, an infectious good humor, sexy delivery and an extremely clever style. This is Dorothy Dandridge, the most exciting new sepia singer." When they went to London to perform at the Café de Paris, her billing was twice the size of Phil's. As a result they would soon part.

In England, she was entertained by Randolph Churchill and was chatted up by Prince Philip.[1]

"I was naive enough at the time not to know who he was," she said.

One night at the Café de Paris, Dorothy was visited by a baron, who brought armfuls of long-stemmed roses and a gold and jade bracelet. Each night he met her at the stage door with more flowers and new gifts. Dorothy found him handsome. He had just been through a divorce case that had made headlines worldwide. His six-year marriage, he said, had been due to his wife's possessiveness. Dorothy made a mental note, if this relationship led anywhere, not to make the same mistake. After a couple of dates in town, he took her to his stately home, which greatly impressed a poor girl who had been brought up in Watts. She thought how wonderful it would be to be the mistress of this baronial hall.

But once inside the castle, she found that all the servants were midgets – odd, but then these English aristocrats had a reputation for being a trifle eccentric. However, he was the perfect host and disarmed her with his charm, even though she was usually on her guard with white men. He called for some red wine from his own winery that was so dark it was almost black. Dorothy was a little suspicious but, as he sipped the wine, she drank some, too. Soon she found herself becoming woozy.

Then a phalanx of midgets came marching in. They stripped the baron naked and dressed him in a sheer and silky woman's nightie. Dorothy wanted to flee, but found she could not move. The baron then told her that he loved her and offered her a lot of money to make love to him. She refused, but she had to watch as two female midgets performed all sorts of perverted acts on him. This went on for hours. Eventually Dorothy regained her strength and insisted that he take her back to her hotel, which he did after the midgets had dressed him again. Dorothy later discovered that he had no intention of making love to her. His turn-on was to have her watch while unspeakable acts were being performed on him and she wondered how many women had witnessed a similar performance. It certainly opened her eyes. She had not known that men could be like that. She never saw her baron again, though he later wrote to her saying that he had added a "Negro dwarf" to his staff. Very politically correct.

Back in the States, Dorothy was being promoted as "a volume of sex with the living impact of the Kinsey Report." *Life* magazine called her: "The most beautiful Negro singer since Lena Horne." And, in 1954, she would became the first African-American to appear on *Life*'s cover.

Flowers now piled up in her dressing room, along with all sorts of expensive gifts and hand-tooled calling cards. They often came from older men, who were wealthy and wanted to be seen out at nightclubs with such a beauty.

"You can't be pretty and colored without innocently inviting half of all the men you come into contact with to lust," she said. "From my early teens, I wanted a romance to be just a simple and idealistic thing, but instead it was always a game of fox and hounds, with me as the fox."

Her huntsmen wanted a one-night stand, a brief encounter, a week-long affair or a short holiday at a swanky resort. She gave them short shrift. She turned down a racing driver, the owner of a department store who kept a stable of mistresses, a producer who wanted to show her his casting couch, a baseball star and any man who wore flashy jewelry.

"As soon as I learned a man was after some rapid weekend boffing, he was out," she said. "Finding a man who wanted to go to bed was the easiest thing in the world. Finding a serious man was one of the most difficult."

With those lovers she did entertain, discretion was their keynote. They avoided nightclubs and eschewed publicity. She did not want her romances in the newspapers. While she was appearing at *La Vie en Rose* in New York, she met the actor Harding Allbrite, who had played secondary roles in a number of Broadway plays. He was handsome and fancied himself as one of the "sweater boys," a group of talented young men from Long Island who wore casual sweaters into their 30s. Dorothy was puzzled by him. All he seemed to want to do was to kiss. After several weeks she took this situation in hand and "brought the relationship to where it belonged." It was her first romantic involvement with a white man and it lasted for several years. The newspapers knew nothing of it, but Dorothy was hurt when black friends accused her of selling out.

They spent time together whenever she was in New York and once or twice they met up in Los Angeles or Las Vegas. Otherwise she ran up huge phone bills. The problem was that Allbrite had no money and had his heart set on marrying a millionnaire.

"Had I been worth a million dollars and could have said to Harding, 'Marry me and we'll go to the bank and open up a joint account,'" she said, "I think he would have. Moreover, life with him would probably always have been pleasant."

They enjoyed each other's company, cooking together in the kitchen, drinking wine, snuggling up on the couch. She could hardly condemn him for his fecklessness. After all, she wanted exactly the same thing as he did – to marry someone who could pay the rent. They were birds of a feather. He would tell her of the latest heiress he had his eye on and she would cheer him on. Eventually he succeeded in bagging a wealthy women and spent the rest of his life on a prolonged vacation in expensive resorts. Of course, what was sauce for the goose was sauce for the gander – or the other way around – and Dorothy had numerous amusing adventures with wealthy admirers.

*

After appearing in the suggestively named *Pillow to Post* (1945) and *Ebony Parade* (1947), she got her first starring role in *Tarzan's Peril* (1951), also released as *Melmendi, Queen of the Ashuba, Jungle Queen, Tarzan and the Jungle Queen*, and *Tarzan's Mate in Peril*. She was the eponymous mate, the jungle queen herself. It was her 19th movie.

"I was surrounded by muscles and cackling monkeys," she said.

She lost the monkeys later that year when she played a wife in *The Harlem Globetrotters* (1947). An engagement at El Rancho in Las Vegas brought her to the attention of Columbia studio boss Harry Cohn[2] who, though he had failed to bed Rita Hayworth,[3] had succeeded with Marilyn Monroe[4] and many others. Now it was Dorothy's turn. One night she was invited up to the King of the Casting Couch's office, only to find that there was no casting couch in it. Instead, Cohn was in his pyjamas and a purple dressing gown. He said he was delighted to see her in the flesh and paid extravagant compliments to her beauty – her "fine bones, delicacy and lovely soft flesh."

It was plain the way the conversation was going and, offended that he hadn't even provided a couch to seduce her on, Dorothy took umbrage.

"Because I'm an attractive Negro does not give you, or anyone, the license to take me to bed five minutes after you shake my hand for the first time," she said.

Then it was Cohn's turn to play the shocked innocent. He pointed out that he had 40 beautiful women under contract and if he laid them all once a week he would have no time to make pictures.

"Why is it that there are so few girls left you can pay a compliment to without them taking off their clothes?" he asked. He then lashed the desk top with a riding crop.

His manufactured outrage was all the more amusing because he was in his pajamas in his office. He had had a long day, he explained. He had been dictating letters from his steam bath and "I didn't feel I had to put on white tie and tails for you," he said.

He called for something to eat and she joined him, but he did not even offer her a drink. This puzzled her. Why was he not plying her with alcohol, she asked, "You know, we colored girls are just naturally supposed to drop our panties when we get some alcohol in us."

Cohn parried this by saying that what was destroying African-Americans was not the way they were treated, but the way they expected to be treated. Then he boasted about how Columbia had forced pictures with African-American actors in them into the South over the objections of the distributors. Then he made a confession.

"When I first saw you on-screen, I had a hard-on for you," he said. "Who the hell wouldn't? All that quiet sex wrapped up in a cute brown bundle."

He walked her to the elevator. But realizing that, by leaving his office without responding to his advances meant that her career at Columbia was over, she hesitated when it came to pushing the button. He smiled and pushed it for her. When the elevator came, he took her by the hand and led her back to his office.

"When you didn't push that elevator button, it was just as if you said, loud and clear: 'Harry, I want you to go to bed with me. I want to make you happy so you will make a famous actress out of me,'" he said.

When she began to deny it, he said he had heard every word. Up until that point they had had an honest relationship.

"Don't spoil it," he said. "Not pressing that elevator button was just like taking your clothes off."

Then as a token of honesty on his part, he admitted inviting her to his office to lay her and that everything he had done was to that end. But he was tired and wanted to go to sleep. However, the following night he would be in bungalow AA at El Rancho and would be delighted if she visited him there. There is some dispute over what happened next. In her autobiography, Dorothy intimates that she did not go to bed with him.

"I was supposed to reach a sympathetic hand across the table," she said. "But I never reached out a hand … I didn't have to crawl into a strange bed with a strange-looking little man for it to happen."

However, Earl Mills, her manager, said that she did go to his bungalow. She found Cohn a fascinating human being, though she never worked for Columbia Pictures again.

Next she fell for the English actor Peter Lawford.[5] She liked the fact that he seemed to pay no attention to her color. When she protested that the club he was taking her to did not allow Negroes in, he expressed disbelief and took her in anyway. Afterwards, he drove her to lovers' lane, put his arm round her, and "kissed me in a delightful, gallant, English style, if kisses can have nationality." I'm an Englishman and English kisses do have nationality. All you Dorothy Dandridge look-alikes out there, please take note.

Dorothy felt a natural affinity for the English and loved the way they spoke. Peter was dashing, always a gentleman, and had zest for living. He liked to party but she felt she got too much of that on-stage. She spent her working life in smoky nightclubs. When she was not working, Dorothy preferred a quiet domestic life and she told him she would rather spend more time alone with him.

"Then that's the way it shall be," he said.

In their time together they never had a single argument.

"Sometimes it has seemed strange to me how people emanating from traditions so remote from each other could be so harmonious together," she said, "but we did consort together with the most unimaginable ease and comfort."

There was only one bone of contention – chitlins. Peter had never come across them before and could not stand the smell of them cooking. However, once Dorothy chopped them finely, sprinkled them with paprika, and served them in long-stemmed glasses with Tabasco sauce and garnished with parsley, and he asked for more.

The problem was that chitlins and pigs' feet and black-eyed peas made Dorothy feel that she was staying close to her roots. Eating soul food meant that she was not just another elegant lady singing white songs for white listeners. Cooking it up in her kitchen, she felt at home again with her own people, but ham hocks and collard greens did not sit too well on Peter's sophisticated European palate.

Like many Americans, she found it difficult to read the insouciant English manner. Blunt-speaking Americans can never tell whether the phlegmatic English are saying what they genuinely think or just being polite. Although she had freely entered into a sexual relationship with him without ties, she now longed to hear him say: "Marry me." But she did not expect to hear those words from his lips, nor did she feel she had the right to expect it.

At the same time two other white men were after her, father and son. They were Elmer Tyler, who owned several huge hotels in San Francisco and was planning to retire, and George Tyler, who was taking over management of the chain. Both were married.

"So many white men think there is nothing sweeter than having a brown boff on the side," she said, "under wraps, taken in the dark or kept behind the scenes."

Elmer had false teeth and, consequently, drooled. She dreaded kissing him, fearing that his dentures would slip down her throat. Still, he offered her a 14-storey building, worth three-quarters of a million dollars back then, if she'd… Elmer's wily and possessive wife befriended Dorothy in the hope that she would take pity on her and not seduce her husband. Instead Dorothy felt sorry for the old man, whose life was slipping away from him. He had a sense of beauty and felt that getting his hands on some of it might help prevent his life slipping any further.

On the other hand, the son had nicer lips. Kissing him was good, but he did not know how to handle an affair the way his father did. In neither case was marriage mentioned. Dorothy fled to New York where, unbeknownst to one another, both father and son called her. This was okay but, during the father's phone calls, she could not help visualizing the foam breaking around his mouth. Dorothy's problem was that, although she liked wealthy men and all they had to offer her, she liked handsome men more.

Playing in racially segregated Florida, Dorothy had heard of a man named Frank Gabriola, though he also went by a number of other names. He owned a hotel in New York with an associate where she got a four-week engagement at $8,000 a week. Gabriola was a man with a complex business with interests in property, entertainment, prize fighting, horse racing and other sports. His love life was just as complicated and "he liked a change of ladies now and then."

The gang of henchmen who hung around the club and ran errands for him introduced themselves to her by diminutives – Abe, Joe, Sam, Tony – but they called each other Bull, Butch, Dutch… It goes without saying that you should never trust a man whose middle name is "the."

Gabriola watched her perform in the club and, on her fourth day, Sam, the manager, came to her dressing room and told her that the boss liked her, but if she was going to be a star, he said, she needed the "gingerbread and whipped cream."

"Yeah, all the trimmings," said Sam. "You gotta be dressed like a million bucks, see? Different dresses. They gotta be like this…" and he held his cupped hands against his own flat chest as if offering up a pair of prize breasts.

Dorothy was already housed in the bridal suite of the hotel and she was told what was expected of her "clearly and horizontally." A week later, a party was held in her honor. Gabriola and his henchmen sat around with the chorus girls, four girls to each man. Dorothy pointed out that the girls looked a little uncomfortable.

"I thought you'd like a big party," said Frank.

"With girls?" asked Dorothy.

Within ten seconds they were gone. Frank then spelled out how he intended to make her a big star. He would give her a rhythm section and cut a slew of records. His brother, Harold, was in the music business and, with payola, her records would get played on every radio station in the US. The next night, at an intimate dinner after the show, Gabriola offered her a contract of $1,500 a week for the next five years. She did not even have to sing, just sit next to him, look pretty, mix him a drink, and light his cigar sometimes. He already had a wife, children and grandchildren, and there was no chance of marriage. It was a tempting offer but, as a gangster's moll, she feared she might end up being notorious rather than famous. She was also afraid that being under contract to one club for five years would kill her career. And Gabriola was not in a very secure profession. If he was killed or sent to jail, she had to consider who would inherit her contract. Besides, she wanted to see other men.

At the time she was being pursued by numerous admirers. She had two or three phone calls a day from suitors across the country and overseas, and she had little time to judge their intent. Were they serious about her or did they just want to bed her? Marriage is what she wanted, though it would have to be to the right man. Mr Right would, naturally, come with "money, position, and charm." She met many men like that and one of them might be serious. Later she discovered that there were countless men with money and position who simply pursued women to get them into bed. Shocking! Worse still, back in those days, she noted:"Often white men had a deep-seated fear of intimacy, even association, with a Negro woman."

In many states, sex across the color line was still illegal, though few observed the law in this respect if they could get away with it – that is, in the South white men frequently slept with black women, but if a black man went sniffing around white women he was liable to find himself castrated or lynched.

Dorothy discovered a deep block in the mind of the white American male.

"They don't know what to expect from a woman of color," she said, "but they think they should expect something different."

They expected a black lover to be sexier, wilder, less inhibited. In my own experience I find this to be true, but then black male friends of mine say that they find white women sexier, wilder and less inhibited than black women. I think it has more to do with crossing the color line than an attribute of one race or the other.

Despite this mental block – and we are talking the 1950s here – Dorothy became determined to marry a white man.

"In my romantic little brain, I visualized someone rich, famous, handsome, charming," she said, "and he might even love me for my color."

Meanwhile, her daughter Lynn's periods had started. Afraid that she might have sex and have a baby of her own which she could not take care of, Dorothy had her tubes tied just in case.

In 1953, Dorothy played opposite Harry Belafonte in *Bright Road* (1953), but she began going out with Jerry Mayer, the director of the movie and the nephew of studio boss Louis B. Mayer.[6] Dorothy soon realized that he was not the marrying kind. Ironically, Dorothy had to "black up" for the role as she was not considered dark enough and being involved in a movie that touched on "the Negro question" attracted the attention of the House Committee on Un-American Activities. Strange times.

When *Bright Road* came out, a scandal magazine ran the story that a white musician had asked her out for a walk in the woods near Lake Tahoe and she had cheerfully succumbed to his alfresco advances. The studio did not want her to make a fuss over it, considering such stories to be good publicity, but Dorothy sued and won. She wanted to show that a woman of color could be talented and successful – something other than just a quick lay.

Louis B. Mayer took a personal interest in the picture because of Dorothy, who he called the "sexy, sultry, satiny nightclub singer." This pleased her very much. He was not concerned that, in the movie, she was supposed to be playing a prim schoolteacher.

"I don't care about sex appeal," he said. "Some girls have it and some don't. You do. But here's what I want you to do. I want you to look prim and proper just like you've been doing. But I want you to think sexy."

Dorothy said that she would practice, though she thought she knew how to think sexy already. Then Mayer explained his vision of the future.

"The industry is ready for a Negro actress," he said, "a sexy one with class."

Lena Horne had had it, but she did not want to become a movie star. Mayer said that Dorothy had the perfect qualities for success – "placidity, beauty, refinement and sex." He predicted that she would become the highest-paid African-American in movie history.

After *Bright Road* was completed, her relationship with Jerry Mayer could not stand the strain of her constant traveling while Mayer was stuck in Hollywood. One of her engagements took her to the Copacabana Hotel in Rio de Janeiro where, at a party after her first show, she met Juan Alvarez de Costigliana Freyre Vivaldi Martinez. In his 40s, he was olive-skinned, suave, well dressed and charming. She accepted his invitation to show her around the city. The next day, he picked her up in a chauffeur-driven limousine. After a tour of the sights of Rio, the chauffeur drove them around his extensive estate, then back to the business section of Rio to show her the banks he owned.

He was the richest man she had ever known. That evening as she got ready to go on stage, she found that she had forgotten all about Jerry, Peter and even Lynn. She was falling in love again. That night she put on a particularly sensuous performance, hoping that somewhere out in the audience he would be watching. Though she was, as ever, cool and ladylike.

They had known each other for just a few hours when he took her to an apartment of his in a downtown building. In a sumptuous, dimly lit room, there was a four-poster bed. They sat on it and sipped Brazilian wine. It went to her head and she began to giggle. He put his arms around her and said: "What are you afraid of? Am I so ugly?"

He was not ugly and this only made her laugh all the more.

"Let yourself go," he said, letting her go.

"Juan," she said, "don't men feel that you are common or cheap if you know what to do too well?"

"But you are an actress," he said.

Up until that point, she had always played the lady on screen. In that bedroom that night she discovered the wanton she would later immortalize in *Carmen Jones* (1954) and *Porgy and Bess* (1959). It was Juan who brought it out in her. He started calling her "cat," for he loved his pussy.

"My little cat," he said the next morning, mixing his metaphors, "you are the first woman I have ever met who really is a lady in the parlor and a bitch in the boudoir."

Suddenly Dorothy found that she was cured of the problems that had dogged the whole of her singing career. She felt none of the paroxysms or other physical symptoms she usually suffered after her shows. They would go out after even the most strenuous performance, have fun and make love. Juan had straightened her out both emotionally and physically.

One night after the show, he took her to the macumba, where black-skinned Brazilians performed voodoo rites to the beat of cat-skin drums. At the end of a dirt road in the interior hills, they found the locals dancing around a fire and chanting.

They worshipped figurines of the Virgin Mary and Christ, though their rites were "orgiastic."

"Once more Juan knew how to enliven my senses and prepare me for the succeeding hours in his apartment," she said.

On another occasion he took her to the "lover's leap" where many disappointed couples threw themselves to their deaths on the rocks below.

Juan would stay with Dorothy each night after her performance. No matter how late they stayed out or what they got up to when they returned home, he would be up by ten or 11 o'clock and head off to one of his offices. Then a huge bouquet of flowers would arrive. By the end of her two-week engagement, the apartment looked like a florist's.

Dorothy had no reason to rush back to the States. She had no pressing engagements, but they did not discuss their plans. There was nothing on the agenda except "incessant lovemaking." They were doing it so much that he stopped going to his office and spent all his time, day and night, with her. And whenever a business associate called, he said: "That can wait."

On the rare occasions that they were not hard at it in the bedroom, they went out on trips in the car. Away from the splendor of the Copacabana, she saw dark-skinned people living in squalor and abject poverty. This drove a rift between them.

Then the story of their affair broke in the Brazilian newspapers. Dorothy had the maids translate for her. Juan, she learned, was a big shot, not just in Brazil, but throughout Latin America. According to the newspapers it was scandalous that such a man should fall for a North American entertainer - a gringo. Dorothy was, in tabloid speak, a sexy siren, luring him to his doom.

To escape the publicity, Juan took her out to one of his smaller country estates, where the *residência* had just ten rooms. Attended by only four servants, "it was like being alone," said Dorothy.

There Dorothy began to figure things out. How come this guy needed so many houses? How many women did he have? For that matter, she did not even know if he was married or single.

Even on the *estância*, the phone rang. Business associates called to discuss the growing scandal. Juan explained that, in Latin America, men in his position were not supposed to have relations with actresses – and she, as far as the Latin American press were concerned, was just a saloon singer. The affair was hurting his business. It had even made the front pages in neighboring Argentina, where he did a lot of business. His colleagues were afraid that he might do something foolish, like marry her. She came over all noble and said that perhaps they should not see each other so much any more. His response was to whisk her off to Estado del Paradiso, a vast mansion he owned set in acres of gardens and looking down on 50 miles of virgin forest. Over an intimate dinner served by a vast retinue of staff, Juan told her that, although he was separated from his wife, as a Catholic, he could not remarry.

"I can't marry you, Dorothea," he said, "but I can give you the benefits of marriage."

He made a vast sweeping gesture that took in the house, the staff, the gardens, the forests...

"Everything you have seen," he said, "is yours for all time, and this can be your home if you will be my *concubina*."

She realized that their affair would have to go underground. He would go about his business while she waited for his return in splendid comfort at Estado del Paradiso, but they could never be seen in public again. She asked to be taken back to her hotel. They agreed that she would have five days to think it over. When the time was up, she would meet him in São Paulo and tell him her decision.

Back in Rio, Dorothy was suicidal. She was realized that she was being offered the same arrangement offered by so many white men in the US. She tried to contact Juan, but could not reach him. A doctor had to be called to give her a shot to calm her. When the week was up, she arrived at São Paulo to find that Juan was not there to greet her. Instead she was met by his chauffeur who, she noticed, was not wearing his cap. Nor was he driving the usual limousine, but a much more anonymous car. She felt that she was already dissolving into the background. The chauffeur took her to Juan. They talked over the situation, but she decided that the arrangement offered her no security. What happened if he died or found a new *concubina*? Would she have to start back in show business all over again? The following day she was on a plane back to Los Angeles.

During the flight, she reviewed the situation once again. Despite the sensuality and beauty of the love affair, she felt that she had been psychologically raped by a man who not only cared nothing for her but also cared nothing for his own people – particularly the black-skinned Brazilians who lived in abject poverty. Not only was Juan a bastard, he was a fascist bastard. Once again, she chastized herself, she had failed to find the right man.

Dorothy studied at the Actors' Studio with Marilyn Monroe. They would pour out their hearts to each other about their failed relationships. It always fascinated Dorothy why white men thought that black women were better in bed. She was intrigued by a price list circulated by a Hollywood madam at the time which quoted: Whites $50; Orientals $75; Negroes $100. Was it because black women were supposed to be more uninhibited in bed? Or was it because they were the forbidden fruit?

One story particularly cheered Dorothy. A slim and pretty girl she had known in Watts made her living as a prostitute. She had little to look forward to in life, but one night she was called to a poker game where she met a white stockbroker who took a shine to her. He set her up in a nice house. Then, to everyone's surprise, he married her. To Dorothy, this meant there was still hope.

After long sessions at the gym, Dorothy slimmed down to 34-22-36, went on the road again, and poured all the money she earned into glamorous gowns. At the Mocambo, "the swank crowd cheered loud and long for her songs of SEXperience," as one reviewer put it. "Every number had a thin lining of sex."

Her dressing room was full of flowers and cards, and men were drawn to her like moths to a flame. She saw dozens of them, while keeping in contact by phone with Jerry Mayer, Peter Lawford and Harry Belafonte – though not with Juan. She never spoke to him again. Her relationships with men fell into a set pattern. They would make contact with her via her room, the maid, her pianist or the club manager. They would meet and spend a couple of hours or a day together, but when it became clear that she was wanted a serious relationship and, more than anything, to get married, their interest cooled. Dorothy put this down to America's attitude to color. She found herself the "tragic mulatto" of fiction – too light to be accepted by the growing number of politically conscious African-Americans and too dark to be accepted into white society, with the movie roles and marriage to a white man that went along with it. No matter how beautiful or talented she was, the color barrier was still there.

She also recognized that her beauty stood in her way. Plain girls, both black and white, could find husbands who were faithful and supported them. But with everything that nature had endowed her with, she only encountered bad faith, vacillation and men who ran away. Beauty, she decided, was a curse. However, she thought it might help her get the title role in *Carmen Jones*, the movie version of Oscar Hammerstein's Americanized version of Bizet's opera that was then casting. When she went up for it, the producer-director Otto Preminger was unimpressed.

"You can never play the Carmen role," he said. "You are too sophisticated. You could never play a whore."

Dorothy was determined to prove him wrong. She went out and bought a low-cut blouse and a provocatively short skirt. Then she returned after taking the precaution of removing her underwear. She barged into his office during a conference and leaned forward over his desk so that everyone present could see that her magnificent breasts were natural, unpadded and completely unsupported. Then she put one leg up on the chair beside Preminger so that he could clearly see that she was not wearing any panties.

By way of an audition he asked her to open and close the draws in his desk. She had to bend down low to do this. Then he asked her to open and close the draws again, this time from the other side of the desk. He liked what he saw.

Preminger was nothing if not a compassionate man. When he saw that the poor girl could not afford any underwear, he took pity on her and scheduled a screen test, which he directed himself. It was a bedroom scene which involved a number of "frank shots." The action was red hot and Preminger was quite overcome with the sexual excitement Dorothy generated. By the end, she lay back on the couch exhausted.

"Well, young lady," he said, well satisfied, "you've got the part."

The day before shooting began, Dorothy decided she did not want to play Carmen Jones after all. She feared a backlash in the African-American community if she, a black woman, played a whore. Otto Preminger knew how to handle this. He went around to her apartment on Sunset Strip and they drank some champagne together. He told her that she must let him take charge. She was more than equal to the part and, together, they would make the best picture of the year.

As the evening drew on, she became fascinated by this man who was already a Hollywood legend. He had been an actor in the famous Max Reinhardt Theater in pre-war Germany, before coming to America to direct some of the classics of the 1930s. He was 20 years her senior, but she let him put his arms around her. Although he was bald and stout, he was definitely all male. During the making of the movie, he explained, it was good if the director and the star did a "two-to-two for the duration of the picture." It was good for both the picture and the people involved, he said, if they got to know each other body and soul. Impressed by his argument, she sacrificed herself for the sake of the picture and that night they became lovers.

During the shooting of *Carmen Jones*, Preminger did everything to smooth Dorothy's path. In the evening he would have dinner at her apartment and drink champagne – he had it delivered by the case – then he would stay the night so that they could work at producing the best possible movie. As the filming progressed, Dorothy grew afraid that their affair would end once he had the movie in the can. Otto, however, hinted that this might not be the case. He contemplated divorcing his wife.

Carmen Jones opened to rapturous reviews, particularly for Dorothy whose name was moved up the billing.

"I bathed in the glorious reviews of *Carmen Jones*. I felt I had made a name for myself," she said. But then she read a review that said: "Sometimes she threw around obvious sex." Sexual remarks about her always hurt and outweighed all the other compliments written elsewhere.

She was nominated for an Oscar, the first African-American to be nominated for a major acting role. Preminger warned her that she would not get it.

"The time is not ripe," he said. Just as the time was not ripe for him to marry or even to be seen in public with a black woman.

Although the movie was over, they continued to be lovers and drank more champagne. Off-screen he taught her how to be a movie star.

"Drink the richest and the best," he said. "Never settle for anything less."

He dictated what she wore, who she saw, where she went

and who she was seen with. As well as her lover, he was the daddy she never had. He also taught her how to approach Darryl Zanuck,[7] head of 20th Century Fox, who agreed that she would not be used merely as "a Negro actress."

"I see you as a rounded-out actress who can do anything," he said. "You can appear in a variety of castings, as Italian, Brazilian, Puerto Rican, Mexican, anything."

Preminger insisted that she ask Zanuck for more money than he wanted to pay. It was the only way to win his respect. She got a three-year contract at $75,000 a year. The problem was he also began to interfere in her nightclub act, a medium he knew nothing about. He wanted to dress her in black and light her with a single spot on her face. She knew that nightclub audiences wanted to see her boobs and watch her wiggle her ass. She hated him turning up unannounced at her engagements.

While in New York, she was feeling low and the hotel doctor was called to give her a vitamin shot. The following Sunday he took her to see some old movies at the Metropolitan Museum. They liked each other from the off, but Dorothy was concerned about his unpredictable mood swings. She discovered that he was alternating uppers and downers, and began substituting placebos. She told her manager, Earl Mills, that the doctor had been practically impotent from drug taking when she first met him. That was why his wife had left him. Now he was virile again and Dorothy admitted to helping him out on that score. She liked helping people.

Despite this romantic interlude, she still wanted to marry Preminger and she asked him to give her a child. He said no. It is thought that she had an abortion that upset her for a long time.

"I should have gone ahead and had that child anyway," she said.

She sought solace with Edward Cheyfitz, a red-headed Jewish lawyer and prominent Washington Democrat. She always got on well with Jews. Although Cheyfitz and his wife had separate bedrooms, he refused to sleep with Dorothy. He did not want to have an affair with her, and would only sleep with her if they could marry. And he did not want to get a divorce.

She was on the verge of breaking up with Preminger, and flew to New York to see Cheyfitz. But when she arrived at Idlewild Field - now JFK International Airport - she was paged. It was Preminger, who ordered her to come home. She did so. He picked her up from the airport and drove her home to Hollywood, but he did not say the words she longed to hear. She thought that he was afraid of what marrying a black woman might do to his career. When she got out of the car the relationship was over.

Dorothy began to see that, although she had not grown up with the racism of the South, she still faced an insurmountable race barrier.

"God, if God was a beautiful black woman, probably couldn't surmount it," she said.

In frustration, she began to wreck her life, turning down starring roles and throwing money about.

"Some people kill themselves with drink, others with overdoses, some with guns; a few hurl themselves in front of trains or autos," she said. "I hurled myself in front of another white man."

When she had sung at the Riviera in Las Vegas, a bouquet of flowers came from a Jack Denison. By now, she ignored stage-door johnnies, but Denison was persistent. A Canadian of Greek origin and the owner of a small nightclub, he sent flowers every day and kept in touch when she was out of town. He told her that he had been in love with another Negro woman. They had planned to marry, but she had died. Dorothy only found out later that the girl had died shortly after giving birth to his daughter, who had to be supported by Joe Louis and other prominent members of the African-American community when he failed to provide child support. Still, he had mentioned the magic word "marriage" and, when she split with Preminger, she simply phoned him and said: "Jack, I'm coming to Las Vegas. Your apartment needs a woman's touch."

She moved in and they lived as man and wife. Dorothy admitted that she simply "invented a married life" for herself. They stayed together for over a year.

Meanwhile she was making the movie *Island in the Sun* (1957), which dealt with a love affair between a white man and a black woman. No one was quite sure how far they could go with interracial lovemaking on-screen. The story was set in the Caribbean and a British actor, John Justin, was used for the lead, but still the dialogue was constantly being watered down, to Dorothy's constant frustration. Her character, who had been demure in the book, turned out to be a whore on-screen, who did little but sit around on a big brass bed with her stockings rolled down.

"It's so hard for them to think of a Negro island girl as anything but a prostitute," she said.

While filming on location in Jamaica, the cast paired off – with the exception of Dorothy, who was constantly on the phone to Denison, and her former beau, Harry Belafonte. Belafonte, naturally, wanted to take up where they had left off, but Dorothy insisted that she was a one-man woman. In frustration, one night, he broke her door down. His desperation deepened when she won a limbo competition and went swimming with James Mason. Belafonte eventually called a white girl he knew, Julie Robinson, a former Katherine Dunham dancer. She flew in to keep him company. Later, they married.

In *Island in the Sun*, Dorothy Dandridge proved once again that she had on-screen sizzle. Next came *Tamango* (1957), in which she played an African slave loved by a white ship's captain. It was aimed at the European market, although diluted love scenes were filmed for a US version. However, it was an unwritten rule of the Motion Picture Producers' Association that there should be no intimate interracial love scenes, and the movie got little exposure in America. Another attenuated interracial love scene appeared in *The Decks Ran Red* (1958) which also starred James Mason and Stuart Whitman. And both Dorothy and Trevor Howard[8] – an accomplished ladies' man – were frustrated when their on-screen kiss was cut from *Malaga* (1960).

Dorothy got to play a whore again in *Porgy and Bess* (1959). She received hate mail accusing her of demeaning African-Americans and asking: "Why do you always play prostitutes?" Harry Belafonte pulled out of the picture, but Otto Preminger, directing, called her and urged her to take the part.

"It'll make you as big a star as you were when you did *Carmen*," he said.

On the sound-stage, their relationship was professional. Preminger gave her a hard time like the other actors. He was so tough with them and so tough in his portrayal of African-American life – for the times – that he was accused of being prejudiced. However, the studio warned her against going public about their affair to rebut the charge.

Eventually the frustration of filming got to Dorothy and she decided to quit show business once more.

"Jack," she said to Denison, "don't you think we ought to get married?"

"Sure, honey," he answered. "Why not?"

The ceremony was held at St Sophia's Greek Orthodox church in Los Angeles. That evening they flew to San Francisco. In the bridal suite on the top floor of the Fairmont, Dorothy was just slipping into a negligee she had bought especially for the occasion when Denison revealed that a new club he had opened in Hollywood was in trouble. Before even consummating their marriage, he wanted to cut their honeymoon short and fly back to Los Angeles. He said that if she did not start singing in his club right away and save it, he was going to jump out of the window.

"Jump," she said, pulling off the negligee. She dressed and went down to the lobby where she met some friends and joined them for drinks. Later, when she returned to the suite Denison had calmed down, but it did not make her feel any better.

"The note on which we started our honeymoon was a banknote," she said.

Reluctantly, she played his club, but it was too small to exploit the business she generated and it went out of business anyway. Denison sat around at home drinking. They rowed. There were no more movies on the horizon and the fees she could command for singing engagements dropped off sharply. Then she was hit for taxes and lost a packet investing in an oilfield in Arizona. In November 1962 she filed for divorce. Four months later, as the decree absolute came through, the bank foreclosed on her house. Just as she was getting kicked out of her home, her daughter Lynn was returned to her. She had missed a few payments to the woman who looked after her. Dorothy found that she could not take care of her daughter. The state stepped in and took her away.

Dorothy continued her singing career. She had an appreciative white following, but she became more and more concerned about the American attitude of white American men to black women and the fallacies black and white people invented about each other.

"One of the fondest notions whites seem to have is that Negro men have a larger phallus than white men," she said. "This is unproven, and it can't be proved by me."

Dorothy would certainly have been in a position to know and I for one, as a white man, find that a comfort. When it came down to it, racial prejudice, she concluded, was basically sexual. Although she had done well in life, she felt that white men had treated her little better than those men in the South who kept a black woman in a shack so that he could use her for sex now and again, without any thought of marriage.

She began to play smaller and smaller rooms. Her debtors and the IRS pursued her and she began to drink too much – Otto Preminger had left her with an insatiable thirst for champagne. Her sex life fell on hard times, too.

"In Toronto, my morale was so low … I threw myself on a few men, thinking I might as well have an orgasm as there isn't much else," she said. Even her search for the "big O," it seems, was not often successful.

Denison had taken over as her manager during her marriage. Now she called back Earl Mills. He whisked her off to a health farm in Mexico where, he claims, they became lovers. Her career was just on its way up again when, on September 8, 1965, she died from an overdose of the antidepressant Tofranil. It is not known whether it was an accident or suicide. She was just 42 years old.

According to Earl Conrad, who wrote the foreword to her autobiography *Everything and Nothing*, certain friends unintentionally hastened her death by warning her that if she told her life story she would hold back the march of black womanhood.

"Dorothy Dandridge wanted to tell of her friendships and romances that crossed the color line," he said. "But her friends attacked her in full force, telling her that her autobiography was a disgrace and should be kept quiet."

Certainly her autobiography is far more sexually explicit than Earl Mills's biography, which was made into the movie *Introducing Dorothy Dandridge*. Strangely, Dorothy always thought that a white actress would to be cast to play her in her life story. Instead she got the incomparable Halle Berry. Sadly, we will have to leave the sex life of Halle – and that of the gorgeous Robin Givens – for future volumes of *Sex Lives of the Hollywood Goddesses*. They are on my wish list, but, for now, they must be considered work in progress.

As for Dorothy, she wanted the story of her friendships and romances that crossed the color line to reach a wider audience. I hope I have helped. She went to her grave still puzzled by what white men saw in black women. I wish I could have been there to tell her. America hasn't got it yet, but with the rate of interracial marriage in the UK soaring, I am proud to say we Brits understand.

4

Wuthering to New Heights

Although Dorothy Dandridge was known as the first Hollywood goddess of color, that accolade properly belongs to Merle Oberon. But she hid it. She allowed people to believe that she was born in Tasmania, like Errol Flynn.[1] Actually she was born in Bombay of mixed parentage. This attempt to obscure her past in the racist Hollywood of the 1930s encouraged all sorts of tantalizing rumors to spring up around her – that she had been a streetwalker in London and Calcutta and that she had been sold into the brothel cages of Bombay as a child. The truth is that she was an extraordinarily beautiful woman who used her sex and her exotic background to her advantage.

Merle was a true child of the British Empire. Her mother, Charlotte Selby, was a Eurasian girl from Ceylon, now Sri Lanka, half Singhalese, half Irish. She had just turned 14 when she was impregnated by an English tea planter. He went through the motions of marrying her to legitimize the child, but divorced her immediately. With money from her husband's family, she moved to India with her daughter, Constance. She worked as a nurse but, a pretty young woman, she spent much of her time entertaining dashing young English officers. One of her lovers was an army engineer named Arthur Terrence O'Brien Thompson. Not only did he enjoy the favors of Charlotte, he rarely missed an opportunity to molest Constance, who was now a pretty 14-year-old. Charlotte fell pregnant and they married. Leaving Constance behind in Poona, they moved to Bombay, where they lived in the Khetwadi district, famed for its nautch girls and just a few steps from the red light district of Kamathipura where young girls sold into the brothels were displayed in bamboo cages for all to see.

Estelle Merle O'Brien Thompson – known in the family as Queenie – was born on February 19, 1911. Three years later her father died of pneumonia on the Somme. She never knew him. By the time she was a teenager, she was following in the footsteps of her mother, going to the movies and nightclubs with young military men and brokers who might help her scale the social ladder. At the age of 17, with her dark hair, smokey eyes, full lips and ravishing figure, she was so much in demand that she was accused of being a prostitute. In fact, encouraged by her mother, she was a giddy young thing in love with love and a glutton for the firmness of the male body. Her beaux included Jimmy James, Oswald Maitland, David Hammersley, and Gordon McDonell, who wrote the story for Alfred Hitchcock's *Shadow of a Doubt* (1943).

At Firpo's in Calcutta, where young Anglo-Indian women could rub shoulders with British businessmen, she ran into Mark Hanna, head of Paramount Pictures in India. One night in his apartment, he introduced her to Colonel Ben Finney, a 28-year-old big game hunter, the heir to a Virginia fortune and a great catch for Merle. For the next week, he was her constant companion. They went dancing at Firpo's and the Great Eastern Hotel. Merle looked ravishing in stunning backless dresses with her body powdered to pass as white. She tried hard to seduce Finney, but he was cool and prim. Then one night when he took her home he noticed that the light on the stairs of her apartment block was out and offered to walk her up. This was Merle's big chance. She got him into the flat, but before anything untoward could take place her mother appeared, her brown skin looking conspicuously dark against the white of her robe. Although Merle dissembled, it was clear that Charlotte was not the maid. The cat was out of the bag. Finney was from Virginia where interracial sex was illegal until 1965, but he was too much of a hypocrite just to drop her. He said if she came to see him in Antibes, where he was spending the following summer, he would introduce her to the movie director Rex Ingram, who lived nearby in Nice.

Merle raised the fare for herself and her mother from the rich merchant Sir Victor Sassoon, but before they left, Constance turned up. It is not clear whether Charlotte ever told Merle that Constance was her half-sister, preferring to pass her off as a foundling. However, the two girls got on. One day Charlotte returned to find Constance praising Merle's beautiful 18-year-old body, as Merle stood admiring herself naked in the mirror.

"What if the sweeper should come in?" asked the furious Charlotte.

"Lucky sweeper," said Merle.

In July 1929, Merle and Charlotte sailed for Marseilles on an Italian freighter, while Constance went to a nunnery. Meanwhile, Mark Hanna sent a telegram to Finney who was staying at the Hôtel du Cap, saying: "Merle Sailed For Marseilles – And You." Finney became uneasy. With all the prejudices of his slave-owning forebears, he was concerned about being seen with a girl whose brown limbs would show up against the white sand of Eden Roc, the famous beach at the end of the hotel garden. He told the front desk that, when Merle turned up, they should tell her that he had left for Paris. Again, not wanting to leave her entirely in the lurch, he called Rex Ingram in Nice and told him that a young hopeful was on her way from India to see him and to be sure to give her an audition.

While Merle disembarked at Marseilles, Charlotte went on to London. Merle called the Hôtel du Cap to be told that Finney had left for Paris. She refused to believe it and hurried to the hotel, only to find that Finney had fled. But Rex Ingram was not going to get away.

Ingram had been an ace in the Royal Flying Corps, before emigrating to the US at the age of 19. At 32, he launched Rudolph Valentino's[2] career with *The Four Horsemen of the Apocalypse*. Now 36, he had his own studio, the Victorine, in Nice and a mansion, the Villa Rex, which hosted a year-round party for the rich and famous. He was pursued by women and surrounded himself with beturbaned Africans, veiled dancing girls, midgets, dwarves and giants... With his taste for the exotic, he took one look at Merle and hired her on the spot, casting her in *The Three Passions* (1928), a movie about love, money and religion. With the money she earned, she headed on to London, where she caught up with Charlotte. They took a flat off Baker Street, which Merle paid for by taxi dancing at the Hammersmith Palais. Her stunning good looks, gorgeous figure and flawless dancing meant that she was soon whisked off to the West End, dancing at the Café Anglais in Leicester Square, the Café de Paris in Coventry Street and at the legendary Embassy Club in Bond Street, where she saw the Prince of Wales, the future Edward VIII.[3] During the day she worked in a flower shop or did extra work at Elstree Studios where, in the commissary, she met a young man named Reginal Truscott-Jones, who became the great Welsh womanizer Ray Milland.[4]

"She was the most exotically beautiful creature I had ever seen," said Milland. "She was like an advertisement for Singapore Airlines before the airline existed. I didn't take my eyes off her for the next nine months."

Her beauty won over the actor Edward Ashley, who agreed to make a screen test with her. She then approached a young man who worked for Alexander Korda, the Hungarian-born movie producer who was the leading light of the British film industry at the time. He also crumbled, but the test was actually made for Irving Asher, the head of Warner Brothers in England. It was a disaster. Merle fluffed her lines and began to cry. When the footage was sent to Hollywood, Jack Warner famously telegrammed back: "IF YOU WANT TO SLEEP WITH WOMEN GO AHEAD, BUT DON'T WASTE MY MONEY TESTING THEM."

Nevertheless, Merle continued to work as an extra under various names and let her extraordinary beauty do the rest. She became the mistress of the actor-director Miles Mander, who gave her a bit part in his movie *Fascination* (1931). The production boss of British Paramount, Reginald Denham, remembered her turning up on the set.

"One day Miles brought a young girl on to the set at Elstree whose beauty electrified the whole studio," he said. "Stagehands in platoons whom I had never seen before appeared miraculously from behind scenery to stare. Electricians clambered down from their bridges, and clerks and secretaries sneaked out of their cells."

Still working at the Café de Paris, Merle set her cap at the black crooner 'Hutch'. At the time, Jamaican-born singer Leslie A. Hutchinson was wooing London society with the love songs of the day. Dressed in white tie and tails, he sipped champagne from a glass which he rested on the lid of his Steinway and mopped his brow with a huge silk handkerchief. Though married with children, he was pursued by society ladies who sought the ultimate thrill – sleeping with a black man. He had a number of duchesses and countesses under his belt, and had a well-publicized affair with Lady Mountbatten.[5] By seducing Hutch, Merle climbed another rung of the social ladder. Now she was rubbing shoulders with the rich, the powerful and the titled. And among her new social circle was Alexander Korda.

Merle was two-timing Hutch with the American golfing tycoon Charles Sweeney, who said: "If I'd known that Merle was going out with that nigger boy, I would never have allowed her to." In his autobiography, Sweeney admitted that he was ashamed to be seen entertaining Merle because of her Indian background. He only took her to social events because she wanted to go so badly and because people envied him for escorting such a beauty.

It was Alexander Korda's formidable wife, the silent movie star Maria Corda, who first drew Merle to her husband's attention. This sounded the death knell of his marriage. However, Korda was as ambitious and image-conscious as Merle, and could not be seen to be having an affair with an extra. Before he bedded her, he would have to make her a star. Under her new name, Merle Oberon, she took over the lead in *Wedding Rehearsal* (1933) from Ann Todd, who was injured in a car accident. Then in *Men of Tomorrow* (1933), she got off with her leading man, Maurice Bredell, though she fell out with the mannish German director Leontine Sagan – famed for her first movie *Mädchen in Uniform* (*Girls in Uniform*, 1931), a lesbian tale set in a suitably strict German girls' school.

Soon after, Merle fell ill. She had been experiencing pain during intercourse with the numerous men she was dating. Then she began bleeding. It was discovered that she had cancer in one of her Fallopian tubes. The operation to remove it was a disaster, not least because she came round halfway through. While operating, the surgeon discovered cancer in the other Fallopian tube, so he whipped that one out too. He did not tell her, pretending that he had merely tied it. He feared that the psychological shock of becoming infertile at such an early age would imperil her recovery. Peritonitis set in. This was in the days before antibiotics, but Merle pulled through. She was convalescing in Margate when Korda decided to give her her big break. She was to play Anne Boleyn in *The Private Life of Henry VIII*[6] (1933). This was, at last, a credible role. Merle was certainly the sort of beauty that a king would dump his queen and get excommunicated for. The part made Merle Oberon a star.

After bedding Merle, Korda made her sign her to a long-term contract to prevent her going to Hollywood, where producers were showing considerable interest. Merle herself was showing considerable interest in marrying into the British aristocracy. She had been introduced to these vaunted circles by Douglas Fairbanks Sr[6] and Jr,[7] who she met during the filming of *The Private Life of Don Juan* (1934). To improve her chances of marrying a duke, she took elocution lessons to mask her lilting Indian accent, caked herself in white make-up and introduced her mother as her maid to anyone who visited their flat. She also expressed gratitude that her Fallopian tubes had been tied. She was afraid that if she married a man with a title, her husband would not want to risk having a "black" child. Korda's publicity department at London Films came up with the story of her Tasmanian origins. Hobart was so remote, who was going to check? Her father was posthumously promoted to the rank of major. It was true that he had died of pneumonia, but on a big game hunt, not in the mud of Picardy. Her mother became a fair-skinned English rose. Later, when Merle's real mother died, a portrait was painted of this fictitious white woman and it hung above the fireplace in a number of Merle's abodes. Her bogus biography even ended up in *Who's Who*.

Merle was a regular guest at the home of Douglas Fairbanks Sr and his mistress, former chorus girl Lady Sylvia Ashley.[9] There she met the American producer with underworld connections Joseph Schenck[10] who, in his declining years, enjoyed the youthful attentions of Marilyn Monroe.[11] His wife, the silent movie star Norma Talmadge, had recently walked out on him and he was in England looking for a new wife who would bring him a bit of "class." Fairbanks meticulously concealed Merle's background and her reputation for being a bit of a goer from Schenck. All Schenck saw was an upper-class British beauty.

Schenck was hardly her most dashing lover. He was not a handsome man, squat and fat, with thinning hair and heavy jowls. An ill-educated refugee, he had made good in the fledgling movie industry back in the silent days, after a stretch in pharmaceuticals. A ruthless businessman, he had rough manners and a violent temper. On top of all that, he had the beginnings of an ulcer which resulted in indigestion, flatulence, stabbing pains to the stomach, ill-temper and regular vomiting. Merle put up with all of these because, clearly, he was her ticket to Hollywood. He dangled the prospect of a major part in his partner Darryl Zanuck's[12] new musical *Folies Bergère* (1935) opposite Maurice Chevalier.[13] The very thought made Merle's eyes widen – and it undoubtedly had the same effect on her legs.

On a whim, Merle, Schenck, Fairbanks and Ashley flew to Cannes and, at last, Merle got to stay in the Hôtel du Cap. The paparazzi – though yet to be given that name – had a field day snapping the famous lovers. Merle and Schenck were all over the newspapers. Korda was furious.

At a beach party, with Merle in a ravishing white Molyneux number, Schenck announced their engagement and flashed an enormously expensive diamond ring. This did them both a power of good. She got more of the publicity that is the lifeblood of a Hollywood goddess, while he looked like Jack the Lad in macho movie-producer circles.

However, their relationship was already on the rocks. When they married, Schenck wanted Merle to give up the movie business and become a housewife and hostess. Merle would not hear of it. She had something more along the lines of actress Norma Shearer's[13] marriage to MGM's head of production, Irving Thalberg,[14] which had made her a star, in mind. Three days later, pressing business forced Schenck to return to Hollywood. Merle was not sorry to see him go. She already had a contract for *Folies Bergère*. In the meantime, Merle was to star as Lady Marguerite Blakeney in *The Scarlet Pimpernel* (1934) opposite the celebrated cocksman Leslie Howard,[15] who had first made his name playing opposite the voracious Tallulah Bankhead.[16] Their affair began straight away. Howard was legendary between the sheets and Merle could not get enough of him. One day Howard's long-suffering wife, Ruth, walked into his dressing room to find them at it on the floor.

"What are you doing?" asked the embarrassed Ruth, not knowing what else to say.

"Rehearsing," Howard replied without missing a stroke.

"Rehearsing for what?" asked his wife before turning on her heels and marching out. Mrs Howard did not return to the studio. Previously she had turned a blind eye to her husband's myriad affairs, but this one was different. Plainly he was head over heels in love with Merle.

Merle and Howard lunched together behind a screen in the refectory as if no one knew of their affair, which greatly amused the rest of the cast. Meanwhile, Korda had to stand by silently watching as the two engaged in passionate lovemaking on and off the set. It must had been all the more galling as, for all Howard's exquisite Englishness, he was a fellow Hungarian. But Korda was man of the world enough to know that any wound he suffered was self-inflicted.

"The only thing worse than a producer falling in love with his leading lady," he once said, "is a producer falling in love with his leading man."

Hearing of Merle's affair with Howard, Schenck sailed back to England and insisted that they marry right away. She was to forget about *Folies Bergère*, give up her career and come to Hollywood as his wife. She said: "No way," and held 20th Century Fox to its contract on *Folies Bergère*. Then, with the greatest reluctance, she pulled the enormous engagement ring off her finger and gave it back to him.

When asked by a reporter about the breaking off of the engagement, Schenck said: "There's still time. After all, we're both young." Schenck was 54, but he was nothing if not a practical man. That night he sold the ring to Douglas Fairbanks Sr, who promptly put it on the finger of Lady Sylvia Ashley now that his divorce from Mary Pickford[17] was underway.

Reluctantly, Korda gave Merle leave to go to Hollywood to make *Folies Bergère*. She also persuaded Leslie Howard to join her later, talking him into playing the lead in the Broadway play and then the film version of *The Petrified Forest* (1936). Merle traveled out on the *SS Paris*.

Also on board were the French movie star Lili Damita[18] and the young Errol Flynn. Both Korda and Howard worked for British Intelligence – indeed *The Scarlet Pimpernel* can be read as a propaganda film with the Jacobins standing for the Nazi's – and it has been said that Merle was booked on the same ship to keep an eye on Flynn, a Nazi sympathizer. Or perhaps, over dinner at the captain's table, they were supposed to discuss Tasmania, Flynn's birthplace. To her dying day, Merle Oberon hated Errol Flynn.

In New York, she caught up with Ben Finney. Catching sight of him across the dance floor at Jack Ramsey's nightclub, she stalked the big game hunter, crept up behind him, put her hands over his eyes and whispered in his ear: "It's a long way from Calcutta, isn't it, you son of a bitch."

Things did not go well in Hollywood. The studio make-up department spent hours trying to darken her skin while she tried to lighten it. She was supposed to be playing a Eurasian in the picture, though she ended up looking Chinese. She found Maurice Chevalier[19] unattractive, though the script called for her to kiss him passionately. Chevalier himself was somewhat distracted at the time. He was simultaneously filming a French version in which, unlike the English one, the chorus girls neglected to cover their breasts. Merle he dismissed as a "child woman" – presumably because she was not showing her mammaries.

"For God's sake, Merle," screamed the director when Merle gave the Gallic lover a peck on the cheek. "You're a madly in-love, tropical, oriental sex-pot. That's why we hired you." Off-screen, perhaps.

Fearful of blowing her big break in Hollywood, on the next take she threw herself at Chevalier almost knocking him off his feet. Then she swept off back to her dressing room.

That kiss had a profound effect on Chevalier. Finding himself alone at Christmas, he made his way to Merle's house. She, too, was alone and they spent the holiday together, but her thoughts were with Leslie Howard, who was rehearsing *The Petrified Forest* in New York at the time. He could not concentrate on the play for thoughts of Merle and his state of mind was not improved by the arrival in New York of his wife, Ruth. Suddenly, with days to go before the play's opening, he flew to Los Angeles through a violent snowstorm – a hazardous and uncomfortable business in the days before planes flew in the stratosphere above the weather. After one night of turbulent passion, he flew back to New York through the crumps and bumps of another blizzard, arriving just in time for the dress rehearsal. It did the trick. His performance on the opening night electrified Broadway. Merle had no complaints either. In fact, just an hour after filming the final shot of *Folies Bergère* she was on a plane to New York to be with him. She checked into the Gotham Hotel. He checked in too, though he had an apartment where he was living with his wife and children. His wife, knowing what was going on, would constantly send their teenage son, Ronald, over to the Gotham to interrupt their lovemaking. Howard, unashamedly, introduced Merle to his son as his future step-mother.

Ruth Howard was so upset she flew to California, where she planned to get a quickie divorce. This was a mistake. She should have gone to Nevada or Mexico. In Hollywood, old friends persuaded her to go back to New York and fight for her husband. While she had been away, Howard had been so distressed by her absence that he burst out in a rash of painful and hideous boils. Again, in the days before antibiotics, nothing could be done, except to lance each one separately. Merle wanted to nurse Howard through his ordeal, but she could not risk being seen constantly in his suite. If the press got hold of any hint of adultery, it would damage both their careers, perhaps irrevocably. As it was, Howard had to quash press speculation about a divorce by saying that his wife and children were essential to his existence. When Ruth returned to his side, Merle found that their affair was over.

Meanwhile, Merle had come to the attention of the legendary producer Sam Goldwyn,[20] who offered her a part in *Dark Angel* (1935). Back in Hollywood, she met David Niven,[21] who, though penniless, moved in Hollywood's highest circles. There would be no more lonely Christmases for Merle. They would ride, surf, swim and fish together. He was well supplied with invitations to yachting parties and they would sail off for weekends of lovemaking on Catalina or Ensenada, or at Roland Colman's ranch at San Ysidro.

They moved in together in a cottage on the beach, not far from Malibu. She helped him with his acting. Niven had been blacklisted by Zanuck for boasting that he could play polo, then losing a chukka. Merle persuaded Niven to go to a tennis club which had a Turkish bath that Goldwyn frequented. In the steam room, they fell into conversation and Goldwyn offered Niven a test – largely to annoy Zanuck. Merle then used her charms on Goldwyn to make sure the best director and cameraman available were used. As a result, Niven was signed to MGM.

But Merle was rarely content with just one lover. During the filming of *Dark Angel*, Merle formed an intimate relationship with the cameraman Gregg Toland, who flooded her face with white arc light to bleach out any hint of her roots. She also met Gary Cooper,[22] but failed to seduce him. Although one of the greatest studs in Hollywood, his taste in women was unfathomable. He had a long affair with the plump and aging Countess Dorothy di Frasso,[23] who also numbered among her lovers Mussolini[24] and the gangster Bugsy Siegel.[25] Merle's rejection by Coop caused fits of crying. Eventually she broke down completely and Goldwyn closed down the production for several days. She recovered when she heard that Korda wanted her for two new pictures – *Cyrano de Bergerac* with Charles Laughton and a full-scale *Anne Boleyn*. To celebrate, she went dancing at the Trocadero with Niven, who took it in good part when he was addressed by a fan as "Mr Oberon." Also in the party were Marlene Dietrich[26] and her lover Joseph von Sternberg,[27] Joe Schenck and Robert Young.

Merle traveled to London only to find that the two projects Korda had promised her were so much hot air, but Goldwyn called her to say he wanted her back in Hollywood for *These Three* (1936), a bowdlerized version of Lillian Hellman's stage play, *The Children's Hour*, about a child who exposes two women's lesbian relationship. So she headed back to Hollywood and Niven. For Merle, Hollywood life had now become a long round of parties. Leslie Howard was also in California. He was seen chatting to her at a party. Although Niven was too insouciant to care, the hostess slipped Howard a Mickey. He collapsed at Merle's feet and had to be carried out.

At another bash at the home of her agent Myron Selznick,[28] Merle upbraided Selznick for not listening to a word she was saying.

"I'm thinking so hard about what it is like going with you I can't concentrate," he said.

"Well then, let's go upstairs now so you can get it off your mind," she replied.

At a Spanish-themed fancy dress party given by William Randolf Hearst's mistress, Marion Davies,[29] Merle dressed as a flamenco dancer, only to be upstaged by the dancer Tilly Losch who came as Goya's nude, the Duchess of Alba, in a skintight, flesh-colored body stocking that left so little to the imagination she might as well have not bothered.

Merle's close collaboration with director William Wyler precipitated the breakup of his marriage. She played opposite Niven in *Beloved Enemy* (1936). Then the two of them took off on a trip across America. For the trip, Merle used her real name, Thompson, and Niven became Mr Thompson. Goldwyn was furious, not least because Niven left himself open to prosecution under the Mann Act which outlaws transporting a woman across a state line for immoral purposes. And there was no denying that their purposes were immoral. When Niven did not respond to a series of telegrams from the studio warning him of the consequences, Goldwyn fired him. But Merle had Goldwyn in the palm of her hand. She talked him round and Niven was reinstated.

She was called back to London to play the murderous and sexually insatiable Messalina in *I, Claudius* (1937) opposite Charles Laughton. The picture was a disaster. Merle found Laughton's masochistic homosexuality distasteful, nor could she stand working for the cold and sadistic Joseph von Sternberg. The picture was finally halted when she received a cut on the face as the result of a car accident. It was never completed.

By this time, Merle was a big enough star for Korda to be seen with in public. Niven, in the meantime, had hooked up with the blonde actress Virginia Bruce, widow of the silent star John Gilbert.[30] When Merle returned to Hollywood to film *The Cowboy and the Lady* (1938) with, as her choice of director, William Wyler, she forgave Niven for his infidelity and they reconciled. In the movie, she was supposed to play opposite Gary Cooper but, as he was unavailable, she took as her lover George Brent, who had just broken up with Greta Garbo.[31]

Wyler was fired by Goldwyn, but was then recalled to direct *Wuthering Heights* (1939). Although Niven was on hand, playing Merle's husband, the romantic lead of the movie was Laurence Olivier.[32] Naturally Merle wanted to bed him, but at the time he was passionately involved with Vivien Leigh, as we shall see in the next chapter. When Merle turned up in his dressing room he rejected her. Afterward this made their on-screen love scenes a problem. Merle found it difficult to embrace a man passionately on the set who had turned down her advances in private. Nevertheless it was this movie that put Merle at the height of her career. Now she was an irresistible trophy for Korda.

She went back to England with him amid rumors that they had already married in Canada. They were, in fact, engaged. Merle claimed it was the real thing, despite the difference in their ages and Korda's lack of any obvious physical appeal. But Alexander Korda was Britain's biggest movie mogul, equally at home on the sound stage at Elstree and in Buckingham Palace. She had been his mistress – privately, then publicly – long enough. She wanted to be accepted at the palace and one day be, perhaps, Lady Korda.

From England they headed on to the South of France, staying naturally at the Hôtel du Cap. Although everyone knew they were sleeping together, they had the discretion to take separate suites. Also staying there that spring with Joe[33] and Jack Kennedy,[34] along with Marlene Dietrich and Joseph von Sternberg. Merle and Korda planned to marry there. She was to be a June bride, but this presented difficulties. Neither had a birth certificate with them. Korda's was in Nazi-ran Hungary, while Merle's was in India, though she was still pretending that they would have to send to Hobart to get it. What's more, Korda's ex-wife, Maria, was in Hollywood, telling everyone that they had not been legally divorced.

Korda eventually badgered the local mayor into marrying them. One of the witnesses was Suzanne Blum, lawyer to the Duke and Duchess of Windsor.[35] Notably absent from the wedding was Alexander's brother, Zoltan Korda, though he and his wife were staying at the Hôtel du Cap at the time. They did not believe that Merle was attracted to Alex, let alone in love with him. She was 28 and a noted beauty; he was 45, flabby, unfit and physically unappealing. However, they were compatible in another way. She did nothing to conceal her ruthless ambition for money and position, while he loved to flaunt his wealth and power. As a wedding present, Korda gave

Merle a necklace that had once belonged to Marie-Antoinette.[36] But after just two days and one night of marital bliss, they began rowing. The rows continued as they flew home to England.

Merle detested cigarette and cigar smoke, insisted on getting her beauty sleep, rarely drank and ate like a sparrow. Korda constantly puffed on a huge cigar, stayed up all night, drank like a fish and stuffed his huge belly day and night. While he consumed a whole pheasant and other game for breakfast, she nibbled a single slice of toast. They moved into a house near Denham studio with his family who despised her. But being married to Korda did have its fiscal compensations, like when she spent Christmas with the Mayers and gave Louis B's[37] daughter Edie Goetz a Renoir.[38]

When war came, Merle returned to Hollywood to play a young girl who falls in love with a middle-aged composer in *The Constant Nymph* (1943). Before she could start filming, her face erupted in hundreds of bleeding pustules and it was feared that her great beauty would be lost. Korda flew out from England amid intense criticism that he was fleeing the country at its moment of danger, but he could hardly tell the press his real reason for going. He discovered that there was a plastic surgeon in New York who could possibly save Merle's face. She flew to New York with her face veiled. In Manhattan, she underwent a painful procedure where her face was frozen, the skin ground off with a diamond-tipped drill and the flesh stripped. If this was not bad enough, when the skin grew back it caused intense itching. Merle had to have her hands tied to the bed posts to stop her from scratching at it and was fed through a glass straw. She had to endure this three times, and even then she was left with pitting around her mouth. It took years of facials and beauty treatments before this disappeared. As it was, she could not play the young girl in *The Constant Nymph* and the role was taken by Joan Fontaine.[39]

Unable to make pictures, Merle now wanted to make babies. She went to the doctor's where she was told that she had probably lost both Fallopian tubes back in 1932 – though he could not be 100 per cent sure without an exploratory operation.

Disappointed, Merle hoped she would be able to take the role of Lady Hamilton in Korda's 1941 propaganda movie *That Hamilton Woman*, but the part went to Vivien Leigh, who played opposite her new husband, Laurence Olivier. All Merle could do was lust over Olivier in the rushes. The movie was released to protests from the German Consul General in Los Angeles, and Korda was called to testify before a Senate committee investigating the activities of foreign agents in the US.

By this time, the physical side of their marriage was over. Merle made a couple of comedies to cheer herself up, then went to New York to raise money door-to-door for the British War Relief Fund. There she met Richard Hillary, the once-handsome, young Australian fighter pilot who was terribly disfigured during the Battle of Britain. He later detailed his ordeal in his famous book *The Last Enemy* (retitled *Falling Through Space* when published in the US). At the time, he was in New York, trying to stir up anti-German propaganda. Both the British ambassador in Washington, Lord Halifax, and the White House feared that his horrific appearance might backfire as a propaganda tool, making American mothers fearful that their sons might be similarly disfigured if America joined the war. Hillary was deeply depressed when Merle met him in New York. She was determined to help him snap out of it.

Most people could not bear to look at Hillary. His face had been so badly burnt that all that remained of his nose were two holes and his mouth was two pieces of flesh taken from his thigh and sewn in place. His hands were claws and watching him eat or drink was unbearable, even for his friends. Though Merle's beauty was now returning, her brush with disfigurement gave her an instant rapport with Hillary and she was particularly attracted by his beautiful warm voice.

She knew that most women would shrink from the hideously disfigured 22-year-old, but Merle sensed that he was very virile and that sex would restore his self-confidence. She gave him lots of it. It was just what he needed. According to his British publisher, Merle put a twinkle back into his lidless eyes. Hillary was a powerful, frenzied lover whose libido had been suppressed by his long stay in hospital and a shortage of lovers who dared touch him. That, coupled with Merle's insatiable sexual appetite, gave them months of ecstatic nights until Hillary returned to England and the RAF that autumn. Merle stayed on in New York raising hundreds of thousands of dollars for the British war effort by selling kisses.

Merle then returned to Hollywood to make more propaganda films. By this time Korda knew that their marriage was over and accepted his fate. Eighteen years her senior and unfit and out of condition, he knew that he could not satisfy a woman like Merle, and a woman of her beauty was bound to find some younger and more virile man to share her bed. She stayed on in Hollywood, while he began to move his possessions back to England.

But, before they split completely, she became Lady Korda. A joint ENSA-USO tour to entertain the troops meant that she was at Buckingham Palace at the side of her husband when he was knighted. She also spent a weekend with Richard Hillary, confiding to fellow actress Patricia Morison that she aimed to give him two days and two nights of complete happiness, even though he was now involved with an English girl. She met Winston Churchill, who was a fan and had supplied a speech for *That Hamilton Woman*, and General Dwight D. Eisenhower,[40] who shocked her with his racism when he complained of his black troops running off with English girls.

Back in Hollywood Merle was lent out to Harry Cohn[41] at Columbia for the movie *First Comes Courage* (1943). Cohn fell madly in love with her. His approach was anything but subtle. He had a private corridor connecting his office to the actresses' dressing room and he was prone to appearing unannounced with his erect male member out, asking what they were going to do about it. Most actresses had no alternative but to comply with his wishes for fear that he would blacklist them. No one was going to blacklist Lady Korda, however, and she politely declined his crude advances.

Cohn was not her only problem on the picture. The director was the prominent lesbian Dorothy Arzner, who regularly had Merle up at her house for late-night script conferences. During the shooting came the news that Richard Hillary was dead, after the transport plane he was flying was lost at sea. There was no way that she could return to England for the funeral or the memorial service at St Martin-in-the-Fields. Her only consolation was that he was buried in Buckinghamshire, near to the inn where they had spent their last weekend together. She was also comforted by the publication, to considerable acclaim, of *The Last Enemy*, which Hillary had begun writing when they were first together in New York. Soon after, she heard of the death of Leslie Howard. He had been doing some intelligence work in Lisbon and when he flew back to London his plane was shot down.

Korda now spent most of his time in London, while Merle was being squired about Hollywood by her former fiancé Joe Schenck. She was out of town a lot doing war work, visiting the injured in hospitals and doing intelligence work – it seems she made at least two clandestine trips to London, one via Lisbon.

Back in Los Angeles, she began investing in real estate. To keep track of her holdings, she went to business school where she brushed off date after date from fellow students who were barely able to keep their minds on their work with her in the class.

In her next movie, *The Lodger* (1944), she played opposite Laird Cregar, a tortured, overweight homosexual in the Charles Laughton mold. Merle put him on a diet. Under her tutelage, he began to believe that he could give up paying for the favors of Venice Beach hunks and go straight. Unfortunately, Merle's vegetable diet and the heterosexual exertions he endured with a young actress he had picked up did for him. He died of a heart attack at the age of 28.

Short of straight male company, Merle took a young blond carpenter from the set of *The Lodger* back to her place. After a dinner, which was fraught due to the boy's lack of conversation, she tried to seduce him. The youth protested that he was a born-again Christian, recently baptized, and that he had forsworn pre-marital sex. Next day he was missing from the set. That left the way clear for the movie's handsome 35-year-old cameraman Lucien Ballard. They had something in common. He was part Indian – although in his case though the Indian part was Cherokee.

He developed a new, bright white light that bleached out any hint of scarring left on Merle's face. He patented it and marketed it under the name Obie – after Merle – and it became an industry standard. The affair was hinted at in *Photoplay* and Louella Parsons and Hedda Hopper were showered with gifts to keep their mouths shut.

Merle and Lucien spent weekends at her pink stucco beach house named Shangri-La, rising at seven and going to bed at nine. After years with the portly Alexander Korda, it was like reliving her time with the young David Niven. Unfortunately taking up with a cameraman meant that she no longer received invitations from Goldwyn, Mayer or any of the top-flight Beverly Hills–Bel Air crowd.

"Some of us tried to point this out to Merle," said Edie Goetz, "but she would hear none of it. She was completely besotted."

She wrote to Korda asking for a divorce, while his first wife, Maria, crowed with schadenfreude. Alex began to believe that she had never really loved him and the studio publicity department began to put a smokescreen between the happy couple and the women's clubs who would have picketed her movies if they had known she was an adulteress.

Next she made *Dark Waters* (1944). When she got the script, she did not like it, and had it rewritten. The task was undertaken by John Huston[42] who undertook the task simply to get the stake money to back a hot tip at Santa Anita racetrack. The horse lost.

The director André de Toth persuaded her to film without make-up, showing the scarring on her face for the first time. She cried real tears during the scene. Her leading man Franchot Tone[43] bet that he could seduce her, but failed.

Then Harry Cohn was on her tail again to play George Sand[44] in *A Song to Remember* (1945), the story of the composer Frycek Chopin.[45] The film put her back on top as a star.

During her next movie *This Love of Ours* (1945), Merle got her Mexican divorce from Alexander Korda and married her cameraman Lucien Ballard by proxy in Juarez. Ironically, though the film flopped in the US, it was a big hit south of the border. Fortunately, Ballard was away on vacation during the shooting of her next film, *A Night in Paradise* (1946). In it, she played opposite the Turkish heart-throb Turhan Bey.[46] For the first three days he fooled her by hobbling around disguised as a white-haired old man. Then he threw off his disguise and emerged as a virile matinee idol.

"Merle took one look at his bulging biceps and immediately changed her mind about him," said director Arthur Lubin.

Unfortunately, at the time Lana Turner[47] was also madly in love with Bey and turned up on the set to make sure that nothing untoward went on. Merle then insisted that the studio closed the set and Lana Turner was left peeping through the scenery as the action unfolded.

The affair was shortlived as, at 34, Merle still wanted to have a baby. She stuck with Ballard, figuring that if the child turned out a bit dark, his Cherokee blood would be blamed. She flew to the Harvard Medical School to check out the possibilities, but there Dr John Rock confirmed the earlier diagnosis – that both her Fallopian tubes were missing and she would never have children of her own.

Merle now had a $12,500-a-week contract. Written into it was a clause that specified that Ballard was to shoot every picture she made. This made her leading men nervous when shooting love scenes. She made none-too-subtle advances to them off-screen, usually whipping them off to lunch *à deux* and leaving Ballard behind on the set. It did not stop there. During the shooting of *Berlin Express* (1948), actor Charles Korvin recalled that she fell madly in love with her leading man Robert Ryan. He was very much her type of man's man and Ballard could only watch as she became more and more engrossed by him.

"I know that she slept with Ryan both in Hollywood and [on location] in Europe," said Korvin. "Incredibly, Ballard, who undoubtedly knew about it, accepted it all with good humor."

Korvin and the rest of the cast thought it was cruel and unfair of her and strongly objected to the affair. Ballard denied knowing about it, but on the train from Paris to Berlin, Merle would leave Ballard in their sleeping compartment at night and go to Ryan's. Then when they stopped off at Frankfurt for two days, Merle shared Ryan's room when they were billeted in a nearby castle, without a thought for the humiliation she was heaping on her husband. The affair lasted until the end of the picture. But aAfter they returned to Los Angeles, Merle went on a skiing trip to Sun Valley with Ballard. She never saw Ryan again.

To patch up her marriage, she took Ballard on a belated honeymoon to Switzerland and Italy. In Rome, they stayed with the American adventuress Dorothy, the Countess di Frasso. She regaled them with the story of her affair with the Jewish gangster Bugsy Siegel, who she met when he came to Italy to sell arms to Mussolini. Dorothy and Bugsy had then headed off together to the Cocos Islands off Costa Rica, looking for the buried treasure of the conquistadors in a boat hired from Marino Bello,[48] Jean Harlow's[49] stepfather. Bello supplied a crew that was half Jewish and half Nazi, with predictable results. Dorothy spent the war in Mexico, dogged by the FBI because of her investments with the isolationist Senator Robert R. Reynolds in German arms factories. After the war, she returned to her villa in Rome where Hitler[50] and Mussolini used to meet. She liked to show off the huge bath which, she boasted, could barely contain the considerable bulk of Il Duce. Even though Merle was an Anglophile and a committed British patriot, the war was now forgotten.

Dorothy di Frasso hosted a party for them on the island of Capri, where Merle was introduced to Count Giorgio Cini. He was the son of Count Vittorio Cini, an Italian aristocrat who had done the unthinkable in 1918 and fallen in love with a movie star. And not just any old movie star. His siren was the Italian vamp Lyda Borelli, star of the controversial *La Donna Nuda* (*The Naked Woman*, 1914). When she fell pregnant with Giorgio, he had married her. She gave up her career at its height and became a virtual recluse in the Palazzo Loredan Dorsoduro in Venice. Count Vittorio Cini went on to became a minister in Mussolini's government. Eventually he turned against the dictator and brought him down, and found himself imprisoned in Dachau concentration camp. Giorgio grew up to be athletic, charming and handsome. At the age of 30, he was already a millionaire in his own right, owning hotels in Venice and Rome and a shipping line, and he could sweep any woman off her feet.

His latest conquest was the exquisitely beautiful Countess Madina Visconti Arrivabene, daughter of one the richest and most distinguished families in Italy, which could trace its wealth back to medieval times. She had been the toast of Paris before making a brilliant marriage to the distinguished racehorse-owner Count Luigi Visconti, but in 1947 she met Giorgio and fell madly in love with him. There were rumors that they married secretly. However, at the time Giorgio met Merle, he had applied to Pope Pius XII[51] for a special dispensation to marry Madina and she had applied for an annulment.

Despite the presence of Madina and Ballard, they did nothing to hide their mutual attraction and slipped away from the party to make love. The following day, Merle and Giorgio left Capri and checked into the royal suite in the Excelsior, the hotel he owned in Rome. The affair became a massive scandal in Italy, not least because the Pope had chosen that very moment to grant Madina's annulment. She was inconsolable. Ballard was not best pleased either.

According to Hollywood producer Mike Frankovich and his wife, the actress Binnie Barnes, who played alongside Merle in *The Private Life of Henry VIII*, who were staying in the Excelsior at the time, Ballard managed to get onto Merle's balcony. Smashing his way in with a metal chair, he caught Merle in bed with Giorgio, who promptly threw him out. Ballard denied the story.

Powerful forces were at work. Giorgio's father summoned him to Venice and ordered him, now that they had the approval of the Vatican, to go ahead and marry Madina. Giorgio would not listen. Ballard headed back to Hollywood, while Merle made plans to abandon her career and marry Giorgio. She set about getting together enough lire for a dowry.

Alexander Korda was in Rome at the time with his new mistress, the statuesque blonde Christine Norden, who starred as the famous Second Empire Parisian courtesan Cora Pearl[52] in *Idol of Paris* (1948). They too were staying at the Excelsior. Korda was concerned about Merle. His fretting angered Christine and he had to placate her with gifts of diamonds. Giorgio was also plying Merle with jewelry and, Christine said, in the middle of one of the fights that were already marring their tempestuous relationship, he tried to take some of it back. Merle, however, was so intent on holding on to it that she swept up the jewelry and ran out into the street with it naked.

Such antics naturally attracted the attention of the paparazzi, who began pursuing them. To escape them and the growing political instability in Italy, Merle and Giorgio flew to the US. She pretended that he was a hairdresser from Rome, but the gossip columns soon picked up on her Italian count. Merle hoped that he would fit into the social set denied to her during her association with Ballard, but while her friends looked down on Ballard, Giorgio looked down on them. One night when they were entertaining the Zanucks at Palm Springs, Merle insisted that Giorgio wear a tuxedo - she had just had one made for him. He refused. He had just bought three ships for his shipping line that day and he did not see why he could not wear what he damn well pleased at dinner. When the guests arrived, they were still embroiled in a furious row. Giorgio eventually stormed out.

Despite their constant rows over Merle's extravagance, everyone said that she looked wonderful. This was attributed to Giorgio's tireless lovemaking. She called friends for advice on every aspect of her appearance, so that she would look as beautiful as possible for him. She would change as many as six times before allowing Giorgio to see her. Under this pressure, he eventually relented and donned the tuxedo.

They returned to Paris, where they bumped into Korda and Christine again. Her nose was put out of joint even more when Korda gave way to Merle's persistent demands for perfume and gowns. Christine concluded that Alexander was still in love with Merle, and that Merle rejoiced in treating him as her slave. Korda and Christine split and he went on to marry an obscure Canadian girl called Alexa Boycun.

While Giorgio went back to Italy on business, Merle returned to the US, where she tried to raise enough lire, which was not convertible, to marry. They were separated for three months.

They were reunited at a party given by the Zanucks in Monte Carlo, after reports that he had resumed his affair with Madina. The reunion was as passionate as ever. News of it caused Madina to attempt suicide, a mortal sin in the eyes of the Catholic Church. She was saved from an overdose at the last minute – nevertheless, the press blamed Merle.

The rows resumed. In one particularly bruising encounter, Giorgio drew attention to the scarring around Merle's mouth. She underwent plastic surgery once more. To convalesce, they took a Mediterranean cruise on his yacht. One night she found that her jewelry was missing and got hysterical. Giorgio's butler was blamed and was arrested. Even so, Merle continued to carry large amounts of expensive jewelry with her for the rest of her life.

The Cinis were dead set against any marriage between Giorgio and Merle. One evening the couple traveled by gondola to the Palazzo to confront them. Though Count Vittorio Cini was touched by her charm and beauty, he refused to condone the union. Meanwhile Ballard did everything he could to delay Merle's divorce. Eventually, it was granted in August 1949.

By then, Merle and Giorgio were staying at the Hôtel du Cap in Antibes. At a party given by Pamela Churchill, Randolph's wife, where she met up again with Winston Churchill, who promised to teach her to paint. After the party, Giorgio planned to fly back to Venice to try to talk his parents round one last time. Merle watched from the hotel balcony as his small plane took off. To wave goodbye, Giorgio got the pilot to dip the right wing. At that moment the engine cut out. The wing hit a pine tree and the plane burst into flames. Giorgio's burning corpse was thrown clear and landed practically at her feet.

Merle was so shocked and upset, she almost lost her reason. She tried to kill herself. She claimed that she and Giorgio had been married and always would be, and she spent weeks sobbing. She was too weak to attend his funeral and did nothing to counter Madina Arrivabene's claim that she had married Giorgio. Madina inherited part of Giorgio's wealth and Merle got nothing - apart from the blame heaped on her by both the Cinis and the Arrivabene clan. Back in London, she sought to contact Giorgio via a famous medium and did so, she was convinced, successfully.

She was still only 38 and needed earthly consolation, which she found with Earl Beatty, the son of a former Admiral of the Fleet. There was talk of marriage. In the meantime, she signed to star as a glamorous widow in *Twenty-Four Hours of a Woman's Life* (1952). This would take her back to the south of France, but she stipulated in the contract that the shooting must take place in Monte Carlo, not Antibes, where there were painful memories. She would take a short break in California.

Beatty flew out after her to propose marriage, but by that time Merle had met Dr Rex Ross, a handsome Hollywood physician. Beatty would have been the ultimate catch; marriage to him would have made her a countess. But when he arrived she turned him down because she could not have children to continue his line and she did not want to give up her career as she would have had to do if she married into the British aristocracy. Besides, she was already sleeping with Ross, who was prepared to give up his practice and travel with her as her personal physician. Beatty accepted defeat gracefully and returned to London where any number of young women were waiting to comfort him.

Although Merle was not in love with Ross - any more than she had been in love with Beatty or Korda - she talked about retiring after *Twenty-Four Hours of a Woman's Life* and marrying him. They announced their engagement in London that autumn. However, along with marriage would come American citizenship. This meant that she would have to present her papers to the Department of Immigration and Naturalization. She still did not want her Indian background revealed, so she told her lawyer, Greg Bautzer,[53] that she did not wish to proceed. She was staying with Bautzer in Palm Springs, taking mud baths, when Joe Schenck turned up. Merle was now offered a part that intrigued her. She was to play the Empress Josephine – herself of mixed race from Martinique – in *Desirée* (1954) opposite Marlon Brando's Napoleon. She was a little afraid of Brando's new style of screen acting, but the two of them got on famously. Meanwhile, Merle became convinced that Ross was having an affair with the beautiful singer, dancer and actress Liliane Montevecchi.

In pique, she accepted Conrad Hilton's invitation to attend the opening of a new Hilton Hotel in Mexico City. There she met Bruno Pagliari. He was short and far from good looking, but he was one of the richest men in Latin America. He invited her to his home, a construction of white bricks only slightly smaller than the White House in Washington, DC. She arrived in a black stretch limo wearing a white Balenciaga dress, off-set by the Korda diamonds. He took her into the library and showed her a first edition of Dante's *Inferno*. She took him into the bedroom and showed him the inferno itself.

They married in July 1957, only months after meeting. It was a marriage made in heaven. Her career was essentially over and she craved privacy. He was rich enough to build a wall around them $50 million high. For him, she was the ultimate trophy wife that he could parade in front of his business partners – and she had unrivaled contacts both in Britain and the US. Their honeymoon was a Mediterranean cruise, though they missed out the ports of call she had visited with Giorgio. Then they retired to Mexico, alternating between his white house in Mexico City and a palace in Cuernvaca, once owned by the conquistador Hernán Cortez. They adopted two children, a boy and a girl.

Merle soon found that this kind of life did not suit her. Her husband, a busy man with an international business empire to run, had no time to have sex with her. Although it was rumored that she was bedding numerous eligible men, from beach boys to business rivals, she remained celibate for months on end. Eventually she found an excuse to spend more time in Bel Air, where cells from the embryos of cows, pigs and sheep were injected into her to cure the scarring on her face once and for all. The treatment also gave her renewed vigor, enough to have an affair with the married Australian hunk Rod Taylor behind her husband's back.

After a second treatment she became romantically attached to Richard Rush, the young director of *Of Love and Desire* (1963) which was shot in Bruno's houses in Mexico City and Cuernvaca. Merle financed the film with her own money, and in it she played a woman much like herself – one with a tremendous sex drive. Soon after the movie finished, her leading man Steve Cochran met a mysterious end. He sailed from Acapulco on a yacht with three girls hired in Mexico City for what seems to have been intended as an ocean-going orgy, though one of the girls was only 14. A day out to sea Cochran began to experience severe headaches and passed out a couple of times. Pains in his stomach followed and he became completely paralyzed. Then he died. The girls had no idea how to navigate the vessel. A week later, they were towed into port in Guatemala with heat stroke, confused and on the brink of insanity. With them was the rotting corpse of Cochran. They told the police of his agonizing death, which exhibited all the signs of poisoning. However, the coroner concluded that he had died of an infection of the lungs and the girls were released. There was no inquest and no further investigation was made.

Merle now spent much of her time being a hostess. House guests included Ronald and Nancy Reagan,[54] Frank Sinatra,[55] Peter Lawford, Noël Coward,[56] Prince Charles,[57] Lord Mountbatten, George Hamilton, and Lynda Johnson, daughter of President Lyndon Johnson.[58] Merle was close to President Johnson himself and formed a more intimate relationship –

close to love, it is said – with Prince Philip,[59] a great lover of actresses who was another regular house guest. The man closest to her at this time, it is said, was the Cuban designer Luis Estevez. According to Charles Higham and Roy Moseley's biography, *Merle*, they were never lovers and never felt the slightest degree of romantic or sexual feeling for each other.

"Even when Luis, a man of great virility, was close to her flesh, to her velvety skin, beautiful breasts and delicately rounded hips, he felt no sense of the physical," the book says, "and he alone knew of her very occasional romantic adventures, kept utterly dark and hidden because she feared that she might cause pain to Bruno."

You don't say.

Apart from a brief affair with actor Richard Tate and a one-night stand with Eddie Fisher, whose father had advised him never to fall in love with a shiksa, Merle pretty much kept herself to herself. Then, at the age of 69, she met Robert Wolders, a handsome Dutchman 25 years her junior. Her marriage to Bruno Pagliari was now over in the physical sense, so Luis Estevez and the Hollywood hostess Ingrid Ohrbard fixed her up with Wolders, a protégé of Noël Coward and star of the NBC-TV series *Laredo* with a movie pedigree that included *Beau Geste* (1966) and *Tobruk* (1967). He also had a flourishing parallel career as a Hollywood escort. They became lovers. Merle wanted to hide the fact from Bruno, but Wolders insisted that she end her marriage.

Pagliari was crestfallen when Merle told him of her affair. She moved with the children to Los Angeles where they lived with Wolders. Merle and Wolders shared a love of nature, music and art and, when the children were grown, traveled together as man and wife. They made a movie together – *Interval* (1973) – where they played lovers in daringly explicit scenes. Ironically, it was shot in Mexico where, to save Pagliari's face, they pretended they weren't. The result was predictably awful. Merle lost $1 million; Pagliari considerably more. Merle and Wolders then set off on a round-the-world cruise. In Bombay, she was terrified of going ashore in case she ran into her half-sister, Constance.

In 1975, after returning from the trip, Merle and Wolders married. Estevez had succeeded in getting most of Merle's jewelry out of Mexico before the divorce. The newlyweds continued to travel the world but, after attending a civic reception in Hobart, given despite the fact that the authorities there had already discovered she had not been born in Tasmania, Merle had a heart attack. She recovered but died from a stroke on November 26, 1979, still maintaining that she was a white woman down under. But from my extensive study of women of color, they are rarely white down under. They are darker down there and that is the very place that mixed-race women exhibit their ethnic origins. "Pink chocolate" is the term used on Internet porn sites today. Let's not go into that. But were all those guys not paying attention?

5

A Scarlett Woman Named Desire

Laurence Olivier[1] rejected the advances of Merle Oberon preferring the charms of Vivien Leigh. So what did this girl have that Merle did not possess? It is said that she had a love affair with the camera. But she had plenty left over to give to more fleshly lovers.

Like Merle, Vivien was born in India, but in the breezy hill station, Darjeeling. She was also of mixed blood. Her father, Ernest Hartley, was a Yorkshireman. Her mother, Gertrude, was mixed French-Irish and a Catholic – though some said that she was of Armenian stock, which explained Vivien's dark, Eastern beauty, or even that she was half Parsi, making her very similar in make-up to Merle. Her father was required to resign from two exclusive "whites only" clubs when he married.

At seven, Vivien was sent back to England to be educated at a convent school, the Sacred Heart at Roehampton, just outside London. It was strict. The girls were supposed to take their baths wearing long, white calico cloaks so that their naked bodies would not be exposed. Knowing that the nuns would never check, some of the girls stripped off anyway. Vivian Hartley, as she was then known, was not among them. She was a good girl who never wore patent leather shoes lest they reflected what lay up her skirt, and she hid her used undergarments under her white nightdress, topping the pile off with her stockings folded in the shape of a cross.

The only thing this strict upbringing could not squeeze out of her was her precocious desire to be an actress. In plays at school, she played boys' parts, though she was not allowed to wear trousers as they were deemed immodest. Instead she had to wear long coats. Some of the girls who played the female parts opposite her were those who casually stripped off in the bathroom. This little bunch of friends was called the "exquisites" by the other girls for their radiant good looks and their luxurious hair. There were two suspected lesbians in the school and many of the older girls experimented with sex with each other. But Vivian was one of those who eagerly awaited the "real thing." The presence of any man, such as a plumber or a carpenter, at the school caused consternation for the nuns.

When Vivian's parents returned from India, they promptly took her on a Grand Tour of Europe. Her parents traveled in a threesome with John "Tommy" Thompson, who was said to be the love of Vivian's mother's life. The exact nature of their relationship is unclear, though her father said: "When Tommy wants a woman he knows where to find one." The one he found may well have been Gertrude, as Tommy stayed in Europe with her when husband Ernest went back to India. Gertrude had other admirers, who she often entertained into the wee small hours. Vivian teased her about her "beaux," who Ernest always remained on good terms with.

Ernest was no slouch either when it came to infidelity. He took a great many beautiful women as his lovers. Gertrude claimed that she once gave a dinner party where the wives of all those present had been his mistress at one time or another. Vivian said she always knew when her father was having an affair because he brought her bracelets. Ernest and Gertrude later told Laurence Olivier that they had a very happy and successful marriage.

The 14-year-old Vivian attracted her fair share of attention from the boys in the French seaside town of Dinard on the Brittany coast – a resort frequented by Picasso[2] – where they stayed. In letters home to Roehampton, she wrote that she was madly in love and that several boys were madly in love with her. She had more schooling in a convent in San Remo, where the girls went swimming in full-length, long-sleeved bathing suits buttoned to the neck. At a finishing school in Paris, a fellow pupil recalled the 16-year-old Vivian turning up to a school dance in a short dress with no make-up, prompting all the young men to desert their partners and flock to ask her to dance. She kept the picture of a boy by her bed and fell in love with silent screen heart-throb Ramon Navarro after seeing him in *The Pagan* (1929). During the interval she rushed to the loo to put on lipstick, which was considered "fast" in 1929. The story itself concerned a South Sea islander who fell in love with the daughter of a white trader. This may have rung some bells. She was taken out of finishing school when other girls started sneaking out to nightclubs.

During a skiing holiday with a group of friends of both sexes, she came down with a slight chill and stayed by the fireside. Not one of the boys could be persuaded to go out to ski that afternoon. All of them were too busy "finding ways to minister to Vivian's comfort."

In Germany, she listened to music, surrendering herself to the eroticism of Wagner[3] and insisting that she should be allowed to marry immediately, or she would never marry. Now 17, she claimed that she was already engaged to two German boys. And when she saw a good-looking waiter, she told him: "You deserve to be kissed" – in German, then did so. Her mother slapped her.

Back in England she met 31-year-old barrister Leigh Holman at the South Devon Hunt Ball. She had seen him previously only on horseback on the Downs and was struck by his resemblance to her favorite actor, Leslie Howard.[4] She fell madly in love and decided to marry him.

"Vivian was so young and wanted anything she could not get," said a family friend. "And she was going to be so lovely."

She was just 18. Holman was bowled over, too.

"No more enchanting girl than Vivian could have existed," he said.

But her horizons were expanding. He read a biography of Lilly Langtry,[5] which suggested that the life of an actress could be satisfying both on and off the stage. She read *Lady Chatterley's Lover*, when an expurgated edition was published in 1930.

Holman wrote to an old and trusted friend, Oswald Frewen, asking whether he and Vivian could come and stay. Frewen wrote back: "What sex is Vivian?" Holman replied: "A girl. I might even marry her."

Leigh's friend, the publisher Hamish Hamilton, would almost certainly have been a rival for her hand, if he had not just married Jean Forbes-Robertson. Later, his company published the definitive biography of Vivian.

In May 1932, she was accepted at the Royal Academy of the Dramatic Arts after an outstanding audition where she played Lydia's love scene from *The Rivals*. Holman rather looked down on theater people and considered RADA as another finishing school for Vivian, rather than a springboard to a career on stage and screen.

"She did not seem to me at that time to have ambition or the qualities that brought her fame," he said.

Indeed, she gave up RADA, at his request, five days before they married on December 20, 1932 at the Catholic church in St James's, Marylebone. There was little love lost, said one witness. Holman's mother did not approve of his marriage to the daughter of a rather dubious family. Holman himself, a long-term bachelor, was afraid of losing his independence. Vivian wanted to get away from home and her mother was eager to have her "married off, as she had become rather jealous of her," Vivian said.

After the ceremony Vivian slipped the wedding ring off her finger, either to wash her hands or show her friends. Gertrude was aghast.

"Vivian! That's terribly unlucky," she cried. "You must never do that."

They honeymooned in the Bavarian Alps, while Gertrude and Tommy headed for Biarritz. When the newlyweds returned to Holman's flat in St John's Wood, Vivian found there was nothing for her to do there. It was a small place and a maid kept it spick and span. After two weeks Vivian was bored and returned to RADA. Her husband disapproved but she told him that she was only doing it to keep up her French. She was reading and perhaps drawing inspiration from *Colette* at the time. At the end of term she appeared in a RADA production of *Saint Joan*, but that was the end of her stage training. She was already four months pregnant and the pregnancy annoyed, rather than thrilled, her.

When Holman went to Amsterdam on business, Vivian went to stay in the country with Frewen.

"This morning I have been lying practically naked while Oswald has been digging a hole for the cows," she wrote to Holman teasingly. "He assured me I must take everything off, that he won't look, but I must write and tell you so to make you jealous."

In anticipation of the addition to their family, Vivian and her husband moved to a Queen Anne house in the Shepherd Market area of Mayfair, which was then, as now, inhabited by the well-to-do and high-class prostitutes. On October 12, 1933, she had a baby daughter, who she named Suzanne. She soon found herself bored again. She began working as a fashion model behind her husband's back, then as an extra. They fell out when she flew back from a Baltic cruise without him to play the part of a schoolgirl in the movie *Things are Looking Up* (1935). After that, she decided that she was going to dedicate herself to being an actress. An agent suggested that she change her name so she took the stage name Vivian Leigh – adopting her husband's first name as her last. Later she changed her own first name to the unmistakably feminine

Vivien at the suggestion of West End impresario Sydney Carroll.

Carroll was a man who prided himself on discovering new actresses and he was not averse to using the casting couch to do so. He picked Vivien over several other ingénues to play the part of an 18th century prostitute who passes herself off as a virgin to disgrace a French aristocrat in *The Mask of Virtue*.

"He was smitten," said her agent. "She got more than the job. She got Sydney Carroll round her little finger."

She had already been turned down by Alexander Korda, who had no room for her in his stable. Korda considered Vivien an "English rose type." He already had two of those – Wendy Barrie and Joan Gardner. He also had Diana Napier, who he cast as a "high-class beetch," and Merle Oberon, who was his "exotic."

Vivien began to be seen out and about with Sydney Carroll and, when The *Mask of Virtue* opened, the newspapers proclaimed her a star. Korda and Joseph Schenck[6] came to see her and fought over which one was going to sign her. Success on the West End stage propelled her into the glamorous theater set. While there was no more adoring husband than Holman, Vivien flirted outrageously and confided her wildest fantasies to her friends. She told one: "If the Prince of Wales[7] asked me, I would become his mistress." Then she detailed how she would fulfill the role.

She began to feel discontented with her marriage, and told her school friend Patsy Quinn that she felt "tied."

"I'm so young and I do so love the gay life," she said, "and Leigh – though I adore him – is not very social."

The truth is Holman was out of his depth. Vivien was now rubbing shoulders with the likes of Ivor Novello, Noël Coward[8] and the young Laurence Olivier. He had seen her in *The Mask of Virtue* and, apart from finding her looks "magical," said that he felt "an attraction of the most perturbing nature I have ever encountered."

Already it was clear to her that her sexual needs were not being fulfilled within her marriage and she took a lover – the actor John Buckmaster. She felt no guilt about this. It was just that she had to throw off the sexual constraints imposed on her by her religious upbringing. Holman knew of the affair and tolerated it.

Vivien went to see Olivier in Theatre Royal, in which he played a young American matinée idol in the mould of John Barrymore.[9] He swaggered around in black tights with a white shirt gashed open to show his manly chest, delivering suggestive lines with panache and leaping over a balcony like a young Douglas Fairbanks.[10]

"What a virile performance," she said.

He might actually have been satirizing John Gilbert.[11] The year before, he had been summoned to Hollywood to play opposite Greta Garbo[12] in *Queen Christina* (1933), but Garbo snubbed him and the part went to her old flame, the silent star Gilbert who had fallen on hard times.

Vivien went backstage after the performance and, as he sat sweating from his display of physical prowess, she leant over him and planted a kiss on his shoulder. His slim hips and his eyes flashing against his mascara aroused in her sexual longings that she had not known existed. She was instantly enslaved and went to see the play three more times.

But Olivier was no pushover. By his own account he had remained a virgin until the age of 24. He confessed he was dying to taste the pleasures of sex, but would do so "only with the blessing of God." Within three weeks of meeting the actress Jill Esmond, one of the great beauties of her day, he proposed. They married in July 1930. Esmond came from one of the great theatrical families and it was the most fashionable wedding of the season. However, just weeks before the wedding, she told him that "she was in love elsewhere and could not love me as completely as I could wish," he recorded in his autobiography.

"How soon the day o'ercast," he said with typical Thespian flourish. "The indications were that my dreams of high sexuality were not to be realized, which was depressing and soon became oppressive. I was just not imaginative enough to find what might be the key to Jill's responsiveness." Olivier, eager to cast aside his chastity, went ahead with the marriage anyway. But on the wedding night, Olivier claimed years later, he found his bride shared "the same unspoken dread of what was expected of us before going to sleep." After some embarrassed fumbling "we turned away from each other."

And that was that. It was only later that Jill Esmond came out as a lesbian and joined Hollywood's famed "Sewing Circle."[13]

Despite the storm clouds gathering, Olivier took his marriage vows seriously. When he was summoned to Hollywood for *Queen Christina*, women threw themselves at him, but he turned them all down. Such sexual continence would prove no obstacle to Vivien. One night, driving past the Whitehall Theatre where his name was up in lights, she said to a friend: "Someday, I am going to marry Laurence Olivier."

Her friend pointed out that they were both already married.

"It doesn't matter," Vivien replied. "I'll still marry him one day."

She threw her cap at him. She got Buckmaster to take her to the Savoy Grill, where she knew he often ate. Finally, they were introduced and, although his wife was present, she grasped his hand tightly and gave him one of her most devastating smiles. Buckmaster was piqued by this and teased her, drawing attention to the fact that Olivier had shaved off his Ronald Colman moustache to play Romeo in *Romeo and Juliet* – a beardless, though passionate, youth.

"What a silly thing Larry looks without his lip covering," said Buckmaster.

"I think he looks adorable," she said. "He's the sort of man I would like to marry."

Olivier brought a new realism and sexuality to the part of Romeo, after the more fey interpretation that John Gielgud had made famous. Once again, his performance stirred something in Vivien. She went backstage afterwards to tell him how marvelous he was. He confessed that she was the most beautiful woman he had ever seen. She invited him to lunch at the Ivy, but he turned up with Gielgud in tow.

Despite superficial resistance, it seems that they became lovers around this time. The French movie actor Jean-Pierre Aumont recalled seeing Vivien and her husband in the Soho restaurant. Seated at a table not far away was Olivier and a blonde woman. The atmosphere, Aumont said, was electric, but Olivier was still attempting to keep his marriage together.

"I think I will have a son and call him Tarquin," he said to Jill Esmond.

She obliged. She was six months pregnant when the Oliviers went backstage to congratulate Vivien after the first night of *The Happy Hypocrite*. When Olivier introduced his wife, Vivien took one look at her swollen belly and said: "How's little Tarquin coming along."

Jill was taken aback that Vivien knew such an intimate detail of their private life. It was as good as making a public announcement that she and Larry were lovers. But playing to the gallery was important for Olivier. According to his biographer, Roger Lewis, he could not reach an orgasm unless other people were watching him – or he could fantasize that others were doing so. Later with Sarah Miles, he begged her to give him a rundown of her previous lovers so that he could stage a fantasy competition with them in his mind's eye.

He may well have had competition in Vivien's bed when they were first together – and not just from her husband. Maybe it turned him on. Several biographers have said that she was having an affair with Alexander Korda at the time, apparently conducted in fashion model Eve Phillips's flat. It has been said that Korda was too deeply involved with Merle

Oberon at the time, but she was away in Hollywood, and Vivien seems to have stolen at least one of her parts. She was slated to play Roxanne opposite Charles Laughton in Korda's production of *Cyrano de Bergac*, though the movie was never made. It was noted at the time that Vivien was wearing darker make-up and brighter colors, giving her a more "exotic" look. This got her a part in *Fire over England* (1937) playing opposite Olivier as two young lovers caught up in intrigues surrounding the Spanish armada. Olivier's son was born during the shooting of the picture, but the filming made their affair unstoppable. It brought him into contact with Vivien every day. They had to act out passionate scenes before the cameras and, between takes, spent all their time together away from the cast and crew. One day they turned up together in Korda's office.

"Alex, we must tell you our great secret," said Vivien. "We're in love and we're going to get married."

"Don't be silly," said Korda. "Everybody knows that. I have known it for weeks and weeks."

He even lent them his house for their assignations. A fellow actor complained that Olivier was worn out and blamed the over-ambitious athletic stunts that he insisted on doing himself.

"It's not the stunts," said Olivier. "It's Vivien. It's every day, two, three times. She's bloody wearing me out."

But she was well satisfied.

"I don't think I have ever lived quite as intensely ever since," she told journalist Godfrey Winn. "I don't remember sleeping, ever; only every precious moment that we spent together. We were so young."

At the same time, she was writing to her husband telling him how much she missed him. Knowledge of the affair soon became public. They were seen dining in the Ivy and the Savoy Grill together. In itself this was neither shocking nor scandalous, but they were spotted by an actress coming out of a bedroom suite at the Savoy together early one morning and rumors spread across the West End like wildfire.

Korda encouraged the relationship because the romantic interest in the movie depended totally on Vivien and Olivier, who were actually playing minor parts. Flora Robson, who played the lead as Elizabeth I,[14] said that their love scenes were given full value. Graham Greene, then a movie critic for the *Spectator*, remarked that Elizabeth Tudor would hardly have allowed "so much cuddling and kissing in her presence."

Olivier was wracked with guilt. He called himself a "worm-like adulterer, slipping between another man's sheets" and hated his "two years of furtive, lying life," which he dismissed as "sneaky." Even so, he turned up at her house to nurse her when she had flu, paying more attention to her than to his wife and newborn son. Both Vivien's husband and Olivier's wife knew what was going on, but did nothing to stop the affair.

Olivier even turned up to Tarquin's christening party with Vivien. They were unmistakably together. After a few minutes they disappeared. Vivien did not come back, and when Olivier did, he had lipstick on his cheek.

After the filming of *Dark Journey* (1937), Vivien took a holiday in Italy with Oswald Frewen – Holman was tied up with the beginning of the Michaelmas law term at the Bar. They ended up in the Hotel Quisisana on Capri in the suite adjoining that of the Oliviers. When they met in the corridor, Frewen was quite taken back by the kisses, hugs and cries of "darling" exchanged between Vivien, Larry and Jill in this patently contrived encounter. After that, the doors between their suites were permanently open. Vivien even cabled home asking her husband if she could stay on longer, even though this would mean missing his birthday on November 3. She said that this was because the sun was "divine." In fact, the weather was bad, but Holman cabled back agreeing.

*

Frewen found the whole thing impossibly awkward as he was primarily a friend of Holman's. He was hurt that Vivien had used him in a plot to see Olivier as he had fallen for her himself. The uneasy situation continued. Holman, Vivien and Frewen went to see Olivier in *Hamlet*. Olivier, naturally, would turn up for her openings. The Holmans and the Oliviers even spent a weekend together in Sussex. They dropped by for a picnic at Frewen's house in Brede. In the visitors' book, Olivier was forced to sign his name above the date, so that his billing came above those of Jill and Vivien. The boy had star quality. He even took time out to talk to Frewen, trying to persuade him that Vivien would be better off with him than with Holman. He did not get a sympathetic hearing.

Next, Olivier was to play *Hamlet* at the Old Vic. He wanted Vivien as his Ophelia, but this time he was thwarted. The director Tyrone Guthrie sympathized with Olivier's "conflict between his violent, immature love for Vivien … and his more mature, subdued attachment to Jill," but Vivien was already up for the part of Scarlett O'Hara in *Gone With The Wind* (1939) which David O. Selznick[15] was casting. She had been obsessed with Scarlett since first reading the book. They decided that they could not risk any whiff of marital infidelity and broke off their affair. Things got even more fraught when Jill returned to the stage, playing Olivia opposite Olivier – ho, ho – in *Twelfth Night*.

Then, courtesy of Alexander Korda, Vivien and Larry were reunited on the set of *Twenty-One Days* (1937), in which Olivier's character kills Vivien's caddish husband and they start a new life together. Being in such close proximity they abandoned their struggle and resumed their affair. Afterwards, Olivier was due to play *Hamlet* in Elsinore. Guthrie offered the part of Ophelia to Jill, but Olivier insisted on Vivien. This time he got his way.

While Holman had to make do with reassuring telegrams, Jill Esmond went to Denmark to keep an eye on her husband.

Olivier found acting love scenes with his mistress in front of his wife almost impossible.

"We could not keep from touching each other, making love almost within Jill's vision," he said in his autobiography.

Alec Guinness, who was with the company, was delegated to distract Jill so that the lovers could have time alone together. But given Larry's need for an audience for his lovemaking, Guinness wondered whether Jill's presence was not simply adding fuel to the fire. However, the tension of the situation in the gloom of Elsinore seemed to unhinge Vivien. She became depressed, spoke to no one, her eyes appeared blank and she fortified herself with aquavit.

Back in London, Jill visited Vivien at her Mayfair home to confront her. Since the birth of her baby, Jill had, it appears, fallen in love with her husband for the first time. It was too late.

"Do you mean to marry Larry?" she asked.

"I do," said Vivien. "And he intends to marry me. One day, when all the hatred and resentment is finished, we will marry."

Vivien ordered champagne and enquired about all sorts of domestic details. How did Olivier like his boiled eggs? she asked Jill over a flute of bubbly. Did he prefer the yolks runny or hard?

Ten days after returning from Denmark, Vivien eloped with Olivier. They moved in together, before heading off for a vacation in Venice. Vivien promised to write to her husband after a month to tell him whether her new living arrangements would be permanent. She did and said they would be. Frewen, meanwhile, counseled Olivier not to marry Vivien, telling Holman that Olivier was "inconstant and unballasted," and that the relationship "won't last ten years – perhaps not five."

The couple were putting the finishing touches to *Twenty-One Days*, when a journalist commented that Olivier would make a great Rhett Butler. Vivien said: "Larry won't play Rhett Butler, but I shall play Scarlett O'Hara. Wait and see." Someone else suggested Clark Gable[16] as Rhett Butler, but Vivien would not countenance that. She did not like him.

While Vivien's mother, Gertrude, stepped in to look after her daughter Suzanne, Vivien sought to re-establish friendly relations with her husband. She sent him *A History of Furniture* for his birthday. (I think I should let that pass without comment.) But it did not soften his attitude towards divorce and he still hoped, wooden-headedly (sorry) to win her back. A visitor to their Mayfair home noted that he left her nightgown laid out for her, so she could return whenever she wanted. Similarly Jill Esmond refused to give Olivier his freedom and Vivien was constantly afraid that he would leave her to return to his wife and son.

They moved into a new house together, Durham Cottage, a love-nest with a small, high-walled garden hidden away off Christchurch Street in Chelsea. Vivien was getting offers from Hollywood, while Olivier took Ralph Richardson's advice to play more Shakespeare at the Old Vic, on the grounds that, if the scandal broke, it would do him less harm if he bore it with the dignity of a distinguished Shakespearean. Richardson also urged Vivien to join the Old Vic. The Queen took the two princesses to see them, indicating that gossip had not yet reached the palace. With war looming, they took off to France, traveling alone together, as Olivier put it, with "the glowing fulfillment of every desire of wayward lovers." Along the way he planned to stage the four great Shakespearean tragedies – *Hamlet*, *Macbeth*, *Othello* and *King Lear* – with Vivien as his co-star. The plan came to nothing. Instead they were both offered parts in *Wuthering Heights*. Olivier accepted and headed for Hollywood. Vivien declined and stayed behind – because she felt guilty that she had neglected her daughter after her elopement with Olivier and because she was holding out for Scarlett O'Hara. Three weeks later she followed Olivier. Sailing on the *Majestic*, she bumped into Hamish Hamilton who asked her why she was going to America. She said: "Partly because Larry's there, and partly because I intend to get the part of Scarlett O'Hara."

Hamilton laughed and bet her ten pounds that she would not get it. Fifty years later, he admitted that he had never paid up. Olivier's agent in Hollywood was Myron Selznick,[17] who just happened to introduce Vivien Leigh to his brother David with the line:"Meet Scarlett O'Hara."The rest is history.

Olivier was against her taking the role. He burst into Selznick's office and told him that he would not allow Vivien to play the part. After Olivier was rejected by Garbo he had persuaded Jill Esmond to turn down a role in Selznick's *A Bill of Divorcement* (1932), curtailing her Hollywood career, and go back to England with him. This time Selznick simply dismissed the great Thespian's objections by saying: "Larry, don't be a shit twice."

Holman also refused his permission. Vivien needed her husband's consent under US immigration law, but Selznick simply altered the contract and pulled strings to get her a work permit. He also set about altering the shape of her bust, though he insisted that her appearance should not otherwise be tampered with.

Meanwhile Olivier had finished *Wuthering Heights* – he later regretted being "high handed" with Merle Oberon – and went to New York to perform in *No Time for Comedy* on Broadway rather than go home to England. That way, he figured, if something went wrong for Vivien, he could fly out to Los Angeles on a Saturday night, spend four hours with her, and fly back to New York in time for the Monday evening performance. Twice Selznick summoned him to California to calm her down. Otherwise he went to broadcast concerts on a Sunday night and made sure that he was the last person to remain clapping, so that she could hear him on the radio. He wrote to her mother telling her how much in love he was with Vivien, how his life with her had become "unbelievably beautiful," and apologizing for all the heartache and distress they had caused. Vivien continued to write to Holman begging for a divorce – by that time Jill Esmond had agreed.

After a brief visit to England on the eve of war, Vivien and Larry returned to Hollywood, where Olivier was to play the male lead in *Rebecca* (1940). Vivien longed to play the title role and tested twice, but Selznick turned her down. Olivier was secretly relieved as he was embarrassed by Vivien's constant affection. Joan Fontaine[18] got the part. Similarly, he got out of starring opposite Vivien in *Waterloo Bridge* (1940), where she played a ballet dancer who turns to prostitution opposite Robert Taylor.[19] However, Vivien's secretary, Sunny Alexander, a Texan, said: "It is simply wonderful to be around such a beautiful love as theirs." And those who turned up on time to appointments at their house on North Camden Drive, Beverly Hills, would often find them in bed.

With the opening of *Gone With The Wind* and *Wuthering Heights*, Olivier and Leigh became Hollywood's golden couple. Vivien won an Oscar for Scarlett, and *Gone With The Wind* won best picture. The New York critics voted *Wuthering Heights* best picture and Olivier got an Oscar nomination. They moved into a bigger house, next door to Danny Kaye on San Ysidro Drive. Meanwhile the Second World War had started. Friends were joining up and British actors were heading home. At last, Jill Esmond was granted a divorce and Holman began proceedings. Vivien and Olivier were named as respective correspondents.

They returned home briefly to England, then went back to New York, where they played the star-crossed lovers in Olivier's production of *Romeo and Juliet*. Back in Hollywood they were Nelson and Lady Hamilton in *That Hamilton Woman*, which ran into trouble with the Hays Office as it showed a married man living in sin with another man's wife. A scene was added where a guilt-ridden Nelson was ticked off by a redoubtable clergyman. Nelson confesses penitently: "You are right in all you say. I realize it is a wicked, inexcusable thing to do and I am ashamed at my weakness in surrendering to it."

But it was too late for contrition in real life. Shortly after midnight on August 31, 1940, Vivien and Larry were married at Ronald Colman's Ranch San Ysidro in Santa Barbara, with Katharine Hepburn as a last-minute maid of honor. The "limelight of their adultery," as Olivier put it, was now over.

They returned to England, breaking Vivien's seven-picture contract with MGM. Olivier failed to get into the RAF, but joined the Royal Navy's Fleet Air Arm as a trainee air gunner, while Vivien went on tour with *Caesar and Cleopatra*. In the summer of 1942, they managed a brief holiday together in Wales. For the first two days, they did not get out of bed. Olivier said that no man had ever been made as happy as Vivien made him. Back in London, they had three nights of riotous living – during which Olivier and Holman were reconciled – before they returned to their duties.

Vivien went on a tour of North Africa to entertain the troops. Alec Guinness, then serving in the Royal Navy, jumped ship to see her. Concerned about how he would get back to port, she collared an admiral, caressed his campaign ribbons, and asked him what he was doing for the next few hours. When he said, well, nothing actually, she said that, in that case, he would not be needing his car. It was dispatched to take Guinness back to his ship, while the admiral was rewarded with a kiss. On returning to Britain, along with the rest of the cast, she had to strip to undergo a humiliating inspection for lice. By then Olivier was embroiled in making *Henry V* (1944), though Selznick, who still had her under contract, prevented Vivien from taking a part in the production. However, off-screen, they often rehearsed the "wooing" scene, in front of friends and alone, it seems. Vivien fell pregnant, but during the filming of *Caesar and Cleopatra* (1945) she fell and miscarried.

In February 1945, Selznick sued Vivien in an attempt to

force her to return to Hollywood and fulfil her contract. She contested the action, saying that as a married woman and she was subject to national service regulations, and won. But after the war she became depressed when Olivier's career began to outshine her own and, off stage, she began to feel that she could not fulfil his dream of pure, romantic love. While Vivien retreated to their new Buckinghamshire home, Notley Abbey, he went from triumph to triumph on the London stage, drawing on, it seemed, his personal anguish to the delight of West End audiences. Desperate for money, he even considered returning to Hollywood, but Vivien's problems with Selznick meant that no one there would touch him.

That year Larry was knighted and Vivien became Lady Olivier. But despite a series of triumphs on Broadway, the Oliviers were in such financial trouble that it was necessary for Vivien to go back to work. She returned to the West End stage, but soon her depression closed in again. Olivier was making *Hamlet* (1948) and wanted Vivien to play Ophelia. The producers, Rank, insisted that he use someone younger. The part went to Jean Simmons[20] and Vivien began to suspect they were having an affair. She began subtly to get her own back. The actor Esmond Knight recalled visiting Notley Abbey and seeing Vivien in a flimsy dress, plainly naked beneath it, deliberately posing so that she was silhouetted against the brilliant sunshine. Then she took the title role in *Anna Karenina* (1948), a tale of infidelity.

The Oliviers made a triumphant tour of Australia, but between the two of them something went disastrously wrong.

"Somehow, somewhere on this tour I knew that Vivien was lost to me," said Olivier.

She would flirt with other men in the company to make him jealous. In an effort to relieve himself of the burden of her insatiable sexual demands, he encouraged her interest in other young men – "Oh, quite innocently, at first," he says in his autobiography. For Olivier, some of the energy other men expend in sex had to be reserved for his first love, acting.

"He used to sit there watching her rehearse," said one member of the cast, "and embarrass everyone by getting erections.

Olivier damaged his knee playing *Richard III* in Sydney. On the boat home, he was laid up and Vivien, it seems, embarked on a diverting affair with the actor Dan Cunningham. Worse was to come: Olivier had seen the young Peter Finch in Australia and encouraged him to come to London. Not only had Finch met the greatest actor in the world, he also met "the woman who was to be his greatest passion, his mistress and very nearly the death of him." Those close to Vivien are sure that nothing went on between them in Sydney. When the Oliviers arrived back in London, Finch and his wife Tamara turned up and Olivier put him under contract.

The Oliviers confirmed their star status with a triumphant series of productions at the Old Vic, including *School for Scandal*, stage-designed by Cecil Beaton,[21] and *Richard III*, in which Vivien and Danny Kaye dressed up as specters and came on during the ghost scene near the end. In the midst of all this, Vivien told Larry one spring day in Durham Cottage: "I don't love you any more."

He was numbed. It did not help that she followed up with the same disingenuous bullshit we all say under these circumstances: "There's no one else or anything like that, I mean I still love you, but in a different way, sort of, well, like a brother."

Oh yeah. She was off on *A Streetcar Named Desire*.

The producer of *Streetcar* on Broadway was Irene Selznick, David's ex-wife. The London production was directed by Olivier who, it was observed, was brutal to Vivien during rehearsals. His lighting was particularly cruel. The *Times* noted: "Her fading features are exposed to the merciless light of an unshaded bulb."

The part was harrowing, leaving her white and shaking at

the end of the evening. Her mental state seemed to mirror that of Blanche DuBois. In periods of depression she was plagued by sexual fantasies. She was afraid that if left alone she would pick up a strange man on the street, take him home and seduce him. On one occasion she took a taxi driver home with her. On another, she felt the overwhelming urge to seduce a delivery boy. The idea of having sex with someone from the "working classes" seemed to assuage her guilt. Unlike Blanche, she did not give herself to men out of loneliness. Nor did she do it, at this time, when she was not "ill." She felt that she could not tell Olivier what was going on, or let him into her private world of fantasy. He made her feel clean, young and beautiful, somehow innocent and untouched, while, in fact, she wanted to be dirty.

Even Olivier admitted that *Streetcar* contributed to Vivien's final breakdown. It ran for 326 performances. Then she had to play it again in Hollywood, opposite Marlon Brando, winning her second Oscar.

In Hollywood, the Oliviers were now even greater celebrities than when they left. Danny Kaye spent $4,000 on a "welcome back" party for them. Everyone from Groucho Marx and Louis B. Mayer[22] to Lana Turner[23] and Errol Flynn[24] were there. Even John Buckmaster danced attendance.

A close friend of Vivien's, the dancer Robert Helpmann who, according to his obituary in *The Times*, was "a homosexual of the proselytizing kind," was very much a part of the "ménage" at Notley. In the first draft of his autobiography *Confessions of an Actor*, written in 1982, Olivier described numerous homosexual escapades, though his third wife, Joan Plowright, persuaded him to take them out. Danny Kaye, who was Olivier's lover, was also on the scene. Olivier confided to friends that for a long time he had found Vivien's aggressive sexual demands repugnant and burdensome. With Kaye, he simply abandoned himself to the erotic blandishments of a powerfully seductive man.

Vivien had long suspected Olivier's true nature. He had been a close friend of Noël Coward's and they had stayed at Coward's Jamaican home when she was recovering from exhaustion and depression after taking *Anthony and Cleopatra* and *Caesar and Cleopatra* to Broadway. She had seen pictures of Olivier at an all-male gathering performing a song-and-dance act with Kaye. The two were dressed as bride and groom. This could be dismissed as pure British music hall, but rumors in Los Angeles and New York held that Olivier and Kaye were deeply involved in an affair.

However, like many upper-class women, if her husband was being unfaithful Vivien preferred it to be with another man. Other women posed more of a threat. Meanwhile, they kept up a good front. After dining with Winston Churchill, his wife, Clementine, concluded that the old war horse was in love with Vivien.

Olivier turned down the chance to play opposite Vivien in *Elephant Walk* (1954). Instead, he suggested Peter Finch who he had under contract, so Vivien and Peter went off together to Ceylon, now Sri Lanka, to shoot the movie. Finch maintained that their affair began then, but others said that it had been going on since he arrived in England in 1949. For some time, Vivien had been berating Olivier for his performance in the bedroom – well, he could only manage it two or three times a day at the age of 29, remember – and Finch was a well-known stud.

Halfway across the world from her husband, she indulged herself to the full. With the two of them pushing each other to the limit with booze and bonking, the producer, Irving Asher, fearing that Vivien was having a nervous breakdown, summoned Olivier. He flew out and quickly discerned what was going on, but he could not find it in himself to blame Finch.

"Was he not simply doing what I had done to her first husband 17 years ago?" he wrote in his autobiography. He liked Finch personally and never expressed any jealousy over his superior sexual ability. After all, Olivier knew that he was incomparably the greater actor.

With the location shots in the can, the cast flew to Hollywood, where Vivien moved in with Finch and his wife, Tamara. One evening, when Tamara entered the bathroom while Vivien was bathing, Vivien tried to seduce her. The rest of the time, she used every caprice in her formidable arsenal to lure Finch away from his wife. She then went completely mad. David Niven[25] described her walking around her house naked, babbling lines from *Streetcar*. John Buckmaster then turned up fresh from a spell in mental hospital after molesting women on the corner of Madison Avenue and Sixth Street in Manhattan. He joined her in various nude escapades around George Cukor's[26] swimming pool. They tore up money, but he drew the line when she suggested they fly out of an upstairs window together.

Niven and Stewart Granger[27] turned up to rescue the situation and Buckmaster told them that he had been sent by a higher power to protect Vivien. That's okay then, said Granger, who escorted him back to his chalet in the Garden of Allah.[28] Meanwhile, Niven had tried to sedate Vivien, but she outsmarted him. He ate some of the drugged scrambled eggs he'd prepared himself and dozed off. Granger then called a doctor and two burly nurses, and held her down until they injected her with a powerful sedative.

Olivier and Kaye arrived to oversee the situation, but it was Cecil Tennant, an old and trusted friend, who took charge. They decided that they must take Vivien back to England. Her American doctors were legally obliged to report her condition and, once committed to a mental asylum in the US, it would be difficult to get her out. Heavily sedated, she was bundled onto a plane to New York. There she was spotted turning up for her flight to London lying across the laps of Olivier and Kaye. Meanwhile, Elizabeth Taylor[29] took over her role in the film.

In England, Vivien was hospitalized, put to sleep for three weeks, and given electric shock therapy. Exhausted, Olivier went on holiday to Ischia. Vivien never forgave him for not being there when she awoke. He, too, expressed regret for "not being more alive to my duties, no matter how painful or how mortally sick of them I was." Noël Coward stepped in and filled her room with flowers and perfume.

She returned to Notley Abbey, where she kept Olivier up till all hours so often that the artist-historian Kenneth Clark, who visited, was heard to say: "She's killing our greatest actor." Peter Finch turned up. He held hands with Vivien at parties, making Olivier a public cuckold. Rumors circulated that they were going to split, and the *Hollywood Reporter* said that, like the Windsors', their marriage was "a marriage in name – and face – only."

Nevertheless, they played opposite each other in Terence Rattigan's *The Sleeping Prince* and holidayed in Italy afterwards, staying with Rex Harrison[30] and Lilli Palmer – though things were far from congenial in Sexy Rexy's Portofino *casa* as he had recently been "bowled over" by Kay Kendall. The Duke and Duchess of Windsor[31] were also there. Harrison ran off with Kay Kendall soon after.

While Vivien filmed *The Deep Blue Sea* (1955), Olivier was shooting *Richard III* (1955), and if Vivien was not impressed by Olivier's masculinity, others were. Claire Bloom playing Lady Anne, who Richard woos beside the corpse of her dead husband – a part that Vivien had wanted for herself – said approvingly: "With Olivier there was sex and excitement, the masculine drive, the electric vibrancy…"

Vivien was still finding comfort elsewhere and Peter Finch even turned up for Christmas at Notley. As Olivier was setting off some fireworks, he noticed that a rocket was pointing directly at Finch. He thought better of it, changed the aim, and the rocket went off harmlessly into the air.

In 1955, the Oliviers went to Stratford where they played before Prince Rainier of Monaco.[31] They triumphed in *Macbeth*. Critics pointed out that in most productions you don't believe that Macbeth and Lady Macbeth are married, but in this production you believed they were – and that their marriage was crumbling. It may have helped, of course, that Lady Macbeth was going quietly mad.

Vivien was on the verge of another breakdown and Olivier confided in Noël Coward that their life together had become hideous. They were trapped by public acclaim, "scrabbling about in the cold ashes of a physical passion that burnt itself out years ago." Coward was fearful of what could happen. The press was constantly hounding them, but that was not the source of the problem.

"The core of the trouble lies deeper," he confided to his diary, "where, in fact, it always lies, in sex. She, exacerbated by incipient TB, needs more and more sexual satisfaction. They are eminent, successful, envied and adored, and most wretchedly unhappy."

Coward thought that they should live and sleep apart, while maintaining a public front. And, for the sake of her mental health, Vivien should confine herself to comic roles. She was spoiled and self-centered. He concluded that: "If Larry had turned sharply on Vivien years ago and given her a clip in the chops, he would have been spared a mint of trouble."

Meanwhile Olivier, who loved to play out his personal tragedies on-stage, put on Shakespeare's bloodiest play, *Titus Andronicus*. During the action, Vivien loses her tongue and hands, while Olivier lets out one of his famous cries of pain when his own hand is severed. It was enough to drive anyone mad, and it pushed poor Vivien over the edge again.

She headed off to the South of France with Finch. Olivier followed. When he turned up just before Christmas at the house where they were staying as guests, their hosts retired to allow Vivien, Larry and Peter to air their differences. Later they heard raised voices. Creeping downstairs, they spotted Olivier and Finch pulling their ties off, each saying: "Dear boy, I forgot to get you a Christmas present."

Vivien refused to chose between them.

"This is between you two," she said. "You must decide who is to have me."

On another occasion, she said simply: "Well, which one of you is coming to bed with me?"

After eight days, Olivier persuaded Vivien to leave with him. They went to a lakeside hotel at Locanda. Inevitably the question of Finch came up. Vivien said that she saw no reason why she should not have two men.

Olivier was not a man to take this sort of thing lying down. He went to New York and signed Marilyn Monroe for the movie *The Prince and the Showgirl* (1957), based on Rattigan's *The Sleeping Princess*. He had met her at a party on Sutton Place and was smitten.

"One thing was clear to me," he recalled. "I was going to fall most shatteringly in love with Marilyn. She was so adorable, so witty and more physically attractive that anyone I could imagine."

But at the press conference announcing the deal, England's greatest living actor was less than pleased to find himself upstaged by Marilyn's bust. Suddenly, surely by accident, one of her bra straps snapped, provoking a stampede of cameramen.

While Monroe was to take the part Vivien had played onstage, Vivien was performing in Noël Coward's *South Sea Bubble*. At one time Peter Finch was going to be in the play, but was discretely dropped – Olivier had had a showdown with him at Notley and he had agreed not to see Vivien any more. Coward noted that Vivien and Olivier had to present a united front to the world and if Finch brought them down in a blaze of publicity it would damage all three of them. Meanwhile Vivien announced that she was pregnant. At 42 she was desperate to have a baby for Olivier. Mysteriously, Coward felt that he was entirely responsible. When a reporter asked them whether Marilyn Monroe, who was arriving in England two days later, would be a godmother, Olivier replied: "That's an interesting idea."

Vivien quickly added: "But, darling, they've already been chosen."

Then they were asked to kiss for the cameras.

"We're too old for that sort of thing," said Olivier.

When Marilyn did turn up, Olivier was disappointed to find that she had brought her new husband, Arthur Miller, with her. Nevertheless there was a huge round of parties to welcome her. Vivien absented herself, claiming that she could not fit into any of her evening dresses now she was pregnant. Marilyn's own dresses were described as being "as tight as the curves will allow – with seams reinforced." And at a press conference in London she was asked the question: "What do you wear in bed?" which brought the famous reply: "Chanel No.5."

Marilyn went to see Vivien in *South Sea Bubble*, which she quit after 276 performances. The following day she lost the baby. Coward was furious, having believed all along that the pregnancy would come to nothing. She went off on holiday where, she said, she missed "Larry boy."

Olivier was having a terrible time filming with Marilyn who could never remember her lines. Worse: every time Arthur Miller appeared on the set "she would run over and jump into his arms and wrap herself around him and they would disappear into the dress-room for about ten minutes – ahem! – and then she would reappear again "refreshed," according to one of the other actors.

One day she did not appear at all. When one of the production staff tracked her down, all she would say was: "Aw shucks, I've got the curse. Don't you English know about that?"

Vivien and Olivier then went on tour behind the Iron Curtain.

In Yugoslavia, she met Tito[33] and, at a formal dinner where no one spoke English, gave a foul-mouthed speech. The secret policeman assigned to guard her fell in love with her, but was run so ragged that he lost two stone in weight. She broke a bedroom window and refused to get on the train when it was time to leave. The chief of police picked her up bodily and put her on board, receiving a sock in the eye for his pains.

Back in London, Olivier and Vivien were embroiled in a fight to keep the St James's Theatre open. It was then that she discovered that Olivier was having an affair – a heterosexual one this time. She lashed out at him, slashing him across the eyes with a wet face flannel. He lost control, seized her, and hurled her onto the bed. She hit the bedside table whose marble top gashed her just above the left eye. Realizing that they might easily murder one another, Olivier left and spent the night in a mews nearby. Fearing a repeat performance, he gave her a wide berth. Vivien went off on holiday with Holman, her first husband, and Suzanne, her daughter who was now grown up. This drew condemnation from Labour MP Mrs Jean Mann, who said on television: "When a woman finds her ex-husband so easy to get on with that she can spend a holiday with him she should have thought a little longer before she cut the knot."

When she returned, Olivier met her at the airport to keep up appearances. He was now living in Walton Street not far from their new flat in Eaton Square. But he was traveling a lot and Vivien missed him terribly. No one, she found, could match him for advice, comfort, companionship and understanding. She had fallen back in love with him.

It was, of course, too late. Olivier had fallen in love with Joan Plowright, who was playing his daughter in *The Entertainer*. One night while he was taking his make-up off, Vivien turned up at his dressing room. He was just stripping off the thick eyebrows he used to play Archie Rice. Without turning around, he said: "I suppose you know that I am in love with Joan

Plowright."

Vivien became hysterical.

"She couldn't believe it when he met a younger girl who thought he was the cat's whiskers," said a close friend.

Olivier and Joan Plowright took *The Entertainer* to America, leaving Vivien to play the faithless wife in *Duel of Angels*. She drew close to the leading man, Peter Wyngarde. One night, he found her running around the garden naked. It was bitterly cold.

Rumors surfaced in the *Hollywood Reporter* that Olivier intended to marry Joan Plowright. Nevertheless, Vivien was delighted when he returned to England and they were seen together at public functions, though she deliberately flirted with every man in sight. When people turned up at Eaton Square they were surprised to find that he was not there. His absence pervaded the atmosphere.

"She constantly referred to Larry as if they were at the glorious height of romantic love," said one guest. But everyone knew he was trying to get out from under. Gertrude took Vivien off to Italy for a soothing break, but she picked up a fisherman. Her behavior became so outlandish that the police were called, and she bit one of them.

Back in England, Olivier took her out for her 45th birthday. He bought her a Rolls Royce and explained that they must part. Even so, two days later, they hosted a star-studded dance at Les Ambassadeurs for Lauren Bacall[34] who had come to London to start a new life after the death of Humphrey Bogart.[35] They still discussed business together, but there were scenes. Olivier escaped to New York, but had to return to England when his brother died. Despite more terrible dramas, Olivier found it difficult to leave Vivien when, with her illness, she needed him most, but he knew he had to go.

Olivier spent more time in the States and returned to Hollywood to film *Spartacus* (1960). Vivien drank too much and missed him more than ever. But she tried to make a new life for herself, and was seen on the town with Lauren Bacall and Kay Kendall, and sometimes with Noël Coward in tow. After her girlfriends left to go filming, Vivien was seen "living it up in London with a young artist who sports a beard and wears sunglasses in nightclubs." She was pursued by a Sussex businessman who owned a plastics firm. When he turned up at a party, she "kicked the casanova," according to the *New York Enquirer*, and "followed the kick with a downward slash against his cheek with her fingernails that drew blood."

Vivien's daughter Suzanne wrote to Olivier telling him that her mother's health had improved and implored him to give the marriage one more try. He replied that he was giving her a wide berth and would lose himself in the South Seas if necessary. Vivien was no longer the woman he had married. He too had changed, he said. He acted enough on stage without having to act in his home life, too – though that is exactly what everyone who knew him accused him of. And he wanted to be alone. Well, not entirely alone, as his daily letters to Joan Plowright indicated. They clearly aimed to find happiness together, though both feared that Vivien might take her life.

Olivier worried that their mutual friends would desert Vivien once he left and was surprised when they didn't. Her first husband, Holman, was particularly steadfast.

"Vivien will get no peace of mind until she recognizes that this break with Larry is final," he said, not without relish. "Let Vivien accept that what she did to me, Larry is doing to her."

But she would not accept it. When Olivier returned to London, she met him at the airport with a kiss. She turned up for the first night of *Coriolanus* at Stratford, though he preferred to stay in a hotel than at nearby Notley. During the run she waited in each night, thinking that he would call her immediately the curtain fell. But at the end of the Stratford run, Olivier headed to Morecambe in Lancashire to film *The Entertainer* (1960) with Joan Plowright again playing his daughter. She took the opportunity to leave her husband,

Roger Gage. They divorced on the grounds of Joan's adultery with Olivier. Vivien took the hint and put Notley on the market, but in her dressing room at the Royal Court, where she was playing in Coward's *Look After Lulu*, she would be seen crying.

A German magazine reported that the Oliviers were no longer living together. This was picked up in England by the *Daily Sketch*. They made an effort to be seen in public together, but when Olivier sailed for New York, Vivien did not go with him. He stayed with Stewart Granger[36] and his wife Jean Simmons[37] for Christmas, where he poured out his heart, telling them that he had decided to file for a divorce. It was plainly contagious. Both the Grangers and the Oliviers divorced in 1960.

The great affair was over. Vivien could scarcely believe it. She had hurt and abused Olivier, thinking he would never leave her because they were the golden couple. But he had. Vivien was particularly surprised that he had left her for the plainer Joan Plowright "when you consider that I am cited as one of the great beauties of the century."

As one friend said: "Any young actress would have done."

However, Joan was a brilliant actress and that was enough to captivate Olivier.

Vivien went off to the States with *Duel of Angels*. On Broadway, the director, Robert Helpmann, insisted that Peter Wyngarde squeeze into a new pair of very tight riding breeches. When Vivien saw them, she said: "Peter dear, if you come on in that on the first night, the audience will not only not be looking at your face but they won't be looking at mine either. Take them off at once."

Also in the cast was the actor Jack Merivale, the step-brother of John Buckmaster who was now in a mental institution. One morning Merivale was having a vodka and tonic in the Oak Room at the Plaza to clear his hangover when he found himself the quarry of a homosexual who liked beards. To escape his attentions, Jack made his way to the Sherry-Netherland Hotel where Vivien was having lunch with Helpmann. They got on famously and Merivale took her to the theater on a couple of occasions. One night, Vivien made it plain that she wanted to be kissed. Merivale obliged, but, unsure of the state of her marriage, he was reluctant to go further. Vivien told him that Olivier had his own fish to fry and invited him to make love to her "properly." Afterwards, she told him that he was only the third man she had ever woken up with.

Merivale was soon head-over-heels in love with her. Vivien told him that she loved him too, but she begged Olivier not to divorce her, telling him that it would kill her. She still believed that he would come back to her. He replied that he wanted her to grant him a divorce, as he did not want Joan Plowright's father to know the sexual nature of his relationship with her daughter. Encouraged by Helpmann and with malicious aforethought, Vivien made a simple announcement to the press: "Lady Olivier wishes to say that Sir Laurence has asked for a divorce in order to marry Miss Joan Plowright. She will naturally do whatever he wishes."

Olivier seized the moment. Vivien had already written to him boasting of her affair with Merivale, presumably to make him jealous. He phoned Merivale and asked: "Any chance of a union?"

Jack had seen the effect Vivien had had on Buckmaster and felt unable to commit himself. Merivale says his noncommittal reply brought "a deep sigh across the Atlantic."

Meanwhile the newspapers in Britain were going crazy over "Sir Larry and the Girl from Scunthorpe." The lawyers were warning Olivier that Vivien's announcement would seriously prejudice any divorce case as it smacked of collusion. And Helpmann, mischievous to the last, was warning Merivale to watch out or the men in white coats would come and get him. But it was Vivien who went to see the men in white coats. She started electro-convulsive therapy again, but quit after the first course of treatment.

When *Duel of Angels* closed, Vivien flew home to England, still hoping to save her marriage. Unfortunately, her travel companion was Helpmann, who friends were now calling Iago. Merivale found an excuse to stay in New York, out of harm's way. In London, Vivien's every move was dogged by reporters. This was not helped by the fact that she lunched with Valerie Hobson, wife of John Profumo,[38] the soon-to-be-disgraced Minister for War, and threw herself into the social whirl. Every time she phoned Merivale in New York, he could hear the noise of parties going on in the background.

She met with Olivier, but he was unmoved by her pleas. A doctor diagnosed her as a manic-depressive who was going through a regular cycle. The depressive phase had been brought on by her separation from Olivier. The manic was characterized by a "marked increase in libido and indiscriminate sexual activity." This "overt sexuality," he said, posed a threat to her reputation and social standing.

As Noël Coward remarked when Marilyn Monroe died, she, Judy Garland and Viven suffered the same plight: "Too much, too soon and too often."

Vivien was feeling much better when she flew back to New York. Jack Merivale was waiting for her at the airport, weighed down by a sense of foreboding.

"Down the steps came that entrancing figure, light as a feather. She looked so wonderful. My fate was sealed," he said.

Duel of Angels went on tour in the States in July. Vivien and Jack were greatly amused that the Pullman car attendant's name was Larry, and "just ring for Larry" became their catchphrase. Also on board was a feature writer conducting a series of interviews for the *London Daily Express*, but they prevailed upon him not to reveal the nature of their relationship. Vivien tried to pretend that everything between her and Olivier was the same, meanwhile Jack wrote to Olivier telling him of his great love for Vivien. Olivier received the letter with relief and gratitude. In his reply, he outlined the signs Jack should look for that would indicate the onset of Vivien's manic phase, absolving himself of all further responsibility.

When they reached Hollywood, Vivien and Jack shared a suite at the Château Marmont and hung out around George Cukor's[38] pool, which must have been reminiscent of her time with Buckmaster. John Mills took his 14-year-old daughter Hayley to see *Duel of Angels*. The next day the Millses received telegrams purporting to come from all manner of august bodies, expressing outrage that such a young innocent should be exposed to such filth. In fact they came from Vivien, who had been egged on by Helpmann.

In San Francisco, Jack found himself a room on the 23rd floor of the Huntingdon Hotel, while Vivien was on the third. She insisted that he be moved. Jack received a call from the very punctilious English manager, saying: "I understand you want to be closer to headquarters." Then he added: "I don't blame you." Afterwards they took a brief vacation at Lake Tahoe.

By the time they reached Chicago, Vivien's spirits had revived to the point that she joked to the press that she might be sending Joan Plowright her visiting card. But, when they reached New York, where both Olivier and Plowright were playing, she did not look in on either of them. Nevertheless, she continued to keep Olivier's photograph with her wherever she went.

Vivien and Jack sailed back to Europe together. At Cherbourg, they experienced the first onslaught of the Continental press, who remarked on Merivale's "attentiveness" and said that Vivien looked ten years younger. However, customs impounded a Renoir she was carrying, despite her protests that she never traveled without it as she needed to have something pretty to look at when she was on tour.

In Paris, Vivien's divorce papers awaited her. They toured France and friends remarked how Merivale had changed since he had found Vivien. Noël Coward noted that Vivien was in much better form than she had been the previous June.

"Inwardly she is still hankering after Larry," he confided to his diaries. "However, she is putting up a gallant performance and seems very fond of Jack, who is constantly fulfilling a long-felt want." That want, as Sir Noël liked to point out, was sex.

Back in London, Vivien had to make an appearance in the divorce courts. Olivier was determined to have his way. She was still reluctant, but bowed to the inevitable and admitted adultery with a handful of unnamed men in Ceylon, New York, London and elsewhere. The marriage was finally dissolved. Afterwards there was a party at Eaton Square. Guests included Lotte Lenya, Warren Beatty[39] and Joan Collins.[40] Lenya and Beatty were to play opposite Vivien in Tennesee Williams's *The Roman Spring of Mrs Stone* (1961). Vivien played the tragic, self-destructive Mrs Stone, who lets herself be seduced by a gigolo and gives herself to a street boy. Beatty used his considerable charm to talk her into taking the role. Joan Collins remarked that Vivien had a soft spot for Warren and, when it was suggested that Alain Delon replace Beatty, Vivien dismissed the suggestion, saying: "He's much too pretty. He's prettier than I am."

Olivier's presence hung over the movie. For one riding scene Vivien's mount was a mare that Olivier had ridden in *Richard III*. Trained for battle scenes, when it heard the clapperboard it charged, heading for a tree. Vivien had the presence of mind to duck, but a branch took her wig off.

She flew to Atlanta, alone, for a Civil War centenary showing of *Gone With The Wind*, and appeared in a daringly low-cut dress. On the way back to England she traveled via New York, where she insisted on seeing Olivier. He agreed to a meeting at Sardi's, provided Joan was present. This achieved nothing and when Vivien stepped off the plane back in

London she discovered that Larry and Joan were now man and wife.

The following day she attended the wedding of her chauffeur at St Michael's, Chester Square. Somehow she managed to keep smiling, though all around her knew her heart was breaking. And, after another round of electric shock treatment, she took Jack on holiday.

First they stayed at Noël Coward's place in Jamaica, where Noël remarked: "Jack is good with her and a gentle, nice creature, but I wouldn't care to change places with him." (Well, no, Noël, that comes as no surprise.) Then they moved on to Tobago, where the press tracked the "two lovebirds" down and were soon predicting wedding bells.

During a tour of Australia Merivale found his performance unfairly slated because he was not Sir Laurence Olivier, but things were more relaxed in New Zealand. They went skinny dipping and the former mayor of Auckland, Sir Ernest Davis, now a nonagenarian, proposed marriage. Although Vivien turned him down, he bombarded her with letters after she left. He even made plans to go to England to press his suit, but died before the steamer left.

When Vivien became ill again, she asked Jack to marry her. He said he would not marry while she was ill. Besides, he was in the States at the time, while she was in England.

While Merivale was away, Olivier visited Vivien at her new home at Tickerage Mill, near Uckfield.

"She just took off like a little schoolgirl meeting her boyfriend," said an observer. "It was beautiful, and they walked by the lake together."

He only left after a sharp phone call from Joan.

Vivien and Jack took another quick vacation in Tobago, before she went to Hollywood to film *Ship of Fools* (1965). She turned up at Tarquin's wedding, though Olivier begged her not to, saying he could not sit in a pew with three wives. Vivien announced that, when she was 60, she and Jack would go and live in Corfu. But in 1967, at the age of 53, she was struck down by tuberculosis and died.

She was not forgotten. In 1986, a visitor to Lord Olivier's home found the old man watching a Vivien Leigh movie on the television. The 89-year-old actor sat there with tears in his eyes, saying: "This, this was love. This was the real thing."

But perhaps a better epitaph came from long-time friend Alan Webb, who said: "If you found yourself naked with Vivien in the Sahara Desert with absolutely nothing, 24 hours later you would be coming out in a Rolls Royce, covered in minks and drinking champagne."

6

Under the Rainbow

Since her death in 1969, Judy Garland has become a gay icon, if not *the* gay icon. Indeed, she had a big gay following when she was alive. William Goldman castigated the "flutter of fags" in the audience at the Palace in the summer of 1967 in *Esquire* magazine, while *Time* spoke disparagingly of "the boys in tight trousers" who came to see her perform. Both publications put forward some psychological mumbo-jumbo about why this should be. Others have suggested that homosexuals of the closet era identified with her because she put up with the same demeaning jokes and dismissive remarks that they suffered. No matter how many times she fell down she always got up again – giving hope and inspiration to those marginalized in society. Here's another theory for you. Perhaps it was because her father was gay. She loved him dearly and it gave her a special empathy with homosexuals. She even married a couple. Okay, it was just a theory.

But it's true. Her father was a fag, in the parlance of those unenlightened days. In 1912, the vaudevillian singer Frank Gumm left Judy's mother, Ethel, standing at the altar in Superior, Wisconsin, while he scooted off on a tour of 28 states. He was used to making hasty retreats from small towns across the US when his advances to young men and teenage boys fell on stony ground. Before renting a room from Ethel's parents, he had been run out of Cloquet, 20 miles to the west of

193

Superior, following accusations of perversion according to his stage partner, Maude Ayres. The news soon reached Superior, too. What Ethel thought no one knows, but she was plainly a tolerant woman. She forgave him. In the fall of 1913, Frank returned to Superior and, on a cold afternoon in January, he went through with the marriage.

They moved to Grand Rapids, Michigan, where they ran one of the town's two theaters, the New Grand. Frank was manager and singer, while Ethel played the piano and provided the sound effects for the new silent movies.

"The public likes Mr Gumm because he not only insists upon an entertaining but also a clean performance," said the *Herald-Review*.

The Gumms knocked out three daughters, who followed their father onto the stage. Only the third was not supposed to happen. Ethel thought two children were enough and tried everything from mega-doses of castor oil to driving along bumpy roads to induce a miscarriage. Frank even asked a second-year medical student to perform an abortion. He refused.

Once Frank and Ethel accepted the inevitable, they decided that the baby was going to be a boy and they would call it Frank Jr. It was a girl, so Frank became Frances. But in the family, Frances Gumm – who would become Judy Garland – was known simply as Baby or Babe. She was adored by her father and she adored him back. A family friend called their mutual adoration a "love affair." Babe was never secure in the love of her mother, something she said she craved more than anything else. All three Gumm girls made their debuts on the stage of the New Grand. Frances was just two when she first walked the boards and, from the beginning, everyone knew she was going to be a star.

He had given her three healthy girls, but Ethel frequently complained about Frank's failure in bed. It was hardly surprising given his preferences. After seven years of trying to play it straight, Frank went back to his old ways. Even at the beginning of their marriage, he had plainly enjoyed the company of younger men, but if anything untoward had been going on he had been discreet about it.

Then he fell in love with the star basketball player at the local high school. They often went away together to nearby towns. They even spent a night together in Minneapolis, but no one, including Ethel and the boy's parents, apparently, thought that anything untoward was going on. But then Frank threw caution to the wind and made unwanted sexual advances to two of the ushers at the New Grand. Nobody made a fuss, but it was made clear to Frank that he had better leave town. So, in 1926, the Gumms sold the New Grand and headed off to California, with four-year-old Frances in tow.

Unable to afford a theater in Los Angeles itself, Frank bought one in Lancaster, which lay in Antelope Valley, on the edge of the Mojave Desert, 45 miles to the northeast. They were not entirely cut off from the world of the movies. Nearby Red Rock Canyon was a favorite location for shooting Westerns. Movie cowboys would tie up their horses to hitching posts in Lancaster. Frances soon began to tell people in Lancaster that she was going to be a movie star. No one laughed.

Before Frances was even ten years old, Ethel was taking her to auditions in Hollywood. Too young to perform on the casting couch, Ethel stood in for her daughter, trading sex for showbiz advancement while Judy played outside for an hour or so. Frances was fed "pep pills" to give her performance a little pizzazz.

The casting couch romps caused ructions at home, with Ethel often taking off with the kids in the middle of the night and staying in a hotel in LA for days at a time. Careless of the sort of scandal that drove them out of Grand Rapids, Frank began to chase after teenage boys, while Ethel took a lover, Will Gilmore, the husband of her best friend. It was a relatively civilized arrangement. The Gumms and the Gilmores spent most of their free time together, playing bridge and going on picnics. When Frank was away, Ethel would take the girls to eat at the Gilmore's house, but Gilmore, a stern and ill-tempered man, would make their time there a misery.

Few objected to Ethel and Will fooling around. It was common enough behavior in frontier towns. But people felt sorry for Mrs Gilmore, who was confined to a wheelchair. Although the affair was common knowledge in the town, Babe remained in blissful ignorance until one day when she was playing hide-and-seek. In an upstairs room in an abandoned pumphouse on the Gilmores' property, she burst in on her mother and her lover. Gilmore bundled her out of the room, but a companion recalled that Frances looked stunned, as if someone had struck her across the face.

Frank assuaged the loneliness caused by his marital breach by indulging his interest in good-looking young men and teenage boys. He would pat them on the rear and say "Boy, those look nice" when they wore tight pants. Lucky ones would be given free popcorn and invited to sit beside him at the back of the Valley Theater, where they indulged in a little mutual masturbation. The young movie projectionist got his brother to stay with him in the projection room to fend off Frank's advances, but two of the local high school jocks boasted of the pleasure Frank gave them through oral sex. He would, of course, be forced to beg them first and they would get free admission to the theater. Frances heard rumors to this effect but dismissed them as lies put about by that "horrible man" – the despised Will Gilmore.

Ethel scraped together some money and moved to Los Angeles with the children. Babe attended the Lawlor School of Professional Children – or Ma Lawlor's as it was called – next to Central Casting on Hollywood Boulevard. There she met Mickey Rooney.[1] In 1964, she told *McCalls* magazine that on her first day there, she had had her first kiss behind the curtains with Rooney. Soon the girls went on the road, changing their name to the Garland Sisters along the way. Frances did not like her given name, nor did she like being called Baby or Babe. She renamed herself Judy after an old Hoagy Carmichael song.

Without his wife and children to give him the veneer of respectability, the rumors that Frank was "pansy" spread unchecked and parents stopped sending their kids to watch movies in his theater unaccompanied. Frank lost the theater and was run out of town. Soon after, he died with the sound of Judy's voice singing on the radio still ringing in his ears.

Judy's two older sisters got engaged, then married, but Ethel was more ambitious for her youngest daughter. With or without mother's help the 13-year-old Judy came to the attention of Louis B. Mayer[2] at MGM. Probably without. A shy man, who failed to exploit the casting couch to sleep with women over the age of consent, Mayer had a weakness for young girls and was particularly fond of Charlie Chaplin's[3] nymphets. He would put a paternal arm around their shoulder while his hand would search out and fondle their incipient breasts. And worse. Years later, when Judy was in England, Mayer's name came up in conversation.

"Don't ever mention that pervert's name to me," she said. "I still get nightmares over what that man did to me."

"Young girls don't need locks if they have nothing to be ashamed of," Mayer told his daughters when they asked if they could have a little privacy at home.

The same attitude was applied to his young wards, who ate, slept and worked on the MGM lot. What Mayer liked, he often told Judy, was that she sang from the heart, and he would invariably put his hand on her left breast to show her where her heart was.

"I often thought I was lucky," she said later, "that I didn't sing with another part of my anatomy."

By the age of 20 she got fed up with this routine grope.

"Mr Mayer, don't ever, ever do that again," she said. "I just will

not stand for it. If you want to show me where I sing from –
just point."

Mayer burst into tears.

"How can you say that to me, to me who loves you?" he said.

"It's amazing how these big men, who had been around so
many sophisticated women all their lives, could act like idiots,"
she wrote later.

And he was not the only one.

"Don't think they all didn't try," she said.

For MGM executives, sex with the actresses they had under
contract was one of the perks of the job. One of Mayer's chief
lieutenants, Benny Thau, also took an avuncular interest. When
she was 17, he spotted her on a hotel tennis court. He had just
come from the swimming pool and called her over. They met on
a grassy bank between the court and the hotel. When she bent
down to hear what he was saying, he tried to kiss her, but lost
his footing and started to slip down the incline. Judy grabbed
him and saved him from what could have been a nasty fall.

Another MGM executive did not employ such subtle tactics.
With Judy, as with other women under contract, he made a
blunt proposition.

"Yes or no, right now. That was his style," she said.

When she replied: "No, sir, I'm sorry," he went ballistic.

"Listen," he said. "I'll ruin you. I can do that. I'll break you if
it's the last thing I do. You'll be out of here before I am finished
with you."

A confident teenager, she simply smiled and said: "You'll be
gone before I will." And she was right. A few weeks later Mayer
fired him, fearing that he was trying to take his job.

Clark Gable[4] also took an interest. Seeing the child star sing,
he went over to kiss her. Judy burst into tears.

"Maybe it was because Gable had such terrible halitosis,"
said Mickey Rooney, who was then playing opposite Judy in his
Andy Hardy movies.

Judy was a podgy adolescent, so Mayer put his prodigy on the MGM diet – well-salted chicken soup, amphetamines and phenobarbital. Even so, when filming the *Wizard of Oz* (1939), her burgeoning breasts had to be strapped down to make her look like a child rather than the full-figured woman she was becoming.

When the movie came out, Judy went on a publicity tour with Mickey Rooney. In New York, she managed to slip out on a couple of dates. One of these dates was with an 18-year-old French aristocrat named Viscount Lawrence d'Yago de la Vernier. The Viscount said he had been commissioned to write an interview for a Parisian youth newspaper. He pursued Judy with flowers and telegrams, until she agreed to have dinner with him. A second date followed. Only later did she learn that his charming French accent had been acquired in high school drama classes. His real name was Lawrence Yago and her chateau-dwelling viscount was, in fact, a dental assistant from the Bronx.

Judy's success, naturally, came to the attention of Will Gilmore, who wanted to cash in. His long-suffering wife now dead, he whisked Ethel – who now called herself Mrs Garland – across the state line to Yuma, Arizona, where they married. Judy was furious when her mother indulged her new husband with her hard-earned cash, even buying a car for his son. But Ethel was no patsy. She would not relinquish control of the family finances to her husband and, after three-and-a-half years, they split.

MGM had a problem, too. As child stars go, Judy was already past her sell-by date. At the turn of the 1940s, she was 18, not 16 as the studio publicity maintained. They wrung another three Andy Hardy movies out of her, with Judy playing the sexless young teenager who gets jealous when Mickey Rooney falls for an older, prettier girl. She told a fan magazine: "Nobody thinks about boys less than I do."

She also said that she did not plan to marry until she was 24. Why 24? "Because it sounds like a good long while away."

In fact, Judy had lost her cherry by the age of 15 and had been interested in boys long before that. She had had her first kiss at ten with Galen Reed, a boy who her father paid a silver dollar to join her on stage for duets. Back in Lancaster, she had fallen for buck toothed Charles Murphy, and was still mooning about him four years after her mother had taken her to live in LA. She was also popular among MGM's male child stars.

"Judy and I were very much in love," said 1930s brat Freddie Bartholomew. They held hands during screenings in Louis B. Mayer's living room. His rival for child stardom, Jackie Cooper, stole kisses from her on the beach – or maybe it was the other way around. But she dropped both of them for Billy Halop, one of Hell's Kitchen's "Dead End Kids" who made a series of movies in the 1930s. This little tough guy confessed to a reporter that Judy was one of his "weaker moments."

Who actually popped Judy's cherry is hard to say. The over-sexed Mickey Rooney was a frequent guest at her new home in Stone Canyon Road. He regularly visited prostitutes and fondled girls in the car on the way to the commissary. However, Mickey became captivated by Lana Turner's[4] breasts which, he said, were "the nicest knockers" he had ever seen. He later claimed to have knocked her up, which she denied, and to have taken Ava Gardner's[5] virginity, which she did not.

At 15, Judy was certainly going to bed with Buddy Pepper, who was just seven weeks older than her. She visited his apartment on several occasions for assignations. "She laughed more than anybody else, and she cried more than anybody else," said Pepper.

She was also bonking another child actor, Frankie Darro, and there were others. Where sex was concerned, Judy saw herself as a free spirit – though she wrote a lot of lovelorn poetry. This may have been because, outside of the closed world of the movie lot, she was completely out of her depth. When a boy asked her to be his date for his fraternity pledge party at USC, she wore a slinky evening dress with a slit up the side and a white-fox stole – the sort of thing a sexy starlet might wear to a première. Her date took one look, discovered he had a headache, and ran.

At the age of 17, she began chasing the 32-year-old songwriter Oscar Levant, who was freshly divorced from a beautiful Broadway chorus girl. He was wooing 20th Century Fox starlet June Gale, described by the studio rather confusingly as the "demure Jean Harlow."[6] This did nothing to discourage Judy. Nor did his coruscating wit.

When out at a nightclub one night, Levant yawned.

"I hope I'm not keeping you up," Judy said sarcastically.

"I wish you were," he replied.

Pressed on what he thought of her, Levant eventually compared Judy to a Mozart symphony. She immediately went out and bought all the maestro's work. She listened to it all and decided that she was nothing like the cool, well-balanced classical music that she heard and felt insulted. Nevertheless Levant was inundated with letters, poems and phone calls. Judy's tireless pursuit eventually brought him to the altar – though not with her. He married June Gale, who admitted that she had been taking Oscar "too much for granted." Levant, like Judy a junkie for prescription drugs, gave another reason for wedding June rather than Judy.

"If we had married," he said, "she would have given birth to a sleeping pill."

Oscar's marriage did not upset Judy. She had other fish to fry, particularly bandleader Artie Shaw.[7]

"Oh my God, what a beautiful man," she said when she first saw him.

Lana Turner, Ava Gardner and Betty Grable had the same reaction.

"I got Ava Gardner, I got Lana Turner, I got whoever was around," he said. "With their cooperation. I didn't 'get' them, they came after me."

Judy certainly went after him with a will. When she saw him perform in New York in 1938 – while his mellifluous recording of Cole Porter's "Begin the Beguine" was topping the charts – she drowned him with praise. He was also enthusiastic.

"I 'dug' her," he said. "That's better than 'loved' or 'cared for.'"

Well, he was a musician.

Ethel objected to Judy getting mixed up with such a well-known womanizer. Shaw had been divorced twice by the age of 30 and Judy had first set her cap at him when she was 15. So Judy would get Jackie Cooper and or some other beard to pick her up for a date, then deliver her to Shaw.

Shaw, perhaps mindful of her age, denied having sex with Judy.

"She was the closest thing to a little sister I ever had," he said. "Sex with her would have been incestuous."

Besides, Judy was not one of the "all-American, long-legged beauties" he bedded. Judy thought he was just playing hard to get and confided her feelings to fellow MGM protégée Lana Turner. But when Shaw turned up on the set of *Two Girls on Broadway* (1940) with Phil Silvers, he asked Lana for her phone number. She gave it to him.

"Zoom," said Silvers. "Like a bee making for honey."

On their first date, Shaw and Turner flew out to Las Vegas and got married. Both Judy and Betty Grable, Shaw's other squeeze, learned about it in the newspapers the next morning. Judy sobbed uncontrollably. Her mother, who had been completely taken in by Judy's elaborate deception, said: "So what?" Judy explained. Ethel, ever one to mix it, called Shaw and said: "You've broke Judy's heart."

For Shaw, marrying Lana Turner was the fulfillment of his American dream.

"Lana is a woman I'll have sex with," he told Judy. "I never thought of you that way."

This afforded Judy precious little comfort.

"I won't marry yet," she told an interviewer in the aftermath of the Shaw affair. "Not for three or four more years."

There were plenty of willing young men her own age. Sidney Miller was one of the crowd who regularly turned up at Stone Canyon Road.

"I wanted to make it with her – oh God," he said. "But to her I was just a friend."

"Hi, sweetie," she'd say, or "Hi, doll" when he showed up.

Nineteen-year-old Robert Wilson made his way across country all the way from Buffalo, New York, to whisk her away to his mountain hideaway. He staked out her place, but then thought better of it and gave himself up to the Culver City Police.

"Every time she wiggles that cute little pug nose of hers, I fall more in love with her," said the mooning movie fan in custody. "She's my dream girl."

"Judy Garland Kidnap Plot Laid To Love," proclaimed the *Los Angeles Examiner*.

But Judy preferred to be seen out with the likes of up-and-coming actor Robert Stack,[8] movie agent Baron Polan, comedian Peter Lind Hayes and even the venerable Spencer Tracy who, at 40, was twice her age and married. After an evening at Ciro, the Trocadero and Coconut Grove, Judy would go on to the Café Gala and other chichi nightspots.

"It was kind of 'in' to go to gay clubs," said one young starlet. "It was considered sophisticated."

MGM did not want Judy to be "sophisticated." They had Lana Turner for that. Judy was supposed to be a nice, old-fashioned girl." They decided to put a stop to it by calling in the big guns – in the form of Louella Parsons, who could make or break any career.

"July Garland's boss, who knows what's best for the lively Judy, has requested that she curtail her night club activities," wrote Louella as a shot across her bows.

But Judy did not want to stay home nights. She did not want to be the girl next door. Like every other young woman in

America, she wanted to be Lana Turner. In fact, she confided to Joan Crawford[9] that, among the beauties at MGM, she felt like a polliwog, a tadpole on its way to becoming a frog. Even Mayer called her "my little hunchback." It did not help that she was cast opposite Lana Turner and Hedy Lamarr[10] in Ziegfeld *Girl* (1940). Once again Judy was cast as the plain and dutiful daughter, while the stagehands wolf-whistled at Lana and Hedy and the public drooled. Nevertheless, in 1940, Judy was MGM's top female box office draw.

The studio continued to team Judy with Mickey Rooney and hinted at a romance. Much to Judy's chagrin – in real life as in the movies – Rooney always kept an eye out for the prettier girls.

"I have always loved Judy without ever being in love with her," he said.

Meanwhile Judy was seeing several men, including the 31-year-old songwriter Johnny Mercer. At last she got the chance to play the *femme fatale*. Mercer was so besotted with Judy that he wandered around in a lovesick daze. Eventually, a friend of the family begged her to give him up, which she did. She was already dating David Rose, another composer who was, again, 12 years her senior.

Naturally Judy wanted to marry him. MGM were implacably opposed. Marriage would destroy the image of their virgin star. What if she was to become pregnant? Ethel was against it, too. Rose was in the throes of divorcing the singer and comedienne Martha Raye. Both Judy's older sisters marriages had run onto the rocks after marrying divorced men – and musicians to boot.

"I wish you girls would find someone who digs a slide rule instead of a slide trombone," she said.

But Judy was smitten. She wrote babyish love poetry which she read to the make-up girls each morning, much to their embarrassment. They had to cope with such immortal lines as:

"Would that my pen were tipped with a magic wand that I could but tell of my love for you."

And:

"That I could but write with the surge I feel when I gaze upon your sweet face."

Don't give up the day job.

Ethel eventually accepted the inevitable, saying: "If I don't let her marry, she'll always say, 'Well, if you had let me marry, I might have had some happiness.'" Judy also managed to talk round Louella Parsons, who had pooh-poohed the idea of the marriage at first. MGM continued to issue threats, but there was nothing they could do about it.

"I want a home wedding with bridesmaids and all the trimmings," said Judy. "I don't believe in silly elopements" – a dig at Lana Turner and Artie Shaw, perhaps – "and since I only expect to be married once. Both Dave and I consider it a very solemn occasion and we want a minister to officiate." (This from a women who was in and out of sexual relations like a shuttlecock, who was marrying a divorcé.)

Actually, a silly elopement was just what it was going to be. At an engagement party on Judy's 19th birthday, which the whole of Hollywood, with the exception of the disapproving Louis B. Mayer, turned out to, they announced that they would wed in late summer when both their work schedules would permit a honeymoon. Instead, one Sunday at the Brown Derby in Beverly Hills, they decided to get it over with. A phone call brought Ethel and Will Gilmore rushing to the restaurant. The four of them took a plane to Las Vegas, where Judy and David Rose were married at 1.20 am. She then telegrammed MGM, begging for a few days off for a honeymoon. The studio was less than sympathetic and insisted that she get back to the sound stage. Returning to LA that afternoon, Judy told reporters: "Even if we don't get any sort of a honeymoon, right now we are the happiest couple in the world." What's more, their marriage was not going to be a regular Hollywood marriage, over in the twinkling of an eye. It was, she said, "the real thing." Oh, yeah.

Moving into a new house on Chalon Road in Bel Air, Judy found that she had no idea about how to cook or clean, or even how to hire help to do such things. Fortunately, mother lived nearby. She stepped in, hiring two maids and supervising them, while David, a railway enthusiast, built a model railroad in the garden. Judy bought him a station as a wedding present. How sweet.

By their first wedding anniversary, it was plain that they were very unhappy together. While Judy was a very young 19, David Rose was a very old 31. He spent more time riding his toy trains than he did riding her. She gazed at him forlornly from the bedroom window at night going round and round his little track. He began to exhibit other eccentricities. One day she came home to find that he had sawn the legs off the grand piano, convinced that he could compose better lying down. Judy herself admitted that she was completely unfitted to be a wife and the studio was still trying to pry them apart.

But David must have taken time off from this model railroad to drive his locomotive into Judy's tunnel because, in the fall of 1942, she was pregnant. When a rumor to that effect surfaced in the *Los Angeles Examiner*, Mayer said: "We simply can't let that baby have a child."

Ethel agreed. After a long talk with David, she badgered Judy into having an abortion. It broke her heart and ended her marriage. Just 18 months after she had told the press that their union was not like other Hollywood marriages, she announced that they had agreed to a "matrimonial vacation" to settle their differences – which is just about as Hollywood as you can get.

Judy loved to be in love and believed that a woman was incomplete if she was not mooning over some swain. So the moment she fell out of love with David Rose she fell in love with 28-year-old Tyrone Power.[11] He was then 20th Century Fox's biggest star and Judy shared her passion with millions of women around the world – and not a few women and men in Hollywood itself.

They met at a party in Brentwood. He had just seen her in her first adult role in *For Me and My Gal* (1942) and found her fascinating. What's more, his wife, the French actress Annabelle was out of town. By the time she returned, they were an item. During his three-year marriage, Power, a bisexual, had had his fair share of dalliances with both women and men, but none that had threatened his marriage before. Within weeks, Judy was demanding that Power divorce his wife and alarm bells began ringing at their respective studios.

Mayer decided that he had been wrong about Judy's marriage. It had not hurt her image and *For Me and My Gal* had been her biggest box office draw so far. To fall for a man who was already on his way to the divorce courts was one thing. To break up a perfectly good marriage was another, especially as America had just declared war on Japan and Germany, and Power had just joined the Marine Corps and was about to go off to defend his country. It seemed downright unpatriotic.

Again the studio took action, but this time they had learned that there was no point in just putting their foot down. Judy could be stubborn. So they employed more subtle tactics, assigning publicity agent Betty Asher to be Judy's mentor. The daughter of a producer at Universal, Asher had secured her place on the corporate ladder at MGM by sleeping with Mayer's chief lieutenant Eddie Mannix. She had also successfully broken up the marriage of Lana Turner and Artie Shaw by being a shoulder to cry on for Lana while bedding Shaw.

When Asher turned up on the set to have a chat with Judy, filming would stop. Pretty soon, they were sharing an apartment in Westwood. Though Asher was not a lesbian and very definitely preferred men, she knew what was expected of her. In the promiscuous movie colony it was not unusual for women to fool around with each other and Asher soon got Judy into bed. This came as a comfort to Judy, who was now having sleepless nights over Power's procrastination when it came to divorce.

Judy forced his hand by announcing that she was pregnant with his baby. Power, now at the Marine Corps' officers' training school at Quantico, Virginia, wrote to Annabelle asking for a divorce. She said no, but when she traveled to Washington, DC, to see him, both Power and Judy assumed that she was going to change her mind. Judy flew to New York to await the call. When Annabelle arrived in Washington, her answer was still no and she would not be shaken. The phone never rang for Judy, who flew back to LA and the tender mercies of Betty Asher – who told her that Power had been showing her love letters to his Marine Corps buddies. If they were up to Judy's usual literary standard, they would have had a laugh. Although this was plainly an Asher invention, Judy believed it and never responded to his letters, even when he went into combat. Judy may have been heartbroken, but poor Tyrone had to suffer much worse. On an outpost in the Pacific, he sat and watched her in *Meet Me in St Louis* (1944) with the other leathernecks.

"She never looked more beautiful," he wrote to a friend.

While Power brooded over his loss on a succession of Pacific islands, Judy found herself a new lover in the form of MGM wunderkind producer Joe Mankiewicz, brother of Herman,[12] who wrote the screenplay for Orson Welles's[13] *Citizen Kane* (1941). Instead of flattering or bullying his actresses as other producers did, he treated them as human beings, even entertaining their interpretations of the roles they were called on to play. They responded by falling into his bed. Joan Crawford[14] and Loretta Young had already succumbed. How could Judy refuse?

"He is the most wonderful man who ever lived," she said.

Marriage was not on the cards. His wife, the Austrian actress Rosa Stradner, was in a psychiatric hospital, and he had two baby sons to look after. Anyway, Mankiewicz did not love her in that way. "I was in love … the way you love an animal, a pet," he said.

Mankiewicz was a devotee of psychoanalysis and Judy was soon on the couch of celebrity shrink Ernst Simmel. When their daily sessions resulted in Judy being more self-assertive, Ethel complained to Mayer. In a chance meeting on the Santa Fe line's luxurious train, the *Super Chief*, Mayer warned Mankiewicz about carrying on with a girl 13 years his junior.

"I'm talking to you strictly as the head of a studio," said Mayer.

"No you're not," said Mankiewicz. "You're talking like a jealous old man."

Mayer had Mankiewicz bundled unceremoniously out of his compartment.

A few weeks later, Mankiewicz was summoned to Mayer's huge white-on-white office in Culver City. This time Ethel was present. Mayer told Mankiewicz to "stop filling Judy's head with all sorts of talk about psychiatrists." Mankiewicz naturally stuck up for psychoanalysis.

"So, my daughter's crazy?" screamed Ethel.

All Judy needed was a mother's love, said Mayer.

"A mother's love, my ass," said Mankiewicz.

The conversation became acrimonious. Mankiewicz ended it with the line: "This studio is not big enough for both of us, Mr Mayer. One of us has to go."

Consequently, Mayer lost one of his most talented producers, who went straight to 20th Century Fox, where he got a pay rise and was allowed to write and direct his own pictures, picking up a shelf full of Oscars along the way. Meanwhile, Judy continued psychoanalysis, and she continued to see Mankiewicz.

The analysis can only be described as a failure and Judy quit it when she went on tour promoting war bonds. When she returned to Hollywood, Mankiewicz's wife was out of the psychiatric hospital and he had resumed married life. But Judy was not content to leave it at that and announced, once again, that she was pregnant. Joe did not believe her. However, knowing that an outright contradiction would be bad for her ego, he went through the motions of arranging an abortion. They traveled together to New York. Mankiewicz's friend, the press agent Mark Hanna, picked them up at the last stop before Grand Central and took them to his upper-east-side apartment. There she took a belated pregnancy test. Joe feigned disbelief when it turned out to be negative. Then they returned by train to California. For Judy the long train journey across the States and back again was like a honeymoon. For Mankiewicz, it was the end of the affair. When they disembarked in LA, for him at least, it was all over.

Judy was at first reluctant to play in *Meet Me in St Louis*. It was just another 17-year-old girl next-door part. But she was persuaded to do so by producer Alan Freed, another MGM doyen of the casting couch. This was the guy who, when welcoming Shirley Temple to the studio after Metro had poached her from Fox, emerged from behind his desk with his penis out. Unaware of what was expected of her, the 11-year-old star simply laughed. Freed threw her out of his office.

Although Judy was still stuck on Mankiewicz, he was advising her to date other men, so she set about bedding her co-star Tom Drake. The problem was that Drake was an all-American boy who liked other all-American boys. Judy got him into bed, but failed to arouse him. After that their on-screen love scenes turned icy. She got sick, turned up late and was impossible to work with. But something magical happened during the shooting of *Meet Me in St Louis*. Viewing the daily rushes, Judy saw that the director, Vincente Minnelli, had done something for her that no other director had done. He had made her look beautiful. It was as if the picture was one long love letter to her. Judy grew in confidence, her behavior straightened out and by the end of the picture she was in love with Minnelli.

But Minnelli was shy and inscrutable, not the type to let his feelings be known or to ask his leading lady out. If she had made an advance, he would probably have run a mile. Fortunately, the dancer Don Loper, a mutual friend, played matchmaker. He arranged a foursome for dinner then he and his date feigned illness and dropped out, so Judy and Vincente dined alone. Soon an affair was underway. A few weeks after the end of shooting, they moved in together. Everyone was shocked. Minnelli was an ugly man, compared by the inmates of Culver City variously to a dinosaur or a goldfish. His unattractive features were plagued with a variety of tics and twitches. What made this match even more surprising was that he was also a well-known homosexual who often wore a full face of make-up. He had had a long-standing relationship with the artist Lester Gaba in New York. Young actors were entertained nightly at his Hollywood home and, on the lot, it was said he was "not marrying material." Plainly Judy was not put off by her experience with Tom Drake, and found that she could work her magic on Minnelli. When she was told that she was bedding an effeminate homosexual, she was adamant.

"That's not it at all," she said. "It's just his artistic flair."

Determined to bag her man, Judy divorced David Rose, then had one last fling with Joe Mankiewicz who, she often said, was the love of her life. Mankiewicz said that he felt that too. While his recollection of his affairs with other women grew dimmer over the years, his experiences with Judy remained forever fresh.

Judy worked with Minnelli on *Ziegfeld Follies* (1944). Then when she got her first straight, non-singing role in *The Clock* (1945, released in Britain as *Under the Clock*) she got the director Fred Zinnemann fired and had him replaced by her beloved Vincente. They were separated professionally the following year when she moved on to *The Harvey Girls* (1946), so they got engaged.

"I think he was truly in love with her," said a friend. "But I think she was in love with the idea that somebody took her seriously."

Like Artie Shaw and Joe Mankiewicz before him, Vincente played Pygmalion, molding Judy culturally and intellectually, a role he had played previously with Lena Horne. Meanwhile, despite the ring on her finger, Judy played around. One of her proudest conquests was Orson Welles, who was deeply involved with sex goddess Rita Hayworth[15] at the time. Welles plied Judy with huge bouquets of white flowers. One day Rita spotted a bunch on the back seat of his car and assumed they were for her. Fortunately their quick-witted secretary Shifra Haran removed the card before she opened it. Judy herself made a similar slip up. She invited Welles over to dinner on a night that she thought that Vincente was out of town. When Vincente's car pulled into the driveway, Judy rushed to the door, said that the stove was bust and insisted that they go straight out to a restaurant.

While Louis B. Mayer had previously discouraged Judy's dalliances with older men, he did all he could to encourage the union with Vincente Minnelli who, at 42, was the oldest of the lot. The reason? Business. Judy had told Louella Parsons that she missed the adulation of a live audience and that, when her contract expired in 1947, she would quit Hollywood for Broadway. Judy was one of MGM's biggest earners. They did not want to lose her and Mayer thought that if Judy married Minnelli he might be able to persuade her to stay on. Mayer not only turned up to their wedding, he gave the bride away. The Reverend William E. Roberts of the Beverly Hills Community Church officiated. At the end of the service, he held up a wooden staff to be grasped symbolically by the bride and groom, and Betty Asher, Judy's bridesmaid, and Vincente's best man, Ira Gershwin. Suddenly a fifth hand appeared on the staff. It was Mayer's.

"We were now man and wife in the eyes of God," said Vincente. "What's more, we had the blessing of the man upstairs who in many instilled far more dread."

Mayer plied the happy couple with expensive wedding presents and gave them three months' leave from the studio for their honeymoon. They headed off on the *Super Chief* for New York, so that Judy could at least visit Broadway. The city was in jubilant mood. Germany had surrendered the previous month and, while they were there, the Japanese capitulated and the war was over. Free from the stress of work, Judy threw the pills she had become dependent on into the East River. Even in New York, they could not escape the dead hand of the studio completely. Nick Schenck, head of MGM's east coast office, took them on a shopping trip around Tiffany's, encouraging them to pick out expensive gifts.

They had Minnelli's former lover Lester Gaba to dinner. He was crushed to see the love of his life so deeply involved – and with a woman. And Minnelli was plainly performing his conjugal duties. Before they returned to Los Angeles, Judy was pregnant – really pregnant, not like with Tyrone Power or Joe Mankiewicz. This time both Mayer and mother were pleased – though, given Minnelli's gay ways, many wags on the Metro lot proclaimed it an immaculate conception.

Metro squeezed her into one more picture, *Till the Clouds Roll By* (1947), before she had the baby. As a special concession, her scenes were shot by Vincente Minnelli. On March 8, 1946, Judy went into the Cedars of Lebanon Hospital and gave birth to Liza by Caesarean section. With her big brown eyes and dark hair, she was undoubtedly Vincente's and the gossips were silenced for the time being.

Judy suffered ill health afterward and for a whole year the studio left her alone. Then they pounced. Their strategy had worked; it was now obvious that Judy was not about to leave her husband and baby to play on Broadway and she signed another five-year contract with MGM. Judy and Minnelli began to work together again on *The Pirate* (1948). This was the kiss of death for their marriage. She began to resent him. Minnelli was the reason that Judy had to stay in Hollywood. Worse, he was a studio man who told her what to do on the set. And he was also there when she got home.

They were an ill-matched couple, especially in the bedroom. Judy needed someone altogether more ruggedly masculine and virile. She found that in Yul Brynner,[16] who also managed to bed Marlene Dietrich,[17] Joan Crawford[18] and Marilyn Monroe.[19] However, his son Rock says that Judy was the only one he really loved. Minnelli knew what was going on and sought comfort elsewhere. One night she came home and was about to climb into bed when she realized that it was already fully occupied. Vincente was in it with the handyman. She fled to the bathroom and tried to slit her wrists, though Minnelli managed to get the razor away from her before she did any lasting damage.

Judy had a nervous breakdown and, as soon as shooting on *The Pirate* finished, she checked into a private clinic. When Judy returned home she continued to share a bed with Vincente, but no longer shared a professional life. She had him bounced from her next picture *Easter Parade* (1948), and she did not even tell him what she had done. She also feared that her husband was bedding her co-star Gene Kelly, but Kelly broke an ankle and was replaced by Fred Astaire.[20] Judy was convinced that she was going to have an affair with Astaire, as part of the Hollywood merry-go-round. However, her marriage was on the rocks and she feared this might be the last straw.

"What am I going to do about Vincente?" she asked Sylvia Sidney.

Nothing had to be done. There was no affair. Fred Astaire was the most famously faithful husband in Hollywood, which was really not playing the game. Although she loved working with Astaire, the fact that she was not getting the loving she wanted made her difficult. She was dropped from their next picture together, *The Barkleys of Broadway* (1949), and replaced by Ginger Rogers.[21] Things were little better at home. The box office success of *Easter Parade* next to the failure of *The Pirate* damaged Vincente Minnelli's career. But when Judy turned to him for help and support in her battles with the studio, he always sided with the studio. She went instead to the actress Sylvia Sidney and her husband, radio producer and sometime agent Carleton Alsop. When the studio suspended her, Alsop fought. Eventually the studio had to give in because preview audiences wanted more than the one number they had filmed with Judy for *Words and Music* (1948).

Judy managed to get through *In the Good Old Summertime* (1949) because the producer Joe Pasternak had a dozen red roses sent anonymously to her dressing room every day. Her spies scoured the lot, but failed to discover the identity of her secret admirer. But then she was dropped from *Annie Get Your Gun* (1950) and suspended again. *Hollywood Nite Life* reported that "Miss G" was a pill head and people started avoiding her at Ciro's and the Mocambo. She checked into a private clinic, this time borrowing the money from the studio as she was flat broke from all the fines they had heaped on her for delaying productions. Vincente called once in a while, but she was sustained by the constant attention of Frank Sinatra[22] with whom, like so many, she had a brief affair.

She went back to work, but the pressure and the pills led to a further suspension and a suicide attempt. In 1950, she left MGM altogether, followed a year later by Mayer. Judy headed for New York, where she was seen out on the town regularly with screenwriter Fred Finklehoffe. The newspapers portrayed Vincente Minnelli as "the most broadminded husband in the land." The break with MGM brought with it a final break from her husband, who was still under contract to the studio.

"I obviously failed Judy," admitted Vincente. He outlasted everyone at MGM by never talking back to those in authority. He was not the strong man she needed to lean on and on December 21, 1950 they announced that their marriage was over.

Judy was already in love again. She had been out with Finklehoffe in an East Side dive called the Little Club when she was approached by Sid Luft, a man she had met when making *Broadway Melody* of 1938. He had been the secretary/lover of the picture's tap-dancing star, Eleanor Powell. They had bumped into each other in a bowling alley 11 years later.

"She thought I was a conceited ass and I thought she was a shrimp," said Luft.

Now here they were again 13 years after they had met. Finklehoffe was less than happy about Luft's intrusion. "Get lost," he said. But Judy said she fell in love with Luft at that very moment.

"Let him sit down, Freddie," she said. And Luft pulled up a chair.

A Jew brought up in Waspish Westchester County, Luft had learned to be a tough guy early on. Arrested for carrying a gun at the age of 12, he went into bodybuilding and beat up anyone who got in his way. At the outbreak of the Second World War he joined the Royal Canadian Air Force and, after Pearl Harbor, became a test pilot for Douglas Aircraft. He had produced two moderately successful B pictures, *Kilroy Was Here* (1947) and *French Leave* (1948), and was, at the time, in the process of getting a divorce from 20th Century Fox starlet Lynn Bari. Here at last was Judy's big, strong man, the man who would fight for her.

"Judy, don't mess with him, he's trouble," warned Finklehoffe.

But after years of the effete charm of Vincent Minnelli, here was a man of action and a man of unrestrained and uninhibited passion.

"Judy was crazy about this guy," said a friend. "Anything he did she would ask for more. He had her hypnotized."

When he flew back to LA, she followed. And there he began fighting for her – twice in Ciro's. The newspapers called him "One-Punch Luft" after he broke the nose of Hollywood columnist Jimmy Starr outside the Mocambo. They also dubbed him Judy's "Mr Wrong."

She began to put her career back together again too, taking a four-week engagement at the London Palladium, the English-speaking world's last great variety house. Before she went, she took her pianist, one-time lover Buddy Pepper, up to Vincente Minnelli's house to give her ex-husband a run-through of the act. He had only one suggestion to make – include "Rock-a-bye Your Baby with a Dixie Melody."

When Judy set sail to England, Sid stayed behind in New York, but after a couple of phone calls, he was persuaded to fly over to give her moral support. The show was a triumph and she toured the rest of the British Isles. Back in the US, her knight in shining armor went in to action. Luft phoned Sol A. Schwartz, the president of RKO Theaters, who owned the Palace on Broadway. This was the last of the big variety theaters on the Great White Way, but had long since been converted into a cinema. Two weeks later, *Variety* announced that vaudeville would be returning to the Palace, with Judy Garland topping the bill. Her response was typical. The night before opening, she went to a party without Sid and spent the night with former lover Johnny Mercer. The show was a smash and, despite a few days off after a drug-induced collapse on stage, it ran well into the next year.

Next she gave it to Hollywood. With Sid by her side she took her one-woman show first to the Philharmonic Auditorium and then to the Curran Theater in San Francisco where she played to sell-out audiences for four weeks. But her plans to take the show on to Chicago and the rest of the country had to be scrapped when she discovered she was pregnant. Halfway through the San Francisco run and two days before her 30th birthday Sid and Judy drove to the ranch of one of Sid's friends just outside the small town of Paicines, where they tied the knot.

"It was a beautiful wedding and a beautiful day," said the tearful bride.

The press did not agree. Luft, they decided, was far from the ideal husband – and certainly not the kind of man young Dorothy would expect to find over the rainbow. Jack Warner said that Sid was a "charming fellow. He's one of those original guys who promised his parents he'd never work a day in his life – and made good."

Judy already knew he was trouble. In London, he had taken charge of her finances, slashing the paychecks of her employees while indulging himself in Saville Row suits. When her make-up artist Dorothy Ponedel complained, Judy said: "I know what's going on, Dottie, but I love the guy." Her unpaid employees complained that piles of cash were coming in to – and going out of – the Palladium's box-office each night.

"All my money is tied up," said Judy, "in an attaché case, and that's tied to Sid's wrist."

Back in LA, a few days before her opening at the Palace, Luft had run a red light and shunted one car into another. He had been drinking. An altercation erupted and Judy hit one of the other drivers, a 17-year-old, breaking his glasses. When a dentist who had witnessed the accident said that it was all Sid's fault, Sid broke his glasses, too – along with the nose they were perched on. He was booked for driving without a valid license, drink driving, drunkenness and carrying concealed weapons – two .38-caliber revolvers stolen from the Douglas Aircraft company when he had worked there. Gradually most of the charges were dismissed and he was eventually fined just $150 for drink driving.

Luft's former wife, Lynn Bari, took Judy aside and warned her about Sid's ways. Judy dismissed her as bitter, so Lynn hammered him for child maintenance. It transpired that the upkeep of three race horses he had bought cost twice what he spent on his own son. Judy was called to testify in the court case and was asked how much Sid received as her manager. She looked blank and said simply that he handled her finances and took as much as he needed. Bari's lawyer put it more plainly.

"All the money Judy makes goes into Luft's pocket," he said.

The judge agreed. Dismissing Luft's testimony as "nowhere near the truth," the judge ordered him to double his child support – so his son was now on a par with his racehorses.

Although all this was publicly damaging, it didn't matter to Judy. Without him she felt she would have been just another washed-up Hollywood has-been. Now she was a star once again, on both sides of the Atlantic. And he had only just started. Next he clinched a lucrative new movie contract with Warner Bros. What's more, Judy would not return to being a wage slave as she had been at MGM, with fines for lateness, illness and other delays. Luft set up a production company which would produce up to nine movies using Warner's studio facilities and cash. If the pictures made money, they would share the profits. If they did not, Warner's alone would take the loss. They went straight into production on *A Star Is Born* (1954), with Judy in the final weeks of her pregnancy.

On November 21, 1952, she gave birth to a baby daughter, Lorna Luft. She now had a new husband, a new baby and a new career. Surely life did not get any better than that? But already things were beginning to fall apart. On the day she brought Lorna home from the hospital, Sid was in San Francisco watching one of his horses race. She forgave him but, a few days later, she went into the bathroom and slashed her neck.

Soon after, Ethel died of a heart attack. Mother and daughter had been estranged for some time. After seeing her mother push Liza the way she had pushed Judy as a child, Ethel had had a violent argument with her daughter. Ethel had tried to commit suicide, failed, and had taken a job for a dollar an hour at Douglas Aircraft. She died in the company's parking lot, aged

59, after rushing to work one day. The rift and the death caused a scandal.

It was off-set, however, by the acclaim surrounding the première of *A Star Is Born*. It was the hit of the year, but there were complaints from the movie theaters that it was too long. Harry Warner, jealous of his womanizing brother Jack who had been responsible for the project, butchered the picture. The public hated the truncated version and they lost money. On the night of the Oscars, Judy was in hospital after giving birth to her third child, Joseph Wiley Luft. An NBC camera was on hand to catch her reaction, but the network never cut to it. The Oscar had gone instead to Grace Kelly[23] for *The Country Girl* (1954). Groucho Marx said: "This is the biggest robbery since Brinks."

Warners pulled the plug on Judy's production company and pretty soon the Lufts were broke. So Judy went on the road again. CBS offered her $100,000 for a TV special, then signed her for a series. Las Vegas offered her a booking at $55,000 a week – $5,000 more than anyone else had ever received. Then she went back to the Palace on old Broadway. Triumph followed disaster followed triumph, but many of Judy's Hollywood friends dismissed Sid as a conman and refused to accept him into their circle. Even though Judy was making extraordinary amounts of money, Sid always managed to spend more and they ended up owing everyone, including the IRS. Meanwhile, Judy piled on the pills and the booze. Something had to give.

In February 1956, Judy sued for divorce, largely on the grounds, as Hedda Hopper put it, that Sid was "a gambling man who can kill $10,000 in an afternoon." But after three days' separation she withdrew the suit, telling Louella Parsons: "I love Sid and he loves me and I don't think we were ever so glad to see each other in our lives."

In Las Vegas, she had to play an extra show just to cover his losses at the tables and, when he heard that people were saying he was stealing from her, he said: "Fuck them. People want to believe what they want to believe. I can't straighten them out."

Rows were frequent and public, and those who witnessed them were often shocked by the level of obscenity they employed. Judy claimed that Luft beat her and locked her out of the house, though those who witnessed their fights said that, small though she was, she often gave better than she got. To avoid trouble, Sid spent even more time at the racetrack away from Judy. This suited Judy as it gave her time to pursue her extra-marital flings. She bedded James Mason, her co-star in *A Star Is Born* and renewed her acquaintanceship with Frank Sinatra. Judy had always been an enthusiastic practitioner of fellatio (one deliciously dirty-minded lover always made her sing "Over the Rainbow" afterward because he loved to hear the song sung through a mouthful of semen), but she became concerned about Sinatra's excessive demands in that department.

"All he wants is blow jobs," she told the Lufts' all-purpose handyman, Harry Rubin.

"What's wrong with that?" said Rubin.

"Well, you've gotta fuck once in a while, too, you know," said Judy. "Are you feeling frisky?" And Rubin duly became one of her lovers. She had several on the go at a time, including two or three women. She was uncharacteristically discreet about what she did with them, but when Rubin asked her about a new girlfriend, she said: "When you've eaten everything in the world there is to eat, you've got to find new things." Hmm.

Despite the other lovers Sid was still number one in the bedroom department.

"At least he does everything the way I want it," she told Rubin.

Rubin observed that conflict was their most powerful aphrodisiac. Sid would go away on one of his disastrous gambling trips, return, and there would be a huge conflagration.

"After the fighting had stopped," said Rubin, "they'd jump in the sack for about three days, and it was 'honey,' 'baby,' and 'dear.' Then they got close to each other and it would start all over again."

In February 1958, Judy returned to the divorce courts for the third time in two years. This time she was alleging physical abuse and obtained a protection order. Six weeks later, she announced that she was going to give her marriage "one more chance." That, of course, is the death knell of any relationship. Slowly Judy began to realize that Sid, who she had turned to as a strong man she could depend on, was, in fact, weak – and his weakness was for her money. She went to Jack Kennedy[24] for consolation, phoning him at the White House. He would give her advice on how to deal with her personal and professional life in exchange for a couple of bars of "Over the Rainbow" sung a cappella down the phone.

Seeing that she was all washed up in Hollywood once again, Judy moved to London where she surrounded herself with gay men, hanging out with Dirk Bogarde and Noël Coward. Sid eventually joined her, but he made a crucial mistake. Wanting to pursue some business opportunities of his own, he relinquished her management to David Begelman. At that very same moment, Judy realized that she no longer loved Sid and Begelman replaced him in her bed as well as in the office.

In the summer of 1961, she took the children on a family holiday to Cape Cod, staying just a few hundred yards from the Kennedy compound, without Sid. He turned up anyway and checked in to to a nearby motel. When he finally made contact, she told him bluntly that she was going to divorce him. He fell apart, but the relationship continued. When she fell ill at the Berlin première of *Judgment at Nuremberg* (1961) that December, he went to collect her and they spent Christmas together. But when Judy decided to return to England, he refused to let her take the children. Eventually the police had to be called.

"My marriage is finished," she said when she arrived in London. "It lasted 11 years and it would take 11 years to tell you what went wrong."

Sid turned up in London determined to take the kids back, but she made them wards of court. In England, she made *I Can Go On Singing* (1962) with Dirk Bogarde, but could not get used to the fact that British star trailers did not boast a lavatory. She used the wastepaper basket instead, leaving some lowly studio gofer to deal with the resulting mess.

In 1963, Judy and Sid were publicly reconciled, though she kept Begelman on the side. Determined to revenge himself on the man who had usurped his position, Sid had him investigated and discovered that, while making love to Judy, he had also been milking her. To Judy, it must have sounded all too familiar. She took no notice of the evidence Sid had unearthed. However, she soon found that, thanks to her prestige, Begelman and his partner Freddie Fields had attracted a number of other A-list clients and she was soon complaining that it was easier to get the President of the United States on the phone than it was to speak to her own agent. Soon bailiffs were knocking on the door again.

She comforted herself with a handful of lovers – her piano player Bobby Cole, the actor John Carlyle, who had been an usher at her first Palace show, and the French singer and actor André Phillipe, who performed his "duets" in her dressing room. Then there was Glenn Ford,[25] one of Hollywood's most enduring leading men. He was very attentive and there were hints they might marry, but what Judy really needed was a toy boy. She found one in the form of 33-year-old actor Mark Herron. Seven years her junior, the newspapers immediately dubbed him a gigolo and he set off on a disastrous tour of Australia with her. Panned by the critics, she tried to commit suicide in Hong Kong on the way home, but was saved by Herron, who pushed the comatose superstar in a wheelchair to a hospital through a typhoon.

Subsequent triumphs in London and New York were ascribed to him.

"I hope it's true," he said. "I love her more each day."

More triumphs and disasters followed. Topless photos were circulated and, when fired from the filming of Jacqueline Susann's *Valley of the Dolls* (1967) – in which one of the characters is based on the young pill-popping Judy – she was found lying comatose on a pool table displaying her delta of Venus to anyone who might pass by.

Finally obtaining her divorce from Sid in 1965, she immediately married Mark Herron, with typical good taste, in the Little Church of the West on the Strip in Las Vegas – all major credit cards accepted.

"I feel like Mrs Herron," Judy gushed. "I'm so happy."

They split up immediately after, with Judy complaining that the marriage had never been consummated. What did she expect? She derided Mark as another "faggot." To marry one gay man may be regarded as a misfortune, to marry two looks like… Although they had lived together for some time, Mark's previous sexual experience had been limited to other men, notably the character actor Henry Brandon and that old faithful Charles Laughton. By this time, as well as the pills, Judy was doing heroin and morphine.

Mark went back to Henry Brandon, while Judy took up with the young publicist Tom Green, a recent graduate from Dartmouth who had been president of his fraternity. By this time she was flat broke again. The IRS were after her and, somehow, her books showed that she owed Sid $150,000 for past managerial services. The few people she could get on the phone refused to help, though the wealthy daughter of a movie mogul made an offer which Judy refused.

"She's just like all the other dykes that wanted me to go to bed with them," she told Green.

She found her consolation in wild and uninhibited sex with Green. On one occasion, she disappeared under the table at a

Santa Monica restaurant and performed oral sex on him while he nibbled his hors d'oeuvre. They passed on the entrée and went home for the main course. She was a little more restrained when she went to spend Christmas with Green's parents in Lowell, Massachusetts. Arguing that the captain of a ship can marry passengers, she got the engineer to perform a cod wedding in the dining car of the *Super Chief* on the way.

"I have the unfortunate habit of not being able to have an affair with a man without being in love with him," she explained. She later promised to marry him properly in the chapel at Dartmouth College. She told his family: "What I am is a very proper lady, and I'd just like to have that recognized."

I am sure they were impressed.

She was so proper that, as a Protestant with a bad reputation, she phoned the local archbishop, Cardinal Cushing, to get permission to attend Midnight Mass with the family.

Green quit his job, sacrificing his career, in order to help her. He ended up borrowing money to keep her afloat. Sid sometimes sent a little food for the children and Alma Cousteline and Lionel Doman, the saintly African-American couple who ran the household, dug deep into their own pockets. But eventually she lost the house.

Liza, whose own career was now skyrocketing, rode to the rescue. She made sure the other two kids, Lorna and Joey, got to school and prevented her mother from killing herself. On one occasion she held Judy's ankles when she threatened to jump from a hotel window and it is said she was the only girl in Los Angeles to own her own stomach pump.

In return, Judy picked out Liza's first husband for her. In Hong Kong, Judy and Mark Herron had caught the act of twenty-year-old Australian performer Peter Allen and invited him to come to London with his partner, Chris Bell. The Allen Brothers, as they called themselves, would be Judy's new opening act.

A ferocious matchmaker, Judy arranged for Peter to be at the piano playing Gershwin's "Isn't It a Pity? (we never met before)" when Liza walked into the room. Liza supplied the words and the duet resulted in a New York wedding.

Three weeks later, Liza came home to find Peter in bed with a man, just like Judy had found Vincente in bed with the handyman 20 years before. Marrying gay men seemed to run in the family. Three generations of women had married fellas who worked the other side of the street, but there was a particular twist this time. Liza's husband's lover was none other than her mother's spouse *du jour* Mark Herron, her own stepfather. It was Peter's performance in bed, not on the stage, that impressed Mark in Hong Kong. The affair had continued in London and on to the United States, behind the backs of both Judy and Liza. Man, you could not make this stuff up.

Liza stayed married to Peter for three more years, largely because she needed someone to field calls from her mother. Although the relationship between mother and daughter cooled, it was never severed completely. However, after hearing Lorna sing in her school production of *The Unsinkable Molly Brown*, Judy said: "Fuck Liza. This one's going to pay my rent."

In the meantime Judy turned back to Sid for advice. He arranged a deal with a man of dubious reputation, who would pick up her day-to-day expenses and pay her a small fee in exchange for the profits from her concerts. Tom Green, meanwhile, was to keep an eye on her drug intake. This worked well enough until Judy had a shouting match with her new sponsor's young wife. She missed a few concerts; he stopped her money. Judy was just about to be thrown out of her suite at the St Moritz on Central Park when, in a desperate attempt to save the situation, Tom pawned two of Judy's rings to stop the eviction. Judy had Green arrested for theft and thrown in jail. How the Dartmouth boy had fallen. Nancy Barr, a fan who claimed to have slept with Judy, bailed him out. Judy plagued her with nuisance calls, threatening to put the Mafia onto her. Barr developed a spastic colon and retired from the field of love wounded.

Judy's behaviour also forced Luft's children out of her life. Several times they had to find sanctuary at Liza's apartment on East 57th Street. One night, Joey fled into the snowy streets of Manhattan after his mother threw a butcher's knife at him. At three in the morning, he found safety with his father in a nearby hotel. Lorna ended up in hospital with a breakdown. She called her father who had returned Los Angeles, begging him to let her live with him. A few hours later, she was on a plane bound for California.

Judy traveled from city to city, staying with friends and former lovers. In the middle of October 1968, she was introduced to piano player and songwriter John Meyer. In just a few minutes they were talking like old friends. In just a few hours, she had moved in with him at his parents' apartment on Park Avenue. In just a few days they were engaged. Meyer was convinced that he could put Judy back on her feet again. And he did. He got her an engagement at Three, the gay and lesbian bar on East 72d Street where he played piano – wouldn't you know it. She got $100 cash for a couple of numbers delivered around midnight to an adoring crowd. Within weeks he had arranged three appearances on national TV and a five-week run in London at the Talk of the Town, the capital's premier supper club, at $6,000 a week.

The problem was Judy "lived in the fourth dimension," he said. She wore him out. After just two-and-a-half months together, he came down with the flu. So she found herself another piano player, 34-year-old Mickey Deans – né DeVinko – the dark-haired, blue-eyed night manager of the Manhattan discotheque Arthur where she spent the wee small hours. Meyer's months with Judy formed the basis of his 322-page book *Heartbreaker*.

Deans was a cool dude, the sort of guy who could get you a bag full of amphetamines if you wanted to stay up all night partying and still catch that early morning plane to LA. He was also Arthur's head bouncer, and bore more than a passing resemblance in manner and build to Sid Luft. They had been seeing each other for some months, despite the fact that Meyer was on the scene. When he heard that she was going to London, he asked the 46-year-old Judy to marry him. She did not have to be asked twice.

"I finally got the right man to ask me. I've been waiting for a long time," she told reporters.

Leaving Meyer sniffling into his pillow, Judy whisked Deans off to England, where they intended to wed. Her appearance at the Talk of the Town was a triumph and the run was extended into the New Year. Even though Judy's divorce papers were stuck in California, on January 9, 1969, they went ahead with the wedding at St Marylebone parish church, where the poet Robert Browning had married Elizabeth Barrett of Wimpole Street. Judy was concerned that they had no witnesses.

"God is our witness," said the Anglican priest.

The marriage was made legal two months later in a civil ceremony at the Chelsea Registry Office. The reception was at Quaglino's, a fashionable restaurant in London's West End, but with the exception of Johnnie Ray, a singer already well past his sell-by date, no celebs turned up. It was the "saddest and most pathetic party I have every attended," wrote one British gossip columnist.

A brief honeymoon in Paris was followed by a triumphant tour of Scandinavia. They settled in a mews cottage in London. Mickey managed her affairs, without conspicuous success and he began to make excuses to spend more and more time away from her. When they returned to New York at the end of May, the marriage seemed to be on its last legs.

"I have to get away from Mickey," she told former lover John Carlyle, to whom she renewed an earlier offer of marriage.

The Deans's marriage revived a bit when he visited with his family in their modest red bungalow in Garfield, New Jersey, and Judy began to contemplate a future on the wrong side of the Hudson. Didn't she know that she wasn't a tunnel-and-bridge person? As it was, Judy returned to London, where she now felt appreciated and at home.

On June 21, she and Mickey had planned to go and see the celebrated female impersonator Danny La Rue. They did not turn up. Mickey was woken at around 10.40 am the following morning by a call from LA. It was John Carlyle, who wanted to speak to Judy. She was not in bed beside him, so Mickey went to look for her. The door to the bathroom was locked and there was no response from inside. Mickey had to clamber across a roof and climb in through the bathroom window. He found Judy dead on the lavatory – a farewell scene favored by the famous. The coroner said the cause of death was "barbituate poisoning" due to "an incautious self-overdose" – under English law this is termed "death by misadventure." Marilyn Monroe had gone the same route two years before.

Judy's body was flown back to New York, where the funeral oration was given by former lover James Mason, her co-star in *A Star Is Born*. This time it was very much "A Star Is Dead" – something the reviewers had said many times before, only to be proved wrong. But this time, Judy Garland really was dead and would, very definitely, lie down.

7

Million Dollar Legs Akimbo

While Judy, Vivien, Merle, Mae, and the gang did their bit for the war effort during the Second World War, it was Betty Grable who was the pin-up of the boys overseas. It was her ass they patted when they scrambled for action. It was her million-dollar legs and blonde, cotton-candy curls that they painted on the sides of their aircraft. And it was her one-piece bathing suit that melted away in their imaginations when they thought of the girl back home. They knew it was okay to think such thoughts because she was looking over her shoulder giving a reassuring, peek-a-boo, girl-next-door, all-American smile. But there was more to Betty Grable than even the most hardened could have handled.

The *New Yorker* once defined entertainment as: "Mickey Mouse's adventures and Betty Grable's legs." Sadly, we know little about Mickey Mouse's sex life, but we do know that Betty Grable's legs were open from an early age. She was a graduate of the Busby Berkeley stable.

The bisexual Berkeley, whose mother was an intimate friend of the notorious lesbian Alla Nazimova,[1] was known for his huge choreographed dance numbers featuring hundreds of beautiful young women. Famously, in *Roman Scandals* (1932), he choreographed a huge licentious bondage scene with scores of totally naked girls in chains. Their modesty was preserved from the cameras and the prying eyes of cinema audiences by long, blonde wigs. Those on set, naturally, saw it all. Off screen Berkeley, who had learned his craft drilling troops during the First World War, choreographed even more extravagant orgies for industry bigwigs. Girls who refused to attend or attempted to evade these command performances would be unceremoniously dumped from the on screen line-up. Betty, who started in the chorus at the age of 13 when her mother lied about her age, saw the whole of Hollywood from the bottom up.

"Those parties were the pits," she said. "You'd come out in the early dawn feeling like a piece of meat dogs had been fighting over all night... The message was that either you played their game their way or you got out of town."

Judy Garland worked under Busby Berkeley in four of her early films. She hated him, though she never talked about it.

Betty was plucked from the chorus line and got a solo singing part in Berkeley's first movie, *Whoopee* (1930). The movie was co-produced by the legendary Broadway impresario Florenz Ziegfeld,[2] another champion of the casting couch, particularly when auditioning chorus girls for his follies. He was known for his preference for young girls – at 17 they were too old for his taste. Marion Davis[3] – later the lover of William Randolf Hearst and Charlie Chaplin[4] – was high-kicking under Ziegfeld at the age of 14.

After appearing in a series of cheesecake photographs, Betty came to the attention of Roscoe "Fatty" Arbuckle[5] who, after a sex scandal ended his acting career in 1921, was eking a living as a director at Educational Pictures under the name William Goodrich. She made a number of short films with provocative titles for him under the pseudonym Frances Dean. These included *Flirty Sleepwalker*, *Hollywood Lights*, *Over the Counter*, and *Ex-Sweeties* (all 1931).

For *Palmy Days* (1931), Berkeley auditioned over 15,000 – picking Betty, Jane Wyman[6] and Paulette Goddard[7] to be among the original scantily clad "Goldwyn Girls." On the movie, 16-year-old Betty met 36-year-old George Raft, former lover of Mae West. After a couple of dates, Raft claimed that he had "tossed her back into the pond." In fact, they began a long affair. At the time, Raft was married to a woman who for religious reasons would not give him a divorce. Betty's mother encouraged the romance. A liaison with an established movie star could do Betty's reputation no harm. The fact that Raft could not marry her was an advantage. It meant she was still available for a more favorable match – and, for the moment at least, mommie dearest was not going to lose her meal ticket.

More films with provocative titles followed – *The Age of Consent*, *The Greeks Had A Word For Them* and *Hold 'Em Jail* (all 1932). Betty's participation in these romps was encouraged by her mother. And when Jean Harlow came to prominence in the early 1930s, Betty went platinum blonde and began plucking and penciling her eyebrows.

Her mother badgered the famous bandleader Ted Fiorito into taking the 16-year-old Betty on as a singer. She went on tour with the band and, even though she was chaperoned by her mother, managed a brief fling with the drummer Charlie Price. Back in LA, Betty had a new boyfriend who took her to the beach. A friend who accompanied them said: "Betty wore a bright pink dance leotard – I think it was a leotard because I don't remember having bathing suits that were as revealing as this one was in those days."

When Betty went into the water, the pink bathing suit promptly became transparent.

"You should have seen the boys gathering from all over the beach when she came out," said an eyewitness.

Her role in *The Gay Divorcee* (1934) earned her a contract at RKO. According to the *Hollywood Reporter*, Betty "had an extra glow when she reported for work – friends say that it was because she was in love…" But who with? She was still seeing both George Raft and Charlie Price, between other romances.

On a cruise to Catalina, Bill Carey, another member of Ted Fiorito's band, introduced her to former child star Jackie

Coogan. They co-starred in the touring vaudeville show *Hollywood Secrets* from December 1935 to April 1936 and made the short *Sunkist Stars at Palm Springs* (1936) for MGM. Then they fell in love, announced their engagement, and moved to Paramount.

"They just sat and looked at each other at parties, then they'd go outside and hold hands, and there was nothing mamma could do about it," said a studio worker. Soon the fan mags were showing Betty's canopied bed, though Betty coyly told reporters that: "My contract has something in it that says I mustn't marry until I am 21."

Two days after her 21st birthday, on December 20, 1937, they married – without mamma's approval. Then the two newlyweds worked together on two feature films – *College Swing* (1938) and *Million Dollar Legs* (1939). The title of this second movie was to prove prophetic, though the legs in question belonged to a racehorse.

Although they were seen out together in all the fashionable spots, the marriage was far from successful. Jackie was a boozer and would disappear for days on end. He was involved in a bitter legal battle with his mother over the money he had earned as a child star, and Betty had to sell her personal possessions to pay his debts. The marriage lasted less than two years.

Eventually her potential was seen by Darryl Zanuck,[8] another movie mogul known for his sexual antics. As a child he had lived with his mother in hotels. She had had a life-long habit of lying naked on the bed and leaving the door open for any passer-by who might care to sample what they saw. Mother used to wear green nail varnish and thousands of young women in Hollywood wore green nails as a badge of honor to show they had graduated from his casting couch. When he first came to Hollywood he fell under the tutelage of Charlie Chaplin and his brother Sydney, and began to work his way through the Mack Sennett[9] Bathing Beauties. When his long-suffering wife protested, he said: "Why get so mad about them? They're just tarts – girls to be fucked and thrown away. You're different. I respect you." That's okay then.

By the time he was head of 20th Century Fox, Zanuck had worked out a system. Every afternoon, a girl – an ingénue trying to get into the business or an established star trying to improve her contract – would be conducted into a secret bedroom built behind a bookcase in his office. They would have precisely 30 minutes of the great man's time to prove their point. Those who performed satisfactorily wore the green nail varnish to show that they were, for the time being at least, the girl on her way up. Betty Grable paid regular tea-time visits to Zanuck's office and, consequently, found a lucrative home at 20th Century Fox.

Betty began dating a number of eligible bachelors, which made Jackie jealous. But on October 11, 1939, she turned up at the divorce courts on the arm of – guess who? – Artie Shaw.

"Betty will be Mrs Shaw when she gets her final decree," wrote Louella Parsons.

However, while her romance with Shaw continued, she began seeing producer Buddy de Sylva and other eligible males, while Shaw began seeing Judy Garland on the side. Both were convinced that Shaw loved them when he took off to marry Lana Turner.[10] On the rebound, Betty got engaged to the rich Canadian chain-store owner Alexis Thompson, but it did not last.

After a stretch on Broadway, Betty returned to Hollywood to become "The Queen of Fox" with *Down Argentine Way* (1940). It was her 52d film. Upon the completion of *Tin Pan Alley* (1940) she was given a brief vacation. She jumped on board the *Super Chief*, where she met the New York – and muscle – bound Victor Mature.[11] Betty was stopping off in Chicago. Mature got off too. He took her to the College Inn to hear crooner Dick Haymes,[12] one-time lover of Rita Hayworth.[13] There she met bandleader Harry James for the first time, though she claims to have been unimpressed. When they arrived in New York, Mature said that being on the arm of a big star like Betty Grable did him no harm. It got him a part on Broadway which kept him in New York for a year.

Betty had to hurry back to LA, though. With the Second World War raging, her on-screen freshness appealed to homesick servicemen and she dashed, scantily clad, from lot to lot turning out pictures. This left her no time to tour outside the United States for the USO, but she raised hundreds of thousands of dollars, auctioning her nylons for the war effort. One pair, accompanied by a certificate of authenticity, fetched $110,000.

On-screen she played opposite all the big male heartthrobs – Don Ameche, Cesar Romero, John Payne and Tyrone Power[14] in *A Yank in the RAF* (1941). Off-screen she was paired with Oleg Cassini[15] and Desi Arnaz, later the husband of Lucille Ball. Both on-screen and off-screen, she was paired once more with Victor Mature, who had returned from Broadway. And, still, there was George Raft.

"I would have married George Raft a week after I met him, I was so desperately in love with him," she told Louella Parsons. "But when you wait two-and-a-half years, there doesn't seem to be any future in a romance with a married man."

Even so, they vacationed together in New York. A friend, Paula Stone, recalled that they had a quarrel, which caused Betty to cut her vacation short, and she asked Paula to take her to Grand Central Station to catch the train home.

"When we reached the compartment, there was a huge bouquet of roses awaiting her," she said. "They were, of course, from George, and as she read the card a big smile broke through the tears. She was so in love."

The two were reunited in Hollywood, where they usually preferred to spend their evenings in. When they did go out to fashionable nightclubs Betty would be seen hugging and kissing handsome actors, while Raft looked on with a jealous stare. Behind closed doors he would slap her, but that did not stop her doing just what she wanted. After all, he could not give her what she wanted, which was marriage.

Raft turned down an offer to do a picture with her.

"I'm too much in love with her," he told a columnist, "and working together might lead to an argument somewhere along the line."

"Does that mean they never have any?" commented the columnist sarcastically.

Even so she was too involved with Raft to entertain Cesar Romero's propositions during the making of *Coney Island* (1943). However, after Artie Shaw, she was plainly left with a weakness for musicians. She fell for Harry James while working with him on *Springtime in the Rockies* (1942). He was married and the father of two.

Insecure in her affections, Raft bought Betty an expensive diamond-studded watch, but in the jitterbugging contest at the Hollywood Palladium, Betty was drawn as Harry James's partner. Raft was not happy with this. James went on to win the competition, but with actress Nan Wynn as his partner – Betty had the good sense not to turn up. Even so, this was the end of their relationship. Betty phoned Raft and told him that it was all over.

When she refused to see him in person, he sent a friend, Ben Platt, to spy on her. Platt climbed a tree and tried to peer into her bedroom window where he expected to see Betty and James making out. In the process, he lost his grip and plunged to the ground.

Raft sent another friend with an expensive stonemarten fur coat. Betty refused to answer the door and he had to leave it on the mat. In all, Raft reckoned his gifts to Betty totaled over $50,000, a tidy sum in those days. But it was all over as the normally teetotal Raft found out when he staggered drunkenly over to Betty's table in a restaurant on Sunset Strip, demanding to speak with her. In the ensuing scuffle, James was pronounced the winner. Now it was over for sure.

Betty told Louella Parsons that there were no hard feelings. She was sure that Raft still loved her and she loved him.

"You can't see a person every day, and have them do all the little thoughtful, attentive things George did, and break off without feeling lonely," she said. "I don't expect to get over George today, tomorrow, or next week. But I do know there's no turning back."

In the interview, she denied seeing James, but Lucille Ball was already convinced they were very much in love.

"I remember I'd go and see her," she said, "and she'd lie on the floor with her radio right to her ear, when Harry was playing in Chicago or some place. Everything else would stop when he was on the radio. It would be blaring, and she'd be listening to that horn."

James played the trumpet and he could offer what Raft could not – marriage. He got a Mexican divorce and in July 1943 they married in Las Vegas. The GIs now had a new catchphrase: "I want a girl just like the girl that married Harry James." Betty was already pregnant, and in March 1944 she gave birth to a daughter. Meanwhile Raft consoled himself with 20-year-old actress Bonita Granville, who was six years younger than Betty.

In 1942, 1943 and 1944, Betty Grable was the movie's number-one female attraction, and she stayed in the top ten for the next ten years. She received more than 10,000 items of fan mail a week and, in 1942 alone, sent out 54,000 autographed photographs to the soldiers at Camp Robinson, Arkansas, in response to their letters. The studio also made a great play on the fact that her famous legs were insured for one million dollars with Lloyd's of London. She was dubbed variously "the girl with the million-dollar legs," "the gal with the gorgeous gams," or "the limbs that launched a thousand sighs."

The famous swimsuit shot – "the picture that launched a thousand dreams" – was taken in 1943 and there are several versions of how the pose came about. Some say that she turned her back to the camera to hide her stomach, as she was pregnant at the time. Others say that Darryl Zanuck had just walked into the still photographer's studio and she had looked over her shoulder to smile at him. Anyway, millions of copies found their way to servicemen overseas.

"A lot of guys don't have any girlfriends to fight for," she said. "I guess you could call us pin-up girls a kind of an inspiration."

For both sides. Her picture also fell into enemy hands, who, like their Allied foe, felt the compulsion to pin them up wherever they went. The studio cashed in with *Pin-Up Girl* (1944).

This only increased her fame. Her marriage had done nothing to diminish her sex appeal and, at a hostile stockholders' meeting called to complain about his overspending, Zanuck pointed to a picture of Betty's legs and told his backers that he had "a sure-fire commodity." However, just to be on the safe side, Zanuck added another blonde to his stable, June Havers. She was known for her strong religious convictions – even disappearing into a convent for a brief period – as well as her Billingsgate vocabulary. Plainly another graduate from Zanuck's casting couch, Betty dubbed her "the only girl on the Fox lot with a crucifix in one hand and a rubber in the other."

Zanuck warned his stockholders: "When the boys come home from the battlefields overseas, you will find they have changed." But one thing would stay the same, he said. "There'll always be a market for Betty Grable and Lana Turner and all of that tit stuff." So it wasn't just her legs then, Darryl.

From 1946 to 1947, Betty Grable was the highest paid woman in the United States, but when she made her first attempt at a serious movie, *The Shocking Miss Pilgrim* (1946), Fox received over 100,000 thousand letters complaining that she did not show her famous "gams." That was quickly rectified by

Mother Wore Tights (1947), her biggest financial and critical success. As she explained: "They paid me for raising my shirt, not playing Sarah Bernhardt[16]." She was a girl who knew what it was all about. During the filming of That Lady in Ermine (1948) with Douglas Fairbanks Jr,[17] she presented her co-star with an ermine-lined jockstrap. He returned the compliment with an ermine-lined chastity belt.

Constant filming, meant that Betty was stuck in Hollywood, while James toured the country with his band. Newspaper gossip columnists frequently reported that James was bedding young fans. When Betty asked him about it, she was met with angry silence. Fortunately, she was co-starring with her old flame Victor Mature in *Wabash Avenue* (1950) at the time. After that, she avoided confrontations with James and simply turned the other cheek.

During the filming of *My Blue Heaven* (1950), persistent rumors circulated of a fling with her co-star, Dan Dailey. It is said that James burst into Betty's dressing room unannounced and caught them in the act. A fight broke out, as a result of which Betty had a black eye. She told the studio that she had been riding in the car when James braked too heavily. Dailey's wife divorced him soon after – but that could have been because he signed into a clinic in an attempt to cure himself of his transvestism. He sent a note to Betty from the clinic which read: "Hi, Queenie, I'm getting better," but it is thought that his confinement did nothing to cure him of his compulsion to dress in women's clothing, though he later remarried.

In *Gentlemen Prefer Blondes* (1953), Betty was cast opposite Marilyn Monroe,[18] who would eventually take over her position as "The Fox Blonde." She had already been given Betty's dressing room, but they became friends. However, after the movie was in the can, Betty tore up her contract in front of Zanuck's face and left the studio weeping. At the same time, thanks to Harry James's drinking, gambling and womanizing, her marriage was on the rocks. They divorced after 22 years of marriage. She turned down a number of movie roles, preferring more lucrative television appearances. She also toured in cabaret, starred in musicals and surrounded herself with compliant young men. But wherever she appeared in the US or the UK, older gentlemen would appear at the stage door, clutching her old pin-up picture for her to sign.

In 1968, Betty became romantically involved with one of her young posse – Bob Remick, a dancer from *Hello Dolly*. He was 22, the age of her eldest daughter; she was 50. Betty was an old-fashioned girl with strict Victorian morals. When they were at home in Las Vegas, he was required to leave the house discreetly before dawn, even though this meant scaling a wall and crossing the Desert Inn golf course to avoid the neighbors' prying eyes. Later, he was allowed to stay in the house, but in a separate bedroom for appearances' sake.

She would always give him – or for that matter any other young male escort – two or three hundred dollars when they went out so he could pick up the tab. But when she was drunk, she would abuse him. She was also very jealous.

"Bob never looked at another woman, as far as I could see," said her manager Kevin Pines, "but Betty probably did not believe that. But can you imagine the ribbing that boy took when he came out of the chorus line and started dating Betty? He really did adore her."

Pines thought they would have married if Betty had not feared her fans' reaction to her marrying a man half her age. Before Betty and James divorced, the three of them would be seen around town together. On one occasion they were dining with Pines when Betty and Bob had a row. Betty stormed out of the restaurant. They decided to let her go, then Bob relented. He got in the car and followed her down the street.

"As Betty walked, her pants started falling down," said Pines. "We couldn't very well let Betty Grable walk along Las Vegas streets with her ass showing, so we pulled alongside and told her what was happening."

But Betty was sensitive to Bob's feelings. She told friends not to mention George Raft when he was around and she was deeply embarrassed when Lita Baron named her as correspondent – along with 77 other women – when divorcing Rory Calhoun, who Betty had played with in a couple of movies in the 1950s and the teenage Jayne Mansfield had caught with his trousers down.

As usual, when a younger man was smitten with an older – and richer – woman, she was very much in the driver's seat, at first. But gradually Remick took control. He had some money saved and used it to treat her, and whatever he was doing to her, it made her feel young again. The actor Art Kassul saw them in Jacksonville, Florida five years after they had got together.

"I was happy about it," he said. "Bob seemed to have a real feel for her."

By then, Remick had also made some radical changes to Betty's act.

"Initially she was subdued in her dress, as though attempting to tone down the sex image – she wore only one dress that showed off her legs," said Kassul. "But at Jacksonville she wore a sexy black nightie. It was as though she were saying, 'It's still there kids … look it over.'" However, Betty confided to Kassul that she still loved Harry James and probably always would.

In 1973, she was struck down with cancer. In the hospital shortly before she died, her hospital gown fell open exposing her backside.

"Don't worry, no one's looking," said one of the nurses.

"They would have done once," Betty replied.

8

I Could Have ****ed All Night

There was still a demand for virginal screen heroines after the Second World War, and the most virginal of all was Audrey Hepburn. In 1961, she was – you would have thought – scandalously miscast as a call girl in Truman Capote's *Breakfast at Tiffany's*. But the hard-drinking, chain-smoking, twice-divorced Audrey was much more like Holly Golightly than her adoring public imagined.

Born in Brussels in 1929, she was educated in England. Her parents were fascists and she spent the war years in Holland, where her mother thought they would be safe. Unfortunately, they chose to stay in the small industrial town of Arnhem, which became the scene of heavy fighting in September 1944. Her father had been left behind in England, where he was interned and it was years before she saw him again. Her mother, in occupied Holland, was the lover of a German general.

A plump child with uneven teeth, Audrey thought no one would ever want to marry her. However, she slimmed down with age and wartime food shortages, and had sex appeal from early on. Her dance teacher, Winja Marova, said: "When she was on-stage, you immediately saw that a flame lit the audience." Even the local paper, the *Arnhemse Courant*, singled the 13-year-old Audrey out for her "beautiful figure."

With the liberation though, Audrey, as an English girl, became quite a star locally, and her mother took her to see a

British film unit who were operating in the area. Mother and daughter moved to Amsterdam, where Audrey continued with her dance classes. Fellow student Anneke van Wijk recalled her as a "normal Dutch girl with chubby cheeks" and she must have put on some weight as a result of the improvement in post-war rations.

"I remember that because I used to take showers with her after the lessons," she said. "It wasn't until later, when she started to act, that she became so skinny."

An older dancer Loekie van Oven took the "shy and withdrawn" 17-year-old under her wing.

"Love or *érotique* do not play an important part in it," she said. "It had nothing to do with sexuality. We flirted sometimes, but that was it."

Two Dutch filmmakers were making a low-budget travelogue on Holland for the British Rank movie company. They auditioned Audrey and gave her a part because of her big eyes. After a little modeling work, she got the money to take up a ballet scholarship in England. There she did more modeling and became a chorus girl, often picked to wear the skimpiest outfits.

"I can't stand it," said fellow dancer Aud Johanssen. "I've got the best tits on-stage, and yet they're all staring at a girl who hasn't got any."

In fashion shoots, she would wear falsies, obeying the 11th commandment of the fashion industry: "What God's forgotten, we stuff with cotton."

British comedian Bob Monkhouse, once a gag writer for Bob Hope and Jack Benny,[1] thought that her appeal lay in her innocence.

"Everybody in the audience thought, 'I want to look after little Audrey,'" he said. "She seemed to be too pretty, too unaware of the dangers."

But she was not innocent at all. When she adopted a stray cat, she named it "Tomorrow." It was a neutered tom – the joke was "Tomorrow never comes."

Audrey was self-conscious about her flat-chestedness.

"I was too thin and had no bosom to speak of," she said.

But the young French crooner Marcel le Bon, who played alongside her in the show *Sauce Piquante*, had no complaints. They began dating and he fell desperately in love with her. By the end of the short run of the show, he was filling her dressing room with flowers. There were rumors of marriage, until the producers pointed out the "no-marriage" clause in her contract. Nevertheless, reports of the affair surfaced in the tabloids.

After the run ended, Audrey and Marcel planned to take a cabaret act on the road. But after a short cabaret run at Ciro's in London – where Tallulah Bankhead[2] had memorably tipped a glass of champagne over Gladys Cooper's head – their bookings fell through. Blaming himself, Marcel took off for the US, leaving Audrey to take bit parts in second-rate British movies, including the tantalizingly entitled *One Wild Oat* (1951) and *Young Wives' Tale* (1951). She was also in the running for the lead in *Lady Godiva Rides Again* (1951) with its consequent nude role, but was rejected after the audition for being too thin. She made her first real impact as the scantily clad cigarette girl in *Laughter in Paradise* (1951), but what she was now after was a "serious relationship," which she found in the person of John Hanson. Six years her senior, he was a dashing war hero and socialite who liked beautiful women and beautiful actresses in particular. Immediately before Audrey, he had been Jean Simmons's[3] escort.

"We met at a cocktail party in Mayfair at Les Ambassadeurs and we were attracted to each other right away," he said. "I invited her for lunch next day. We soon fell in love and became engaged a few months later. She was a one-man woman, and it was a relationship of that kind."

At the time Hanson – later Lord Hanson – was away a lot, building up what would become a $17-billion global conglomerate. But Zsa Zsa Gabor was there at the beginning. "Audrey and I started together in London," she said. "She was a beautiful Dutch girl, engaged to James Hanson. I was making my first movie, *Moulin Rouge* [1952]. His partner Gordon White was chasing me, and Jimmy was chasing her. They were dahling – such a handsome couple. Jimmy was not only rich, but charming."

The relationship flourished for about two years. Audrey felt that her mother disapproved, describing her as "a lady of very strict Victorian standards." Plainly Dutch Victorian standards were very different from those in Britain and America.

"It was the first time in my life," said Hanson, "I had ever slept in the same bed as my fiancée – with her mother bringing the breakfast in. She was a very earthy woman."

The author Colette herself picked Audrey as the trainee cocotte in the stage version of *Gigi* – a precursor to Holly Golightly – and Paramount signed her for *Roman Holiday* (1953). Hanson paid a flying visit to New York for the première of *Gigi*, proffering a diamond ring to formalize their engagement, and an announcement appeared in the "Forthcoming Marriages" column of *The Times*. They were to be married after the shooting of *Roman Holiday* which was delayed several times. Audrey announced that she would take a year off to be a wife to Hanson, but it would be impossible to give up her career completely. However, those in the know noticed that the framed picture of Hanson had disappeared from her dressing table at the Fulton.

"So many people whom I hardly know asked me what was his name and when were we going to be married, that I simply had to put the picture into a drawer," she said. "My private life was my own."

Plainly there was plenty of traffic through milady's boudoir.

She took Hollywood by storm. Hers was a new kind of beauty. She did not have the heavyweight languor of the other sex goddesses – Elizabeth Taylor,[4] Sophia Loren[5] or Marilyn Monroe.[6] She even refused to pose for the usual cheesecake photos.

"I think sex is overrated," she said.

On the set of *Roman Holiday*, the director, William Wyler, said he thought she should wear falsies.

"I am," said Audrey.

On seeing the picture, veteran director Billy Wilder said: "If that girl had tits, she could rule the world." Her bust size was given as $32\frac{1}{2}$A.

According to her friend, the Australian actor John McCallum, Hepburn's sex appeal came from her huge eyes.

"Sex starts in the eyes," he said. "A film close-up of an attractive woman's face is far sexier than a close-up of naked breasts." Which was just as well. "There is an expression to the effect that men make love to women's faces, and I think there is a good deal of truth to it."

Audrey herself said: "Sex appeal is something that you feel deep down inside. It's suggested rather than shown … I'm not as well stacked as Sophia Loren or Gina Lollobrigida, but there's more to sex appeal than just measurements. I don't need a bedroom to prove my womanliness. I can convey just as much appeal fully clothed, picking apples off a tree or standing in the rain."

But hold hard here. A pair of big gozongas and some gratuitous nudity can't hurt.

In fact, when she was first in Hollywood, Audrey put her sex appeal to the test. She was at a studio party packed with gorgeous young starlets disporting magnificent figures who were, naturally, surrounded by men. She picked up a drink and withdrew to a corner of the room to see how much man-appeal she could generate.

"I just stood there whispering to myself that I was the most desirable creature in the world," she said, "that I was somebody men could not resist – and it worked. Before the party was more than halfway over I had more men around me than I'd ever thought possible."

It was all in the eyes. And when she wanted a man, she knew how to use them.

"There's never any need for any woman to ogle any man," she said. "Ogling puts the men off. It scares them away. In fact, the faintest flutter of an eyelash should be enough. The truth is that I know I have more sex appeal in the tip of my nose than many women have in their entire bodies. It doesn't stand out a mile, but it's there."

It did not work on everyone, though. One movie mogul turned her down for a part with the words: "Heck, if I wanted to look at bones, I could always have my foot X-rayed."

Hanson traveled to Rome during the filming of *Roman Holiday* to guard his investment. But when the shooting was over, there was no wedding. Audrey had to go straight back to the States for a tour with *Gigi*. Halfway through the eight-month tour she broke off her engagement.

"When I couldn't find time to attend to the furnishing of our London flat," she told Anita Loos, "I suddenly knew I'd make a pretty bad wife." She told the press that it would be unfair to Hanson to marry him when she loved her work so much. Naturally the studio were putting pressure on her not to marry, especially to someone outside Hollywood. Hanson took it well, and they spent Christmas together in Chicago before going their separate ways. There were already other men in her life. At the end of the tour, she was asked whether she had always had "beaux buzzing around her." She replied: "Well, I'll say this. I have never wanted for one – not since I was 17 anyway."

One of the latest crop was 62-year-old Groucho Marx, who was spotted dining with her. When asked if they were engaged, Groucho replied: "I don't want to be ungallant, but Audrey's too old and wrinkled for me."

Roman Holiday was a huge hit. John F. Kennedy[7] said it was his favorite movie of all time, and it put Audrey on the cover of

Time magazine. Meanwhile, the *New York Mirror* was speculating that Greta, the wife of her co-star Gregory Peck, was "giving him the bounce because of his affection for the sylph-like nymph, a willowy boyish miss."

Audrey denied any such thing.

"I saw her coming out of Romanoff's the other day and she asked me to spend next Sunday swimming in the pool at her home," she said. "Does that sound like I'm a homebreaker."

Soon Audrey was involved with Mel Ferrer, an actor, director, producer, writer and co-founder of the La Jolla Playhouse. He was a friend of Gregory Peck, and 12 years her senior. He also had a complex marital record. After having a son and a daughter by his first wife, Frances Pilchard, an artist he had met at Princeton, he divorced her and married Barbara Tripp. He had a son and a daughter with her before divorcing and remarrying Frances Pilchard. Nevertheless, Gregory Peck had given him Audrey's number and, when he was in London, he called her.

Audrey had seen him in *Lili* (1953), one of her favorite films, and fallen for his sensitive portrayal of a crippled carnival puppeteer opposite Leslie Caron and Zsa Zsa Gabor. When actor James Coburn worked with Audrey on *Charade* (1963) she told him about their first meeting and how they had fallen in love. Coburn knew Ferrer from the La Jolla Playhouse and asked what the attraction was.

"The way he looked me in the eyes," she said. "The way he penetrated me with his eyes."

Leslie Caron was a bit more down to earth.

"Mel is very complex," she said. "On the one hand, he was very generous and very paternal to Audrey and to me when we worked on *Lili*. On the other hand…"

Audrey was very much in love with Ferrer, but there was a downside to their affair. She felt guilty about being involved with a man who, back home in America, had a wife and kids.

In her next picture, *Sabrina* (1954), Audrey played the daughter of a chauffeur who falls in love with the two sons of her father's employer. In the movie Humphrey Bogart woos her and wins – commenting on the age difference, one reviewer said: "Every time Bogie pitches the woo, you feel like calling the cops."

On-set, Wilder kept trying to push them into bed together, but Audrey resisted, as she had on *Roman Holiday*.

"Billy," she said, "that will ruin everything. No one sleeps with anyone in fairy tales."

In reality though, it was William Holden who got the girl. And the fact that Audrey was "giving Holden a tumble" heightened the tension on the set. After shooting the picture on Long Island, they returned to Los Angeles, where they were often seen together in a secluded booth in Lucey's Restaurant, sipping cocktails. Afterwards they would go back to her two-room apartment on Wiltshire Boulevard. Friends said that she never went to bed with Holden, claiming she had "very little sex drive," but Holden was not a man to take no for an answer. He was notoriously promiscuous and flaunted the fact. Bizarrely, he would even take mistresses back to meet his wife, actress Brenda Marshall, whose real name was Ardis Gaines. Even so, his marriage lasted for over 20 years.

Like the rest, Audrey also got the home visit.

"We both felt terribly guilty sitting at the dinner table," said Holden. "We felt sure that Ardis knew what was going on."

Audrey, Holden declared, "was the love of my life," and he was very much her type. She liked men who were bold, buccaneering and a little rough around the edges. Holden was a bluntly spoken, heavy drinker who used crude language in his cups.

There was a problem, though. Audrey wanted to have children but, after the birth of their second son, at his wife's behest, Holden had had an irreversible vasectomy. Brenda told director Billy Wilder's wife that the doctors had told her that it would be dangerous for her to have any more children, so Holden had done the decent thing and got the vasectomy.

"Why didn't you have your tubes tied?" asked Mrs Wilder.

"The minute you do that to a guy, he's going to try to screw everybody," said Brenda.

In Holden's case, it seems academic.

Another tale is told in Ian Woodward's 1984 biography of Audrey – that the vasectomy was provoked by Audrey herself.

"Audrey was 11 years younger than me," Holden is quoted as saying. "She kept asking me to settle down, talking of the babies we could have together. The constant talk of marriage and babies was getting on my nerves, so I went out and got a vasectomy – I was half drunk at the time. I did it to shut up her talk about babies."

Audrey was shocked. She broke down and cried. It was the end of the affair and he regretted it later.

"I was really in love with Audrey but she wouldn't marry me," he said. So after the movie was finished, Holden set off on a worldwide publicity tour. "I was determined to wipe Audrey out of my mind by screwing a woman in every country I visited," he said.

He succeeded, even though there was some danger involved. He was trying to screw a Thai girl in a boat on one of the canals in Bangkok, when the boat overturned and he fell into the filthy water. Worried that he might catch an infection, he poured alcohol into his ears back at the hotel. He took more orally.

Back in Hollywood, he visited Audrey in her dressing room and told her what he had done.

"Oh, Bill!" she said.

"That was all," said Holden. "It was as if I had been a naughty school boy."

But Holden was not the only one in love with Audrey.

"She was so gracious and graceful that everybody fell in love with her," said Billy Wilder. "Me included. My problem is that I am a guy who talks in his sleep. Fortunately, my wife's name is Audrey as well."

Wilder's most famous pronouncement about Audrey was: "This girl, singlehanded, may make bosoms a thing of the past." Later he amplified this statement, explaining: "Henceforth, the director will not have to invent shots when the girl leans way forward for a glass of Scotch and soda."

William Holden may have taken some drastic action to get Audrey out of his system, but Mel Ferrer had not. He came up with a way for them to be together. He sent her the script of a pre-war French play he had discovered – *Ondine* by Jean Giraudoux. She agreed to play a water nymph in it. She offered to co-star with him, split the billing and share her percentage with him.

"If this isn't love," said a friend in the business, "what is?"

During rehearsals Audrey and Mel moved in together in an apartment in Greenwich Village. This sent Frances Pilchard scuttling back to her lawyers. Ferrer did not care. His plan was to make the two of them into the next Leigh and Olivier. However, in that partnership, Olivier's talent balanced Leigh's looks. Ferrer, good though he was, was not up to the job – especially as Audrey wore a costume that was little more than a wisp of fishnet and a few strategically placed leaves. It would have been indecent on anyone else – someone with a fuller figure, perhaps. The play was a triumph for Audrey, though there was a mini-scandal when she shared her curtain calls with Ferrer.

"The audience went wild, applauded, screamed – but she would not turn until he came out," said Eva Gabor. "I don't know of another actress who would have done that. She was in love with him."

Apart from her performance, the show was written off as a bore. Ferrer, it was said, was not up to the part.

"If he played his scenes on top of her, you'd have the feeling that he was laying a corner stone," said the director. "Personally, I call the whole show a fucking failure."

Nevertheless, the box office did good business. "Nymph Mania" it was called by the *Saturday Review*. *Photoplay* called her "flat-chested, slim-hipped and altogether un-Marilyn Monroeish." "Is Hollywood shifting its accent on sex?" asked a worried *Silver Screen* after *Sabrina* came out.

"She's changing Hollywood's taste in girls," the magazine continued, "from the full-bosomed, sweater-filling type with more curves than the New York Central Railroad, to the lean, umbrella-shaped variety."

Audrey admitted that she was not very voluptuous.

"It may be that the accent has gone off sex slightly," she volunteered, "and gone on to femininity."

About a year after she had left Holden, Audrey was at a dinner party with Holden and his wife Ardis when she announced her intention to marry Mel. Holden was filled with a jealous rage. After the run of *Ondine* finished, Audrey and Mel went to Switzerland where they wed. Gregory Peck could not make it due to filming. James Hanson also sent his regrets. They honeymooned in a farmhouse outside Rome as he was filming at Cinecittà. When the couple returned to their new flat in London, Audrey was pregnant. A few months later, she miscarried.

Audrey and Mel were close. Some said too close. The allegation was made that he would not let her appear in movies where there was no part for him.

"You couldn't get near her unless he was taken care of somehow," said Tony Curtis. But Audrey insisted that she did not want to be separated. If they were parted just once, even for a few short months, "then the once becomes twice – without realizing it, we might have let material success ruin two lives." She did not want to take any step that might jeopardize her marriage, she said.

Her leading men were no threat – Fred Astaire[8] at 57 in *Funny Face* (1957) and Gary Cooper[9] at 55 and *Love in the Afternoon* (1957) could be mistaken for child molesters on-screen.

"The charge is unfair to Coop," she told the *New York World Telegram*. "In *Love in the Afternoon* he's not trying to fool

"only had 11 lovers – not counting anything that happened before I was 13." This is missing from the movie.

Nevertheless, the movie did well domestically and better abroad. And it won an Oscar for Henry Mancini's score and for the song "Moon River," whose lyrics were supplied by Judy Garland's old flame, Johnny Mercer.

Next Audrey played the lesbian lover of Shirley MacLaine in Lillian Hellman's *The Children's Hour* (1962), the part previously played by the smouldering Merle Oberon. The movie was condemned for condoning sapphism – by showing that "those who choose to practice lesbianism are not destroyed by it – a claim disproved by the number of lesbians who become insane or commit suicide," said *Films in Review*.

With both their contracts about to run out at Paramount, the studio put Audrey and Holden together again in *Paris When It Sizzles* (1964). Audrey was apprehensive because Mel was away a lot filming *The Longest Day* (1962) and *The Fall of the Roman Empire* (1964). She had heard rumors that Holden was still desperately in love with her, even though he was having a fitful affair with the beautiful French actress and model Capucine – French for nasturtium, would you believe? The director Richard Quine, who had just broken up from Kim Novak,[20] calmed her fears.

Someone else was hot for her, too. Soon after she left to film in Paris, her chalet in Bürgenstock, Switzerland, was burgled by 22-year-old science student Jean-Claude Thouroude, who stole her underwear and her Oscar for *Roman Holiday*. He turned himself in and told the authorities that he had been motivated by a passion for Audrey. He was disappointed when she did not appear at his trial. He was fined and given a suspended sentence. The judge explained his leniency by saying: "Love is not a crime."

When Holden arrived at Orly to face Audrey again, he heard his "footsteps echoing against the wall of the transit lounge, just like a condemned man walking his last mile." His nervousness only increased his drinking, which was already out of control. One night he climbed a tree outside her window. She leant out and kissed him, and he slipped, plunging to the ground. Fortunately, his fall was broken by a parked car. His wife turned up and harangued him, but he took no notice. Instead he bought a brand new Ferrari, which he drove into a wall.

Holden finally signed into the Château de Garche, a hospital for alcoholics, to dry out. Tony Curtis, who was cooling his heels in London, flew over to film a couple of rapidly scripted scenes and prevent Paramount closing down the production. Noël Coward[21] and Marlene Dietrich[22] were also called in to perform similar functions. As a result, the picture went way over budget. The movie stank and the studio shelved it for two years.

Audrey's performance was not helped by the fact that reports were coming from Madrid, where Ferrer was filming *The Fall of the Roman Empire*, that Mel was out and about with various ladies, including the "vivacious" la Duquesa de Quintanilla. Gossip columnists then reported that Audrey had renewed her affair with Holden in retaliation.

That was ridiculous, said Audrey. All she had done was "mother him a little" when he crashed his Ferrari. In response, Ferrer failed to show the proper amount of jealousy and Audrey threatened divorce. Mel promptly flew home to patch things up – or, at least, paper over the cracks.

While *Paris When It Sizzles* was gathering dust on the shelf, Audrey started filming *Charade* (1963) opposite the 59-year-old Cary Grant,[23] who was afraid of looking like one more in a long line of Hollywood child molesters alongside the 33-year-old Audrey – which was weird because his highly publicized current amour and wife-to-be Dyan Cannon, was 25. But the screenplay was rewritten so that she seduces him, rather than the other way around, and their age difference is a running joke.

The best off-screen gag went to Walter Matthau. James Coburn was having a chat about the script with Cary Grant, who he had just met, when Matthau turned up on the set for the first time. Matthau pointed at Grant and said to Coburn: "Hey, Jim, did you ever see anybody do a better impression of Cary Grant?" And he walked away.

"It was the only time I ever saw Cary Grant off balance," said Coburn.

Coburn also admitted to being wild about Audrey.

"Underneath, Audrey was a very sexual creature," he said, "always secretive and goddesslike. It would take some kind of godlike creature to bring her down – but she didn't seem to be too unwilling. She was the gamine goddess."

Maybe Grant was that godlike creature. Later, she described him as "such a lovely souvenir."

Charade was a hit, and another hit with John F. Kennedy who called Audrey to tell her that she was his favorite actress. She reciprocated in 1963 by singing "Happy Birthday" at his 46th – and last – birthday party. It was a year after Marilyn had caused such a stir with her breathless rendition. Audrey's version was altogether sweeter, though her passions burnt no less intensely.

Julie Andrews had been a hit as the star of *My Fair Lady* in London and on Broadway, but she refused to take a screen test when Jack Warner bought the movie rights. The part was offered to Audrey, who wanted to turn it down. She realized that theater goers would be disappointed if they did not see Julie Andrews in the part she had made her own. But if Audrey did not take it, she knew the part would go to Elizabeth Taylor, who deserved it even less than she did. So she accepted the part, even though she couldn't sing and the songs – including "I Could Have Danced All Night" – had to be dubbed.

Warner did not want Rex Harrison for the part of Professor Higgins either. Michael Redgrave, George Sanders and Noël

Coward had all turned down the stage role before Harrison got it. Laurence Olivier, Peter O'Toole, Cary Grant and – of all people – Rock Hudson[24] had all turned down the screen role before George Cukor called Harrison in England and asked him for a screen test. Harrison said he did not do tests, but sent two nude Polaroids.

"They saw that I was not as decrepit as they feared," he said. He got the part, and Cecil Beaton[25] was called in to give the picture the right Edwardian look.

André Previn, the musical director on the movie, said that he and a few of the boys would discuss Audrey in locker-room terms. "But there was almost never anything carnal about it," he said. "You wouldn't look at her and say, 'Boy, would I like to...' She didn't provoke that. My wife once said to me, 'How close were you to Audrey?' I said, 'I was hopelessly in love with her.' She said, 'Good,' because she knew it would never come to anything."

Cukor closed the set of *My Fair Lady* so Mel was excluded. But sounds of quarreling came from her dressing room. To pacify him, the studio gave him a small part in *Sex and the Single Girl* (1964) which was filming on a sound stage nearby. After *My Fair Lady* was finished, Audrey planned a long vacation at their chalet in Switzerland. Instead, she made 16 trips around Europe, following him when he went filming because of persistent rumors that he had been seeing other women. At other times, she cooked, cleaned and entertained for him. Everybody adored her dirty jokes.

According to publicist Henry Rogers, the Ferrers' marriage was becoming increasingly an unhappy one. She wanted to spend more time at home with her husband and son, while he was ambitious for his wife and himself.

"It seemed to me that she loved him more than he loved her," said Rogers, "and it was frustrating for her not to have her love returned in kind. She confided these feelings to me and I always saw the sadness in her eyes."

With her marriage now in a parlous state, Audrey was cast in *How to Steal a Million* (1966) opposite Peter O'Toole, a leading man her own age for a change. During the filming they spent a lot of time shut in a closet together and there were rumors of an affair. They were false. Next she was cast as an erring wife in *Two for the Road* (1967) opposite Albert Finney, seven years her junior. The script called for nudity and a steamy bedroom scene.

"My mind knew it was acting, but my heart didn't – and my body certainly didn't," said Finney. "With a woman as sexy as Audrey, you sometimes get to the edge where make-believe and reality get blurred."

In this case, make-believe and reality became one and the same thing. This time the rumors were true and their on-screen involvement fanned the flames of passion. She eschewed a body double and performed all the stunts herself, including a scene where she and Finney go skinny-dipping in the Mediterranean.

When they were not making love in front of the cameras, they were doing it in private, or cavorting in discotheques and bistros.

"Audrey cared for Finney a great deal," said another of her lovers. "He represented a whole new freedom and closeness for her. It was the beginning of a new period of her life."

The affair was intense, but temporary. She still hoped to patch up her marriage and the action had to be suspended when Mel visited the set. However, 50-year-old Ferrer was going through a mid-life crisis and was having a thing with a 15-year-old Spanish dancer named Marisol, who he and Audrey had met at a party given by the Duchess of Alba. Nevertheless, they were forced back into professional partnership by *Wait Until Dark* (1967), where Audrey starred and Mel produced. However, as producer, Mel spent most of his time auditioning a bevy of pretty young actresses for five-second bit parts.

"It was only later we heard that Audrey was having a very difficult time in her marriage," said director Terence Young. "Both Audrey and Mel confided things to me. But they were a class act in every sense and very little showed."

It turned out Mel was only practicing with those girls he'd been auditioning. Five months later Audrey was pregnant, but miscarried again. After that, she and Ferrer separated for good.

Thirty-nine and available again, Audrey threw herself into the European jet-set, falling straight into the arms of Prince Alfonso de Bourbon-Dampierre, pretender to the throne of Spain. They were seen holding hands in restaurants and dancing cheek-to-cheek in nightclubs. In Madrid, they shared a suite of rooms in the city's poshest hotel, where they celebrated the New Year.

"They were obviously completely happy in each other's company," reported France Dimanche.

Audrey then went to stay in Rome with the Contessa Lorean Franchetti Gaetani-Lovatelli.

"I would give little dinner parties for her," said the Contessa, "and there was always an extra man, but I won't tell you any names."

Even the maid was scandalized by the Mary Quant frocks Audrey brought with her. Thinking they were blouses she informed Audrey that she had lost a valise with all her skirts in. The miniskirt had not yet arrived in Italy and Audrey was a sensation on the streets.

Cruising in the Mediterranean, Audrey met handsome young psychiatrist Andrea Dotti, nine years her junior, who ran a clinic specializing in "women's problems." He specialized in them because, as a playboy, he had caused more than one or two. They fell in love, he said, somewhere between Ephesus and Athens.

"She did not come to cry on my shoulder about the break-up of her marriage or for me to give her comfort as a psychiatrist," he said. "We were playmates on a cruise ship."

For Audrey it was altogether more serious.

"Do you know what it's like when a brick falls on your head?" she said. "That's how my feelings for Andrea first hit me."

But Andrea had playboy written all over him and others spotted the danger signs.

"I knew Andrea very well," said the Contessa Lorean Franchetti Gaetani-Lovatelli, "and I knew that he wasn't the man for her."

Nevertheless, they spent the summer together in the Contessa's villa on the Isola Giglio, off the coast of Tuscany. A typical playboy, he told her that, at the age of 14, he had rushed up and shaken her hand during the filming of *Roman Holiday*, then run home to tell his mama that he had just met the girl he was going to marry. Apparently, from that moment on, Audrey waded knee-deep through his pubescent dreams. When he grew up, fashionable Roman hostesses would seat him next to heiresses but, his stepfather said, he talked constantly of marriage and having lots and lots of children.

"When he came back from the cruise, you could see he was in love," said *il padrigno*. "He made a film of the voyage and included everybody but Audrey. Love made him too shy even to photograph her."

Her divorce was quickly finalized in what critic Sheridan Morley called "an avalanche of good manners."

"I don't know what the difficulties were," said Ferrer. "Audrey's the one who asked for the divorce and started the affair with Andrea Dotti."

By that time Ferrer was getting down with 29-year-old heiress Tessa Kennedy. Three years later, he married for the fourth time – to Lisa Soukhotine, a 34-year-old children's book editor.

The 40-year-old Audrey was worried about the age difference between herself and her 31-year-old lover, but he preferred to think that love conquered all. At Christmas they got engaged and in the New Year in Switzerland the bans were read. The Contessa tried to talk her out of it, but failed. Even his own brothers warned her not to marry him, but she was not having it. And on January 18, 1969, six weeks after her divorce came through, she married her young doctor with her nine-year-old son looking on. The bride's witness was William Holden's former lover, Capucine.

The newlyweds moved into a penthouse apartment overlooking the Tiber near Castel Sant'Angelo in Rome, which had once been the home of the mistress of a famous 15th century cardinal. Within four months of the wedding, Audrey was pregnant again. But with her history of miscarriages, her Italian stallion found she was no longer the tiger in bed and was soon bonking someone else. Newspapers and magazines were full of paparazzi shots of Dr Dotti on the arms of a bevy of notorious Roman beauties, including the infamous model Daniela Ripetti, who was the last lover of deceased Rolling Stone Brian Jones. Audrey closed her eyes to her husband's peccadilloes and withdrew to Switzerland for her confinement. However, his indiscretions were also all over the Swiss press. Apparently, Dr Dotti was trying an age-old approach to women's therapy.

"My approach is closer to Freud's than to that of Jung," he was quoted as saying, "more physical and emotional than religious."

Just how physical Audrey could easily estimate from the newspapers. She gave birth to a second son in February 1970, reconciled with his doting father, and the loving couple returned to Rome where – despite his promise that "it would never happen again" – he continued to fool around.

Audrey stayed at home, playing the dutiful wife, and occasionally removed herself to Switzerland to give her husband more room to play. But wherever she was she could not escape the humiliating evidence of her husband's infidelity all over the papers. Although this irked her, she did not seek therapy.

"I depend on Givenchy in the same way that American women depend on their psychiatrists," she said. Apparently she had enough trouble with psychiatrists already and Givenchy was more dependable. They kept the same mannequin, made for her in 1954, unaltered in four decades. Around that time she met James Hanson again. Unfortunately he was with his wife.

For nine years, Audrey stayed away from the movies.

"It's all sex and violence," she said. "I'm far too scrawny to strip and I hate guns, so I'm better off out of it."

Then she was offered the chance to play opposite Albert Finney again in *Robin and Marian* (1976). After she agreed, it was found that Finney was not available and she had to play opposite Sean Connery instead.

"Everything I had been offered before then was too kinky, too violent or too young," she said. Disappointed not to be reuniting with Finney, she almost backed out but her two sons pushed her into it so they could meet James Bond – though her youngest could not understand why Dr Dotti was not playing the Prince of Thieves. Audrey explained that he did not look good in tights.

For the purposes of the movie, Sherwood Forest shifted to Pamplona, Spain, as five of the distinguished British cast could not set foot in the UK for tax reasons. Audrey did not get on with the director, Dick Lester, and fought with him when he tried to cut her love scenes with Connery. After all, the movie's promo line was: "Love is the greatest adventure of all." When it came out, the picture was promoted with a 30-second clinch between Robin and Marian during the daytime soaps. Every American housewife, it was assumed, would fantasize that they were in Connery's arms.

Most weekends during shooting, she flew home to Rome to try and keep Andrea under control. His nocturnal antics were still making the newspapers, but she was tolerant to a fault, especially after she had one last miscarriage at the age of 45.

"He's done it all his life," she said. "It's not as if all of a sudden he's breaking out at the age of 37 to go to nightclubs. It's his way of relaxing, and I think it's important for him to feel free. I don't expect him to sit in front of the TV when I'm not there. It's much more dangerous for a man to be bored."

And Andrea, if the press reports are anything to go by, was never bored.

Moving with the times, Audrey appeared in Sidney Sheldon's *Bloodline* (1979), besmirching her pristine image in a trashy film about pornographic snuff movies. She consoled herself with a brief affair with her co-star Ben Gazzara, which precipitated his divorce. This made the press and gave Dotti a dose of his own medicine. He was hurt, but not enough to cut down on his own nighttime activities. Among Andrea's hit list were a couple of countesses, but mostly he stuck to Italian or French actresses – Manuela Croce, Karin Shubert, Marilù Tolo, Dalila Di Lazzaro, Daniela Trebbi, Marinella Giordana, Christiana Borghi, Beatrice Corri, Lupua Yerni, Carol André... He was pictured with an attractive woman on his arm – not his wife – in *Paris-Match*, *Oggi*, *Stop*, *Novella*, *Gente*, *Ava Express*, *Annabella*, *Gioia*... It was amazing that any marriage could survive. Some said it was because, when Andrea was around, he was enormously attentive and he had a huge respect for her. Others, such as David Niven[26] – no mean womanizer himself – said: "He took incredible advantage of her and she gamely played the wife."

Many said that they just did not seem to belong together, but Eli Wallach expressed it most succinctly when he said: "When she married that Italian psychiatrist, she went dotty." Or maybe it was just a pun.

"Andrea and I had what you call an open arrangement," Audrey said. "It's inevitable when the man is younger."

She struggled to make the marriage last for the sake of their son. But eventually she gave up.

"Open marriages don't work," she finally admitted. "If there's love, unfaithfulness is impossible." Though how this squares with her own infidelity, I am not sure.

Andrea had his own opinion on where the blame lay.

"I was no angel," he said. "Italian husbands have never been famous for being faithful. But she was jealous of other women even from the beginning."

Not without good reason I would have thought.

Audrey was reunited with Ben Gazzara in *They All Laughed* (1982), which was written and directed by Peter Bogdanovich who also wrote the script. A friend of Gazzara's, he included a lot of things that Gazzara had told him about Audrey and the parlous state of her marriage. His own break-up with Cybill Shepherd, who had been famously replaced by 1980 Playmate of the Year Dorothy Stratten, was also included in the plot. However, this time Audrey and Gazzara failed to click on-screen or off. He was now in the middle of his divorce and had just started dating the woman who would become his next wife, 33-year-old German photographer, Elke Krivat.

"I think when Audrey realized all that, she was very disappointed," said Bogdanovich.

Gazzara said that he steered clear of her this time because she was the marrying kind and that was the last thing that was on his mind at that point. Nevertheless, Audrey pursued him with a ferocity that amazed the other people working on the movie. She only got the message when he began bringing his other – considerably younger – lady friends onto the set.

Meanwhile, Bogdanovich had fallen for Audrey. They were photographed hugging and kissing and with her sitting on his lap during filming in New York, though he denied that there was an affair. When Bogdanovich returned to California with Stratten, she was murdered by her husband, a cheap hustler named Paul Snider, who then killed himself. Audrey proved a great comfort. However, during the shooting of *They All Laughed* she had met Robert Wolders, the fourth husband of the recently deceased Merle Oberon. Seven years Audrey's junior, he knew how to handle beautiful, if aging, movie stars. And he was a fellow Netherlander.

Two months after Merle died, Wolders had gone to stay with Connie Wald, widow of producer Jerry Wald, whose distinguished career included *Mildred Pierce* (1945), *Dark Passage* (1947), *The Adventures of Don Juan* (1948), *Peyton Place* (1957), *Let's Make Love* (1960) and *The Stripper* (1963). Another house guest was Audrey. They spoke Dutch together, reminisced about Merle, and discovered that they had lived only 30 miles apart in Holland during the Nazi occupation. Audrey made Wolders laugh with some of the more vulgar Dutch dialects.

Dr Dotti soon discovered that Audrey had found someone else. Everyone assumed that it was Gazzara or Bogdanovich. The affair with Wolders was conducted secretly – for her sons' sake, not her husband's.

They met casually for a drink, or some pasta. There were long conversations on the telephone.

"I thought perhaps she was just accommodating me," said Wolders. "We began a kind of clandestine relationship, which she went into very reluctantly."

When she returned to Rome, Andrea remarked flippantly: "You look beautiful – you must be in love."

She said: "I am."

Dotti was consumed by jealousy.

Soon after, Wolders came to Rome where he rented an apartment. But let's get this straight: Wolders was not – repeat *not* – a gold digger who pursued older women for their wealth. Merle Oberon had left him a house, two million dollars and her fabulous collection of jewelry. So that's cleared up then.

They conducted their affair discreetly and decided not to marry, and their cohabitation was a Dutch treat. Audrey's mother, who had opposed both of her marriages, adored

Wolders. Eventually, in 1982, her divorce from Andrea came through. Asked whether another marriage was on the cards, Audrey said: "We are happy as we are."

Wolders said: "Everyone knows how unhappy her marriage to Mel was, and the second, to Andrea, was even worse. It would be like asking someone who just got out of an electric chair to sit back on it again."

"I am sort of married to Robert," she later told the newspapers.

Asked why they did not tie the knot, she said: "Why bother? It's lovely this way."

Audrey was upset by the death of William Holden in 1981, after a long affair with Stefanie Powers, star of TV's *Hart to Hart* with Robert Wagner.[27] Then, after Capucine committed suicide, Audrey made *Gardens of the World* for PBS. For five years she traveled the trouble spots of the world as Special Ambassador for the United Nations Children's Fund, before being struck down with cancer of the colon. Hearing that her hospital room was filled up with flowers, the screenwriter Leonard Gersche sent her Madonna's *Sex* book. It made her the most popular patient in the hospital.

"Doctors I never heard of were stopping in," she said.

She died hallucinating on morphine on the same day Bill Clinton[28] was inaugurated. According to the International Movie Database at www.imbd.com, Wolders went on to date Shirlee Fonda, widow of movie star Henry Fonda.[29] And so the daisy-chain continues.

Notes to Chapters

Chapter One
1. See *Sex Lives of the Hollywood Goddesses*.
2. See *Hollywood Goddesses* and *Sex Lives of the Hollywood Idols*.
3. See *Hollywood Goddesses* and *Hollywood Idols*.
4. See *Hollywood Goddesses, Hollywood Idols* and *Sex Lives of the Presidents* (*Sex Lives of the US Presidents* in the UK).
5. See *Hollywood Goddesses*.
6. See *Hollywood Goddesses* and *Hollywood Idols*.
7. See *Hollywood Goddesses*.
8. See *Hollywood Goddesses* and *Hollywood Idols*.
9. See *Hollywood Goddesses* and *Hollywood Idols*.
10. See *Hollywood Goddesses* and *Hollywood Idols*.
11. See *Hollywood Goddesses* and *Hollywood Idols*.
12. See *Hollywood Idols*.
13. See *Hollywood Goddesses* and *Hollywood Idols*.
14. See *Hollywood Idols*.
15. See *Hollywood Idols*.
16. See *Hollywood Goddesses*.
17. See *Hollywood Idols*.
18. See *Hollywood Goddesses* and *Presidents*.
19. See *Hollywood Goddesses* and *Presidents*.
20. See *Sex Lives of the Great Artists*.
21. See *Hollywood Goddesses* and *Hollywood Idols*.
22. See *Hollywood Goddesses* and *Presidents*.

Chapter Two
1. See *Sex Lives of the Hollywood Idols*.
2. See *Sex Lives of the Hollywood Goddesses and Hollywood Idols*.
3. See *Hollywood Goddesses* and *Hollywood Idols*.

4. See *Hollywood Goddesses* and *Hollywood Idols*.
5. See *Hollywood Goddesses* and *Hollywood Idols*.
6. See *Hollywood Goddesses*.
7. See *Hollywood Goddesses*.
8. See *Hollywood Goddesses*.
9. See *Hollywood Goddesses*.
10. See *Hollywood Goddesses*.
11. See *Hollywood Goddesses*.
12. See *Hollywood Idols*.
13. See *Hollywood Goddesses* and *Hollywood Idols*.
14. See *Hollywood Idols*.
15. See *Hollywood Goddesses, Hollywood Idols* and *Sex Lives of the Presidents*.
16. See *Hollywood Goddesses* and *Hollywood Idols*.
17. See *Hollywood Idols*.
18. See *Hollywood Goddesses*.
19. See *Presidents*.
20. See *Presidents*.
21. See *Sex Lives of the Great Dictators*.
22. See *Great Dictators*.
23. See *Sex Lives of the Kings and Queens of England*.
24. See *Sex Lives of the Great Artists*.
25. See *Kings and Queens*.
26. See *Great Dictators*.
27. See *Hollywood Goddesses* and *Hollywood Idols*.
28. See *Hollywood Idols*.

Chapter Three
1. See *Sex Lives of the Kings and Queens of England*.
2. See *Sex Lives of the Hollywood Goddesses*.
3. See *Hollywood Goddesses*.
4. See *Hollywood Goddesses, Sex Lives of the Hollywood Idols* and *Sex Lives of the Presidents*.
5. See *Hollywood Goddesses* and *Hollywood Idols* and *Presidents*.

6.   See *Hollywood Goddesses* and *Hollywood Idols*.
7.   See *Hollywood Goddesses* and *Hollywood Idols*.
8.   See *Hollywood Idols*.

Chapter Four
1.   See *Sex Lives of the Hollywood Goddesses* and *Sex Lives of the Hollywood Idols*.
2.   See *Hollywood Idols*.
3.   See *Sex Lives of the Kings and Queens of England*.
4.   See *Hollywood Goddesses*.
5.   See *Kings and Queens of England*.
6.   See *Kings and Queens of England*.
7.   See *Hollywood Goddesses* and *Hollywood Idols*.
8.   See *Hollywood Goddesses* and *Hollywood Idols*.
9.   See *Hollywood Idols*.
10. See *Hollywood Goddesses* and *Hollywood Idols*.
11. See *Hollywood Goddesses* and *Hollywood Idols* and *Sex Lives of the Presidents*.
12. See *Hollywood Goddesses* and *Hollywood Idols*.
13. See *Hollywood Goddesses* and *Hollywood Idols*.
14. See *Hollywood Goddesses* and *Hollywood Idols*.
15. See *Hollywood Goddesses* and *Hollywood Idols*.
16. See *Hollywood Goddesses*.
17. See *Hollywood Goddesses* and *Hollywood Idols*.
18. See *Hollywood Goddesses* and *Hollywood Idols*.
19. See *Hollywood Goddesses*.
20. See *Hollywood Goddesses* and *Hollywood Idols*.
21. See *Hollywood Goddesses* and *Hollywood Idols*.
22. See *Hollywood Goddesses* and *Hollywood Idols*.
23. See *Hollywood Goddesses*.
24. See *Sex Lives of the Great Dictators*.
25. See *Hollywood Goddesses* and *Hollywood Idols*.
26. See *Hollywood Goddesses* and *Hollywood Idols*.
27. See *Hollywood Goddesses*.
28. See *Hollywood Goddesses*.

29. See *Hollywood Goddesses* and *Hollywood Idols*.
30. See *Hollywood Goddesses* and *Hollywood Idols*.
31. See *Hollywood Goddesses* and *Hollywood Idols*.
32. See *Hollywood Goddesses* and *Hollywood Idols*.
33. See *Hollywood Goddesses* and *Presidents*.
34. See *Hollywood Goddesses* and *Presidents*.
35. See *Kings and Queens of England*.
36. See *Sex Lives of the Great Composers*.
37. See *Hollywood Goddesses* and *Hollywood Idols*.
38. See *Sex Lives of the Great Artists*.
39. See *Hollywood Goddesses* and *Hollywood Idols*.
40. See *Presidents*.
41. See *Hollywood Goddesses*.
42. See *Hollywood Goddesses*.
43. See *Hollywood Goddesses* and *Hollywood Idols*.
44. See *Great Composers*.
45. See *Great Composers*.
46. See *Hollywood Goddesses*.
47. See *Hollywood Goddesses* and *Hollywood Idols*.
48. See *Hollywood Goddesses*.
49. See *Hollywood Goddesses*.
50. See *Great Dictators*.
51. See *Sex Lives of the Popes*.
52. See *Kings and Queens of England*.
53. See *Hollywood Goddesses*.
54. See *Presidents*.
55. See *Hollywood Goddesses, Hollywood Idols* and *Presidents*.
56. See *Hollywood Goddesses, Hollywood Idols, Great Artists* and *Kings and Queens of England*.
57. See *Kings and Queens of England*.
58. See *Presidents*.
59. See *Kings and Queens of England*.

Chapter Five

1. See *Sex Lives of the Hollywood Goddesses* and *Sex Lives of the Hollywood Idols*.
2. See *Sex Lives of the Great Artists*.
3. See *Sex Lives of the Great Composers*.
4. See *Hollywood Goddesses* and *Hollywood Idols*.
5. See *Sex Lives of the Kings and Queens of England*.
6. See *Hollywood Goddesses*.
7. See *Kings and Queens of England*.
8. See *Hollywood Goddesses, Hollywood Idols, Great Artists and Great Composers*.
9. See *Hollywood Goddesses* and *Hollywood Idols*.
10. See *Hollywood Goddesses* and *Hollywood Idols*.
11. See *Hollywood Goddesses* and *Hollywood Idols*.
12. See *Hollywood Goddesses* and *Hollywood Idols*.
13. See *Hollywood Goddesses*.
14. See *Kings and Queens of England*.
15. See *Hollywood Goddesses* and *Hollywood Idols*.
16. See *Hollywood Goddesses* and *Hollywood Idols*.
17. See *Hollywood Goddesses*.
18. See *Hollywood Goddesses* and *Hollywood Idols*.
19. See *Hollywood Goddesses* and *Hollywood Idols*.
20. See *Hollywood Goddesses*.
21. See *Hollywood Goddesses*.
22. See *Hollywood Goddesses* and *Hollywood Idols*.
23. See *Hollywood Goddesses* and *Hollywood Idols*.
24. See *Hollywood Goddesses* and *Hollywood Idols*.
25. See *Hollywood Goddesses* and *Hollywood Idols*.
26. See *Hollywood Goddesses* and *Hollywood Idols*.
27. See *Hollywood Goddesses* and *Hollywood Idols*.
28. See *Hollywood Goddesses*.
29. See *Hollywood Goddesses* and *Hollywood Idols*.
30. See *Hollywood Goddesses* and *Hollywood Idols*.
31. See *Kings and Queens of England*.
32. See *Hollywood Goddesses*.

33. See *Sex Lives of the Great Dictators*.
34. See *Hollywood Goddesses*.
35. See *Hollywood Goddesses* and *Hollywood Idols*.
36. See *Hollywood Goddesses*.
37. See *Hollywood Goddesses*.
38. See *Presidents and Kings* and *Queens of England*.
39. See *Hollywood Goddesses* and *Hollywood Idols*.
40. See *Hollywood Idols*.
41. See *Hollywood Idols*.

Chapter Six

1. See *Sex Lives of the Hollywood Goddesses*.
2. See *Hollywood Goddesses* and *Sex Lives of the Hollywood Idols*.
3. See *Hollywood Goddesses* and *Hollywood Idols*.
4. See *Hollywood Goddesses* and *Hollywood Idols*.
5. See *Hollywood Goddesses*.
6. See *Hollywood Goddesses*.
7. See *Hollywood Goddesses*.
8. See *Hollywood Goddesses*.
9. See *Hollywood Goddesses* and *Hollywood Idols*.
10. See *Hollywood Goddesses*.
11. See *Hollywood Goddesses* and *Hollywood Idols*.
12. See *Hollywood Goddesses*.
13. See *Hollywood Goddesses*.
14. See *Hollywood Goddesses* and *Hollywood Idols*.
15. See *Hollywood Goddesses*.
16. See *Hollywood Goddesses*.
17. See *Hollywood Goddesses* and *Hollywood Idols*.
18. See *Hollywood Goddesses* and *Hollywood Idols*.
19. See *Hollywood Goddesses, Hollywood Idols* and *Sex Lives of the Presidents*.
20. See *Hollywood Goddesses*.
21. See *Hollywood Goddesses*.

22. See *Hollywood Goddesses, Hollywood Idols* and *Presidents*.
23. See *Hollywood Goddesses*.
24. See *Hollywood Goddesses* and *Presidents*.
25. See *Hollywood Goddesses*.

Chapter Seven

1. See *Sex Lives of the Hollywood Goddesses*.
2. See *Hollywood Goddesses* and *Sex Lives of the Hollywood Idols*.
3. See *Hollywood Goddesses* and *Hollywood Idols*.
4. See *Hollywood Idols*.
5. See *Hollywood Goddesses* and *Hollywood Idols*.
6. See *Sex Lives of the Presidents*.
7. See *Hollywood Idols*.
8. See *Hollywood Goddesses* and *Hollywood Idols*.
9. See *Hollywood Goddesses* and *Hollywood Idols*.
10. See *Hollywood Idols*.
11. See *Hollywood Goddesses*.
12. See *Hollywood Goddesses*.
13. See *Hollywood Goddesses*.
14. See *Hollywood Goddesses*.
15. See *Hollywood Goddesses*.
16. See *Sex Lives of the Kings and Queens of England*.
17. See *Hollywood Idols*.
18. See *Hollywood Goddesses, Hollywood Idols* and *Presidents*.

Chapter Eight

1. See *Sex Lives of the Hollywood Goddesses*.
2. See *Hollywood Goddesses* and *Sex Lives of the Hollywood Idols*.
3. See *Hollywood Goddesses*.
4. See *Hollywood Goddesses* and *Hollywood Idols*.
5. See *Hollywood Idols*.

6. See *Hollywood Goddesses*, *Hollywood Idols* and *Sex Lives of the Presidents*.
7. See *Hollywood Goddesses* and *Presidents*.
8. See *Hollywood Goddesses*.
9. See *Hollywood Idols*.
10. See *Hollywood Goddesses*.
11. See *Hollywood Goddesses*.
12. See *Hollywood Goddesses*.
13. See *Hollywood Goddesses*.
14. See *Hollywood Goddesses*.
15. See *Hollywood Goddesses* and *Hollywood Idols*.
16. See *Hollywood Goddesses* and *Hollywood Idols*.
17. See *Hollywood Idols*.
18. See *Hollywood Goddesses* and *Hollywood Idols*.
19. See *Hollywood Goddesses*.
20. See *Hollywood Goddesses*.
21. See *Hollywood Goddesses*, *Hollywood Idols*, *Sex Lives of the Great Artists* and *Sex Lives of the Kings and Queens of England*.
22. See *Hollywood Goddesses* and *Hollywood Idols*.
23. See *Hollywood Idols*.
24. See *Hollywood Idols*.
25. See *Hollywood Goddesses*.
26. See *Hollywood Idols*.
27. See *Hollywood Idols*.
28. See *Presidents*.
29. See *Hollywood Goddesses* and *Hollywood Idols*.

Selected Bibliography

Audrey Hepburn by Barry Paris, Weidenfeld & Nicolson, London, 1997

Audrey Hepburn - A Bio-Bibliography by David Hofstede, Greenwood Press, Westport, Connecticut, 1994

Audrey Hepburn - A Biography by Warren G. Harris, Simon & Schuster, New York, 1994

Audrey Hepburn - Fair Lady of the Screen by Ian Woodward, W.H. Allen, London, 1984

Audrey - Her Real Story by Alexander Walker, Weidenfeld & Nicolson, London, 1994

Betty Grable by Larry Billman, Greenwood Press, Westport, Connecticut, 1993

Betty Grable - The Girl with the Million Dollar Legs by Tom McGee, Vestal Press, Lanham, Maryland, 1995

Betty Grable - The Reluctant Movie Queen by Doug Warren, Robson Books, London, 1982

Becoming Mae West by Emily Wortis Leider, Farrar Straus Giroux, New York, 1997

Been There, Done That by Eddie Fisher, St Martin's Press, New York, 1999

Confessions of an Actor by Laurence Olivier, Weidenfeld and Nicholson, London, 1982

The Casting Couch by Selwyn Ford, Grafton, London, 1990

The Constant Sinner by Mae West, John Long Ltd, London, 1934

Dorothy Dandridge by Earl Mills, Holloway House, Los Angeles, 1970

Everything and Nothing - The Dorothy Dandridge Tragedy by Dorothy Dandridge and Earl Conrad, Abelard-Schuman, New York, 1970

Finch, Bloody Finch by Elaine Dundy, Michael Joseph, London, 1980

Get Happy - The Life of Judy Garland by Gerald Clarke,

Random House, New York, 2000

Golden Boy – The Untold Story of William Holden by Bob Thomas, Weidenfeld & Nicolson, London, 1983

Goodness Had Nothing To Do With It by Mae West, W.H. Allen, London, 1960

Headline Hollywood edited by Adrienne L. McLean and David A. Cook, Rutgers University Press, New Brunswick, New Jersey, 2001

Heartbreaker – My Life With Judy Garland by John Meyer, Doubleday, New York, 1983

Hollywood Babylon by Kenneth Anger, Dell Publishing, New York, 1975

Hollywood Babylon II by Kenneth Anger, Penguin Books, New York, 1984

Hollywood Death and Scandal Sites by E.J. Flemming, McFarland & Company, Inc., Jefferson, North Carolina, 2000

Hutch by Charlotte Breese, Bloomsbury, London, 1999

In Search of My Father by Ronald Howard, William Kimber, London, 1981

Jane Russell – An Autobiography by Jane Russell, Franklin Watts, Inc., New York, 1985

Jayne Mansfield by May Mann, Drake Publishers, Inc., New York, 1973

Jayne Mansfield and the American Fifties by Martha Saxton, Bantam, New York, 1976

Jayne Mansfield, A Bio-Bibliography by Jocelyn Faris, Greenwood Press, Westport, Connecticut, 1994

Judy by Gerold Frank, W.H. Allen, London, 1975

Judy Garland by David Shipman, Fourth Estate, London, 1992

Judy Garland – A Biography by Anne Edwards, Constable, London, 1975

Judy – With Love by Lorna Smith, Robert Hale, London, 1975

Korda – The Man Who Could Work Miracles by Karol Kulik, W.H. Allen, London, 1975

Laurence Olivier - A Biography by Donald Spoto, HarperCollins, 1991

Little Girl Lost - The Life and Hard Times of Judy Garland by Al DiOrio, Robson Books, London, 1975

Mae West by Fergus Cashin, W.H. Allen, London, 1981

Mae West by George Eells and Stanley Musgrove, Robson Books, London, 1984

Mae West - Empress of Sex by Maurice Leonard, Fontana, London, 1992

Mae West on Sex, Health and ESP by Mae West, W.H. Allen, London, 1975

Maurice Chevalier by Michael Freedland, Arthur Baker, London, 1981

Maurice Chevalier - His Life, 1888-1972 by James Harding, Secker & Warburg, London, 1982

Merle, A Biography of Merle Oberon by Charles Higham and Roy Moseley, New English Library, London, 1983

The Moon's a Balloon by David Niven, Hamish Hamilton, London 1971

The Other Side of the Moon - The Life of David Niven by Sheridan Morley, Weidenfeld & Nicholson, London, 1985

Peel Me A Grape by Joseph W. Weintraub, Futura, London, 1975

Pink Goddess - The Jayne Mansfield Story by Michael Feeney Callan, W.H. Allen, London, 1986

The Queen of Camp - Mae West, Sex and Popular Culture by Marybeth Hamilton, HarperCollins, London, 1995

Queenie by Michael Korda, Collins, London, 1985

Rainbow - The Stormy Life of Judy Garland by Christopher Finch, Michael Joseph, London, 1975

The Real Life of Laurence Olivier by Roger Lewis, Century, London, 1996

Three Plays by Mae West edited by Lillian Schissel, Routledge, New York, 1997

The Tragic Secret Life of Jayne Mansfield by Raymond Strait, Robert Hale, London, 1974

Selected Bibliography

Too Much of a Good Thing - Mae West as Cultural Icon by Ramona Curry, University of Minnesota Press, Minneapolis, 1996

Vivien Leigh by Hugo Vickers, Hamish Hamilton, London, 1988

Vivien Leigh - A Biography by Anne Edwards, W.H. Allen, London, 1977

Vivien - The Life of Vivien Leigh by Alexander Walker, Weidenfeld & Nicolson Ltd, London, 1987

Young Judy by David Dahl and Barry Kehoe, Hart-Davis, MacGibbon, London, 1975

Yul - The Man Who Would Be King by Rock Brynner, Collins, London, 1989

Index

Index

Index